More Praise for *Detrans*

"The stories in *Detrans* are heartbreaking. But you need to read them. Mary Margaret Olohan brilliantly narrates the lives that have been damaged by transgender ideology while highlighting the human costs of getting human nature wrong. The brave young people she profiles in this book are both victims and heroes—the victims of a grotesque medical scandal, and the heroes that will bring it to an end."
—RYAN T. ANDERSON, Ph.D., president of the Ethics and Public Policy Center and author of *When Harry Became Sally: Responding to the Transgender Moment*

"Mary Margaret Olohan's fearless reporting exposes the brutal, horrifying nature of 'gender affirming care' for children and young adults and the medical field's complicity in it. The brave detransitioners she profiles share what it's actually like to gender transition in gripping detail. Their stories, so thoughtfully and sensitively chronicled in *Detrans*, are unforgettable."
—KATRINA TRINKO, editor in chief of The Daily Signal

"While much of the media and medical establishment would rather ignore the devastating stories of detransitioners, Mary Margaret Olohan ensures they're heard. *Detrans* documents a medical scandal of historic proportions, with countless young people manipulated and betrayed into believing they were 'born in the wrong bodies.' Anyone who cares about the well-being of children can't look away from this book and the horrors it exposes."
—KELSEY BOLAR, executive producer of the Identity Crisis series and senior policy analyst at the Independent Women's Forum

"Until recently, no one knew the word 'detransitioner.' It refers to a growing army of victims of the gender quackery that has captured major medical groups. Patients are promised relief through drugs and surgery, but more and more are realizing they were sold a lie. Mary Margaret Olohan's book will introduce you to many young detransitioners. But her book is not just individual biographies. Olohan shows the recurring stages that these young people traverse—from the social pressure and encouragement at the beginning, to the realization, regret, and aftermath. Her account is both moving and infuriating. Let's pray *Detrans* helps put an end to this madness."
—JAY RICHARDS, Ph.D., William E. Simon Senior Research Fellow in Religious Liberty and Civil Society and director of the Richard and Helen DeVos Center for Life, Religion, and Family at The Heritage Foundation

"Mary Margaret Olohan fearlessly reveals the gruesome reality of what prescribing our children puberty blockers, cross-sex hormones, and 'gender-affirming' surgeries looks like. She does a major service to society

by sharing the experiences of detransitioners to spread awareness of the tragedies they have endured at the hands of manipulative activists and bad doctors. Her personal reporting and engaging storytelling make it a must-read as we attempt to destroy this evil enterprise for good."
—MOLLIE HEMINGWAY, editor in chief of The Federalist

"Mary Margaret Olohan uses lived experiences to highlight the severity and harm being done to the victims of the gender ideology movement. To turn a blind eye to the adverse effects of this extreme movement is to be complacent. After reading this book, you will see that the argument is not 'anti-trans'; the argument is pro–child safeguarding, pro-fairness, and pro-truth."
—RILEY GAINES, twelve-time NCAA all-American swimmer, five-time SEC champion, and ambassador for the Independent Women's Forum

"Detransitioners bear the most personal witness to the gender medicine calamity, the worst medical scandal in decades. Olohan tells their stories powerfully and with remarkable compassion."
—ABIGAIL SHRIER, bestselling author of *Irreversible Damage* and *Bad Therapy*

Detrans

Detrans

True Stories of Escaping the Gender Ideology Cult

Mary Margaret Olohan

Since 1947
REGNERY

An Imprint of Skyhorse Publishing, Inc.

Regnery books may be purchased in bulk at special discounts for sales promotion, corporate gifts, fund-raising, or educational purposes. Special editions can also be created to specifications. For details, contact the Special Sales Department, Regnery, 307 West 36th Street, 11th Floor, New York, NY 10018 or info@skyhorsepublishing.com.

Published in the United States by Regnery, an imprint of Skyhorse Publishing, Inc.

Regnery® is a registered trademark and its colophon is a trademark of Skyhorse Publishing, Inc.,® a Delaware corporation.

Visit our website at www.regnery.com.

Please follow our publisher Tony Lyons on Instagram @tonylyonsisuncertain.

10 9 8 7 6 5 4 3 2 1

Library of Congress Cataloging-in-Publication Data are available on file.

Print ISBN: 978-1-68451-501-1
eBook ISBN: 978-1-68451-560-8

Cover design by John Caruso
Cover photograph courtesy of Getty

Mary Margaret Olohan is grateful to The Daily Caller News Foundation for permission to reprint portions of her reporting originally published by them, including, "'It Destroyed My Body': Here's Why This Former Trans Woman Regrets His Gender Transition"; to The Daily Wire for permission to reprint portions of her reporting originally published by them, including, "Catholic Chicago Hospital Chose Ideology over Biology in Treating Biological Girl Who Believed She Was Male"; and to The Daily Signal for permission to reprint portions of her reporting originally published by them, including, "He Went Undercover to Expose 'Rubber-Stamping' of Trans Surgeries."

Printed in the United States of America

*To the girls, boys, men, and women seeking truth in
an age of deceit. To the small but fearless number of reporters,
many of them women, who continue to share these stories
that must be told. And to my late grandmother, Kathy Olohan,
who always told me I would write a book.*

CONTENTS

I was making myself dinner in my dingy little Arlington apartment when I got a notification that a Twitter Spaces event was starting. A young woman I had recently begun following had advertised it as an event where people who had attempted medical and hormonal sex changes were going to share their stories.

It was some time around the fall of 2020, and outside of mostly conservative and academic circles, stories like theirs hadn't really been explored. I listened for over an hour as one after another, people spoke up about their experiences going on testosterone or estrogen, getting surgeries, attempting to live as another sex, and ultimately realizing that they could never fully become a person of the opposite gender.

Hormonal interventions had made their voices confusingly unmatched. One deep-voiced individual articulated that she was actually a biological woman. Their stories were confusing to listen to, and emotional. They described the side effects of hormones: the mood swings, the intense rage, going through puberty as adults, and an overwhelming, almost unmanageable sex drive.

Eventually, I had to stop listening. But I couldn't forget about them. They had been lied to by every institution that they had trusted, and their lives would never be the same.

Now, as their stories are more and more brought to light, we know them as detransitioners.

Detransitioner. That isn't a word that often comes up in daily conversation. To my knowledge, spellcheck and dictionaries don't even fully recognize it yet.

So what does it mean? The word describes a person who has attempted to use surgery or hormonal intervention to change their biology because they believe, or want to believe, or have been told, that they were born in the wrong body. And that nothing will make them happy and content until they have rectified that mistake.

So that person detransitions: They try to reverse the process. They stop taking hormones, they reverse the surgeries (to the extent that that is possible), and they attempt to deal with the mental and physical consequences of such brutal interventions in the physiology and anatomy of the human body.

Not everyone makes it to that point. But this book shares stories of those who have, and who are brave enough to speak out about their experiences.

In March 2023 the Associated Press defined detransitioning as "stopping or reversing gender transition, which can include medical treatment or changes in appearance, or both." Of course, the AP claims that detransitioning is rare. And it is quick to tell readers that the process of detransitioning "does not always include regret" (a laughable claim, considering the circumstances, but one pushed hard by advocacy organizations).[1]

I was surprised to find that the AP would even address detransitioners. Non-conservative media outlets have thus far done their absolute best to avoid sharing the stories of the men and women who have endured this agonizing process.

Any examination of mainstream or corporate media coverage of transgender issues will quickly let you in on a secret: most media is focused on promoting a single narrative when it comes to LGBTQ and gender ideology issues, a narrative heavily informed by the reporting style guides of organizations like GLAAD and the Human Rights Campaign.[2]

GLAAD, formerly known as the Gay and Lesbian Alliance Against Defamation, actively discourages reporting on "negative claims about the transgender community." The organization also urges reporters to "avoid elevating singular voices or rare cases and concerns in equal weight to overwhelming consensus and preponderance of evidence," noting that "doing so is inaccurate journalism and storytelling."[3]

Further, GLAAD offers the media a glossary of terms recommended for reporting on the issue, including the phrase "gender-affirming care."[4] If it is not immediately clear to you what that phrase means, you aren't alone. It is purposefully nebulous, artfully positive in tone, successfully vague, an activist umbrella term used to obscure the grisly details of transition procedures such as hormones, puberty blockers, and irreversible surgeries, even for children.

This "gender-affirming care" language has been widely embraced by non-conservative media outlets, including outlets with massive reach, such as CNN,[5] the *Washington Post*,[6] and the Associated Press.[7]

The use of the phrase has become so standard in coverage of legislation banning irreversible sex-change surgeries and hormones for minors that it is almost impossible for the average reader to know what is being banned, particularly if they are not already familiar with "gender-affirming care."

Most outlets and many activists and lawmakers also use the phrase "anti-transgender bills" or "anti-transgender laws."

Take a look at this March 2023 story from the Associated Press, headlined "Sanders Signs Arkansas Trans Care Malpractice Bill into

Law." The story's first few lines warn that Arkansas governor Sarah Huckabee Sanders signed "legislation making it easier to sue providers of gender-affirming care for children, a move that could effectively reinstate a blocked ban on such care."

Notice the repeated emphasis on the word "care." It is not until the sixth paragraph of the story that the writer addresses what that "care" actually is—and even then he describes it as "gender-affirming hormone therapy or puberty blockers" and "gender-affirming surgery."[8]

He does not mention the growing number of people speaking out about the fact that they regret undergoing their irreversible surgeries (particularly as young girls).[9]

He does not mention the alarming social contagion effect documented by Abigail Shrier in her book *Irreversible Damage*.

He does not mention that the medical establishment does not fully understand the effects that puberty blockers have on a child—or the long-term effects that testosterone and estrogen have upon a young person's body (or an adult's body, for that matter).

His representation of this "care" leaves the uninformed reader wondering: Why would this hateful governor of Arkansas wish to deprive these poor children of "care"?

The reader is given no concept of the grisly realities of what is being banned here. Instead, the reader is left to wonder why Governor Sanders and the lawmakers across the nation who have been pushing similar legislation wish to hurt and deprive young people who identify as transgender of medical care.

That would appear to be the reason the stories are written this way—to obscure the grisly realities of this "care" and portray anyone who objects to it as having a vendetta against the patients who are being transitioned.

And it is not only the media that has jumped on board with this language—many leftist lawmakers and high-profile figures serving in President Joe Biden's administration embrace it as well.

"Gender-affirming care is medical care," claimed Rachel Levine, a biologically male individual who serves as the assistant secretary for health for the U.S. Department of Health and Human Services. "It is mental health care. It is suicide prevention care. It improves quality of life, and it saves lives. It is based on decades of study. It is a well-established medical practice."[10]

A publication from the Biden administration's Office of Population Affairs, released in March 2022, emphasized that "for transgender and nonbinary children and adolescents, early gender-affirming care is crucial to overall health and well-being."

Why? Because this "care," which the messaging acknowledges may include top surgery (to remove or create breasts), bottom surgery (surgery on a girl's reproductive parts or on a boy's genitals), and facial feminization surgeries (surgery to restructure a boy's face into something more feminine), allegedly "allows the child or adolescent to focus on social transitions and can increase their confidence while navigating the healthcare system."

That publication cited a number of high-profile sources in support of its message,[11] including the Department of Health and Human Services' Office of Civil Rights,[12] the Centers for Disease Control and Prevention,[13] The Trevor Project,[14] the Human Rights Campaign,[15] the National Child Traumatic Stress Network's claim that "gender-affirming care is trauma-informed care,"[16] and Columbia University psychologists claiming that gender-affirming care "saves lives."[17]

Activists often make the claim that most major American medical organizations support "gender-affirming care," typically referring to the American Academy of Pediatrics (AAP), the Endocrine Society, and the World Professional Association for Transgender Health (WPATH).

But as researcher Leor Sapir, a Manhattan Institute fellow, points out, "None of these organizations have done systematic reviews of the evidence, a method of review designed to prevent cherry-picking of studies and biased analysis."

He goes on to note that "WPATH is an explicitly ideological organization that now includes 'eunuch' as a valid 'gender identity' that children can supposedly know they have at a very early age."[18]

It seems that all of our influential institutions, from the media and the government to the medical profession, have lined up in defense of "gender-affirming care." But elsewhere in the world, nations that formerly bought this lie are beginning to wake up. Sweden, Finland, and the United Kingdom have each conducted systematic reviews and come to the same conclusion, as Sapir notes: there is no evidence that the benefits of using hormones for treating gender-related distress in youth outweigh the risks of using such hormones.

Consequently, Sweden and Finland severely restricted hormone eligibility for minors and recommended that children with gender distress first be given psychotherapy (and ideally they would only be treated with psychotherapy).[19]

In the United Kingdom, the National Health Service announced in 2022 that it was shutting down England's main gender clinic, Tavistock, after an independent report found that it was "not a safe or viable long-term option" for young people suffering from gender distress because of "the steep rise in referrals" and the lack of peer review for transgender treatments.[20]

That report was conducted by Hilary Cass, the former president of the Royal College of Pediatrics and Child Health, with the aim of ensuring "that children and young people who are questioning their gender identity or experiencing gender dysphoria, and who need support from the NHS, receive a high standard of care that meets their needs and is safe, holistic, and effective."[21]

And soon after that, a legal firm based out of London announced that one thousand families were suing Tavistock in a class action lawsuit, accusing the gender clinic of rushing their children into life-altering and in some cases irreversible treatments.[22]

And yet in the United States, "gender-affirming care" is being presented to young people and their parents as perhaps the only thing that can save their lives.

This is an incredibly sobering reality to face, particularly when so many of the stories we will examine in this book are about young people who were influenced by the messaging of five to ten years ago. Only God knows what will ensue for this current generation.

In 2021 alone, about 42,000 children and teens across the United States received a gender dysphoria diagnosis, according to data compiled by Komodo for Reuters, almost double the number of gender dysphoria diagnoses from 2020 (24,847). Between 2017 and 2021, a total of at least 121,882 children between the ages of six and seventeen were diagnosed with gender dysphoria.

The real numbers are likely higher, since the Reuters data don't include treatment that wasn't covered by insurance or patients who were not diagnosed with gender dysphoria, Reuters notes. (Note that some of the detransitioners interviewed in this book paid for hormones out of pocket.)

And even Reuters admits something that many top media outlets and networks have urgently denied: that children are taking drastic medical steps to change their bodies. "A small but increasing number of U.S. children diagnosed with gender dysphoria are choosing medical interventions to express their identity and help alleviate their distress."

These medical interventions include surgeries, hormones, and puberty blockers, the publication notes, emphasizing that the hormone and puberty blocker treatments begin when the child starts going through puberty, "typically around age 10 or 11," and asserting surgeries are "uncommon" for patients under eighteen.[23] Judging by the interviews in this book, transgender surgeries on underage patients may be more common than the Reuters report admits, but at least it admits they do happen.

It is worth noting here that the Food and Drug Administration has not approved common puberty blockers like Lupron Depot (housed in the class of medications called gonadotropin-releasing hormones, or GnRH agonists) for the treatment of gender dysphoria.

The FDA specifically confirmed to me in March 2023 that Lupron has not been approved to treat gender dysphoria, and when I asked if it was common for medical professionals to prescribe medicine that is not approved by the FDA, they sent me to the Centers for Medicare and Medicaid Services, who sent me to the American Medical Association.

According to David Gortler, a former senior advisor to the Food and Drug Administration commissioner and a current Ethics and Public Policy Center scholar, we don't really know how common it is for doctors to prescribe drugs to treat conditions in a manner unapproved by the FDA (the so-called "off-label" use of medicines).

"We do know, however, that the entire class of drugs that block puberty signals are quite unsafe," Gortler emphasized, "and that's even when they're given for approved indications having nothing to do with transgenderism."[24] These are drugs that can have serious side effects. In June 2022, the FDA added warnings to GnRH agonists about the risk of pseudotumor cerebri, which causes swelling mimicking that of a brain tumor and can result in loss of vision.[25]

But the gender-affirming-care business is a highly profitable endeavor for those who engage in it, raking in vast amounts of cash for surgeries[26] and appointments for renewing prescriptions for hormones, which "you'll need to take…for the rest of your life if you want to maintain the effects…."[27] Those engaged in the business are very aware of how lucrative it is—a good example is Matt Walsh's exposé of a doctor at Vanderbilt University Medical Center bragging about just how big a "money maker" the gender transition surgery business is.[28]

Faced with this type of messaging from the media, the medical establishment, leftist politicians, and even the federal government, it should come as no surprise that the individuals who have gone through the gender ideology rigamarole are typically loath to speak out about their own lived experiences.

And we haven't even touched on the venom of the transgender-promoting community yet. Those who do speak out against this ideology face furious anger and harassment from the very community that convinced them to make these (often) irrevocable choices.[29] They are accused of hating transgender people, of changing sides for political points or financial gain, of seeking attention, and of mental illness. This is particularly true online, where detransitioners face intense backlash from the very community that formerly embraced them, love-bombed them, and urgently pushed them to permanently alter their bodies.[30]

Yet despite this daunting onslaught of criticism, more and more men and women are stepping forward to speak up: to reveal that they, too, were persuaded to attempt crossing that unfathomable divide, that of changing one's sex.

And then they realized they had been lied to, and they turned back.[31]

Researcher Dr. Lisa Littman is the author of a groundbreaking study on detransitioners who went through medical or surgical procedures to treat their gender dysphoria. Littman explains that "the visibility of individuals who have detransitioned is new and may be rapidly growing," noting that as recently as 2014, "it was challenging for an individual who detransitioned to find another person who similarly detransitioned."

Since then, detransitioners' stories have exploded on the internet, on YouTube, Twitter, Instagram, and in the subreddit "r/detrans," leading to media stories and national television appearances by detransitioners. Groups have been founded to promote their stories and spread awareness about the dangers of transitioning.

"In the face of this massive change," Littman writes, "clinicians have called for more research into the experiences of detransitioners."

One huge hurdle that researchers and writers on this topic face is that only a small percentage of detransitioners actually inform their medical providers that they have detransitioned—Littman found that only 24 percent of those in her study had informed the "clinicians and clinics that facilitated their transitions that they had detransitioned.

"Therefore," Littman writes, "clinic rates of detransition are likely to be underestimated and gender transition specialists may be unaware of how many of their own patients have detransitioned, particularly for patients who are no longer under their care."[32]

The fact that so few people reported their detransition to their doctors may be unsurprising given that, as the interviews in this book will show, many detransitioners have found that the medical establishment, including the surgeons who operated on them, have no interest in helping them detransition—or else, perhaps worse, these so-called professionals have no understanding of how to help.

I have had the privilege of speaking with quite a few men and women who made the choice to "detransition." Many of these individuals, including Helena Kerschner and Chloe Cole, I found through social media, where they were seeking to draw attention to their plight through viral posts. I reached out to them via direct message, asking for a chance to hear and share their stories. They were incredibly courteous and helpful—Chloe Cole, for example, connected me with "Abel Garcia" when I asked for her help getting in touch with biologically male detransitioners.

Some of the individuals I talked to were not open to sharing their stories in this book. But the detransitioners whose stories I tell in *Detrans* bravely spent hours of their lives pouring out their experiences so that others can understand what they have gone through—and be warned against doing the same. Their stories, gruesome and heart-rending, border on science fiction, involving manipulative therapy sessions, mental anguish, late puberty, frustration, botched surgeries, attempts to construct phantom body parts, and much more.

Every detransitioner has a unique story. But many of the same fact patterns are present in their stories. These fact patterns often, though not always, include an unhappy childhood or an adolescence fraught with abuse or loneliness. Gender dysphoria at a young age. Discomfort in their own body. Struggles to make friends. Signs that they were on the autism spectrum (often without the confirmation of a medical diagnosis). Adults in their lives, often on the internet, in LGBTQ circles and chat rooms, who pushed them towards transition, hormones, and eventually surgeries.

And almost always, the same driving force: the desperate desire to know who you are and to be happy.

Chapter 1

The Slippery Slope

Prisha

P risha Mosley describes herself as having been "conventionally attractive" when she was a young teen, with long, pretty hair, a small waist, long legs, and an attractive figure. She wore makeup and tried to look like other girls.

"I looked like I was supposed to," she reflects.

Inside, she felt "like shit."

There was a lot going on in her life that could have made her feel that way.

Prisha really began floundering around age twelve, as she entered puberty. She was struggling intensely with her mental health and had developed a severe eating disorder. She began to feel like her life was falling apart around her.

Prisha says her eating disorder was so severe that medical providers recommended she receive inpatient care. She was diagnosed with a personality disorder and a host of comorbidities, she told me—

OCD, anorexia, bulimia, possible schizophrenia, major depression, and more.

"I didn't get enough attention," she explains. "My issues weren't noticed until I was literally trying to kill myself. That's also how I got into the online stuff . . . ," she shared.[1]

According to medical records viewed and reported on by the Independent Women's Forum (IWF), Prisha wouldn't eat for entire days at a time, effectively starving herself. She described herself as being "skeletal" at that time, sharing in an interview with my friend Kelsey Bolar of the IWF: "I could stick my whole hand in my stomach between my rib cage. And my hip bones were sticking out really bad, my hair was falling out and my skin was gray."

Everyone in her life was worried about her, something Prisha was painfully cognizant of. "I made everyone sad."

She was repeatedly hospitalized for attempting to take her own life.

"I just hated myself and my body," Prisha told Kelsey. "Every part of me, I just loathed it. I didn't think I deserved to eat. I was so depressed and so sad."[2]

Prisha was attending a high school in rural North Carolina at the time (a "really bad" school, she told me, with unprofessional teachers and badly behaved students). As she matured, Prisha began to be more and more self-conscious about her breasts, which she said were quite large, drawing inappropriate attention from her peers.

She was touched inappropriately "pretty much every day," she said. Many of us may be surprised by such a statement (I was), but Prisha insisted that the mistreatment was a common thing for her: "People would throw food down my shirt, into my boobs, all the time."

"Just touching me and stuff like that," she said. "Boys and girls."

She didn't really know anyone at school who was transitioning, and she doesn't remember her teachers discussing the topic. But her peers were absolutely starting to explore LGBTQ topics.

"It was ten years ago at this point," she said. "There were a lot of gender-nonconforming people and everybody was some sort of new sexuality every week, the stranger the better, and the [Pride] flags were starting to come out and stuff. So it was starting, but it was mostly online at that point."

Then Prisha faced what was probably the most traumatic event of her young life. At fourteen years old, she told me, Prisha was raped by an adult. And that rape caused her to become pregnant.

Prisha's body couldn't sustain the pregnancy. She was grappling intensely with a crippling eating disorder. The young girl, still reeling from her assault and the knowledge that she was pregnant, found herself miscarrying her infant child.

The miscarriage of her baby was graphic, Prisha told me. She was not only taken unawares—she was distraught.

"I lost the baby because I couldn't eat," she would say. "I had failed as a woman, my body a graveyard...."[3]

She cried as she shared the story with me. I asked her if she had ever named the baby. Yes, she said, she had named her baby June.

One day when she was out walking, she noticed a small rock on the ground that was in the shape of a little baby curled up in the womb. Prisha took the rock home. It reminded her of June. And she still has it, kept safe in a little box that she likes to think of as June's bed, keeping her warm and safe.

Prisha's rape significantly impacted her young mind and her views of womanhood and sex. It would not factor much in the conversations she would have with the gender therapists who pushed her down the road to surgery, but Prisha believes that the rape heavily affected her desire to transition.

"I was so young and ignorant that I thought [rape] only happened to girls," she explained to me. "I wouldn't talk about it.... I feel like [the therapists] should have seen that as a red flag too, but they didn't."[4]

"I didn't want anyone to ever be able to go inside [me] ever again," she told Kelsey. "So I thought atrophy sounded like a good thing as far as I could even understand it."[5]

Prisha is twenty-four years old now. She is very frank about sharing her current struggles to find medical professionals who will help her deal with the medical complications of her transition. She has a boyfriend, detransitioner friends who push her to speak out about her experiences, and empathetic media allies like Kelsey to help share her story.

But there was a time when she thought that transitioning was the only solution to her problems. At age seventeen, she began testosterone injections. And at age eighteen, she went under the knife to remove her breasts. Forever.

On July 17, 2023, Prisha filed a lawsuit against providers and institutions that treated her during her transition. Her legal complaint is available online in its entirety.[6]

Prisha's story, and every other detransitioner's story mentioned in this book, cannot be properly understood without a knowledge of their early life, their families, and what was going on in their social circles and in their minds when they were making these pivotal decisions.

I asked Prisha about all of those things. I asked her about her parents' relationship, and about her own relationship with social media. With pornography. With the therapists she encountered, with the friends in LGBTQ circles that she met along her transition path.

Why? Because she, and others, say that these things massively impacted their choices. And they want to share their stories in the hope that other vulnerable young people can learn from them.[7]

I should add here that most (although not all) of the stories in this book are of biological women who sought to transition to become men. The reason for that is the alarming rate at which young women have begun attempting transitions in recent years, as Abigail Shrier documented in her book *Irreversible Damage*, which lays out evidence that a "social contagion" is responsible for the rapid growth in the number of girls, especially young girls, deciding they want to transition.

Shrier cites a study by Lisa Littman on "rapid-onset gender dysphoria" (ROGD), a study based on parent reports about their children that suggests there has been a dramatic rise in biological girls identifying as transgender boys as a result of social and peer contagion—mutual and often negative influences among young adolescents.

For the study, Littman recruited parents from three different web spaces filled with parents of trans-identifying children. In the 256 completed parent surveys that resulted, the adolescents and young adults described were predominantly female (82.8 percent).

Significantly, Littman's study found that none of the young people described in her study would have met the diagnostic criteria for gender dysphoria in childhood. A good portion (62.5 percent) of the young people were, however, suffering from mental health disorders or neurodevelopmental disabilities (or both) before the onset of their gender dysphoria. And in 36.8 percent of the friend groups that the surveys described, "parent participants indicated that the majority of the members became transgender-identified."

Littman calls for more research on this topic, including data collection from the young people themselves, from parents, clinicians, and third-party informants to further explore "the roles of social influence, maladaptive coping mechanisms, parental approaches, and family dynamics in the development and duration of gender dysphoria in adolescents and young adults."[8]

Shrier's *Irreversible Damage* tells the stories of a number of families whose young daughters went down this path. The parents she spoke with were largely progressive, Shrier shares, accepting many leftist principles and stances when it came to LGBTQ issues. But these parents knew their daughters—and they still found it difficult to swallow the gender ideology pill pushed upon them.

"[Rapid-onsent gender dysphoria] differs from traditional gender dysphoria, a psychological affliction that begins in early childhood and is characterized by a severe and persistent feeling that one was born the wrong sex," Shrier explains. "ROGD is a social contagion that comes on suddenly in adolescence, afflicting teens who'd never exhibited any confusion about their sex.

"Like other social contagions, such as cutting and bulimia, ROGD overwhelmingly afflicts girls," she continues. "But unlike other conditions, this one—though not necessarily its sufferers—gets full support from the medical community. The standard for dealing with teens who assert they are transgender is 'affirmative care'—immediately granting the patient's stated identity."[9]

Luka

Luka Hein is another brave young woman I spoke with.

Luka describes a relatively normal relationship with her parents, though her father and mother divorced when she was in seventh or eighth grade. The divorce made her family life "kind of rocky," she told me.

"At this point, I still had a decent relationship with them, and we would still talk about stuff," Luka said. "I was still living with them, I would go back and forth each week, which definitely was mentally exhausting for me."

She was raised Catholic and went to Catholic school from pre-school until her freshman year of high school. Luka described her Catholic school experience as "nice." Most of the kids at school lived close by and could walk to each other's homes to play, she told me.

But after she stopped going to Catholic grade school, Luka said that she and her mother didn't go to church much anymore. Her father, who was not Catholic, eventually started going to a church

Luka describes as an openly left-leaning, "progressive-Methodist church slash coffee shop place."

Luka has since seen the female minister (as well as her own therapist and doctor) at a transgender-promoting protest.

"I saw her in opposition to the bill that would have protected minors from this kind of medical stuff," Luka said of the minister. She was there in February 2023 in opposition to the Nebraska "Let Them Grow Act."

The legislation, signed by Nebraska's governor in May 2023, banned puberty blockers, hormones, and surgeries for gender dysphoria for young people under the age of nineteen.

"She knew who I was, she knew me," Luka said. "It was quite the feeling to see a reverend you knew, your doctor, your therapist, a youth group leader down there.... I had to go sit down a little after that.

"I should have known...."

Luka went to an all-girls religious school for high school, an experience she didn't enjoy much. This wasn't because of the school itself, she said—she was going through a lot in her own personal life.

Her parents' divorce was a huge change in Luka's life, one that took a toll on her mentally. She eventually, around age seventeen, stopped staying at her dad's house because she didn't like moving back and forth. But before that, Luka endured some traumatizing experiences on social media that would hugely inform her path forward.

Primarily on her cell phone, Luka was accessing a lot of social media sites. Instagram. Twitter. YouTube. And Kik—"for talking to people"—a chat app now renowned for "having a giant problem with predators," as Luka explained to me.[10]

Her parents didn't really understand how these social media sites worked, Luka said. They would occasionally check in and tell her that she had had enough screen time, but that was pretty much it.

She wasn't on Reddit and Tumblr, two websites that are more commonly known as places for young people to consume transgender-promoting content, but Instagram users would post transgender-related content from these platforms, and Luka would see it on Instagram. This included graphics with little statements like, "If you think you're trans, you're trans!"

Online messaging on transgender topics was (and still is) overwhelmingly positive. But unlike today, there was hardly any messaging on the dangers of medically transitioning. "At the time, you didn't really have anyone talking about the negative parts of transition," Luka explained.

And so as she explored the internet more, Luka fell into different internet groups and began spending time in chat rooms filled with adults. These adults preyed upon her, Luka said.

Luka told me that she feels these adults groomed her. They solicited nude pictures from her, sent her sexual communications, and pressured her into making what she describes as "child sexual exploitation material" of herself.

The pressure she experienced included everything from threats to love-bombing, depending on the individual pushing her.

"It was a lot of preying on the fact, at that point, I didn't feel like I had anyone to talk to, and being naive about the damage that would be done with these people."

And for a lonely young girl, these types of attentions were not only meaningful, they were filling a void that she desperately wanted to be filled. Luka was at a new school and had been struggling to fit in, and the adults she met online quickly latched on to her vulnerability.

"It was one of those things where I was almost searching for some kind of connection," she explained. "And they really took advantage of that and took advantage of the fact that I was kind of naive and didn't know any better."

Luka vividly remembers the night her parents found out what was going on—when we talked about it, she almost shuddered as she recalled it. She was staying at her dad's house. That night, through an iCloud update, Luka's mother accidentally stumbled on messages that her daughter was receiving from adult men. Panicking, she called Luka's father, and he freaked out as well.

"Yelling," Luka described the scene. "Getting upset."

The majority of the adults preying on Luka were men who were talking to her on Kik, she said. Many of them identified as transgender women.

By the time her parents found out, Luka felt that she had gotten herself into something that she had no idea how to get out of. She recognized that the relationships with these adults online were wrong.

"It didn't help my mental state when you have these predators saying, 'You're going to get in trouble if people find out, it's going to be your fault,'" she said. And the predators weren't wrong! Luka's parents, understandably horrified and frightened by the revelation, responded very dramatically. Their response further exacerbated the traumatic incident, she told me.

The night her parents found out, they called the police. The female officer checked Luka's body for signs of abuse or self-harm, having her lift up her shirt and take off her pants. The young girl was already having what she described as essentially a breakdown at that point, and her psychiatrist recommended that Luka enter a partial hospitalization program.

Luka told me she was in the program three separate times over the course of the next few months, for two weeks each time. It was while she was in that partial hospitalization program that she encountered therapists who would change her life.[11]

On September 13, 2023, Luka filed a lawsuit against professionals and institutions that treated her during her transition. Her entire legal complaint can be read online.[12]

Chloe

Chloe Cole grew up in a two-parent household, the youngest of six siblings. Her mom was atheist, her father grew up Christian, and her family usually didn't attend church, though she recalls going a few times.

She describes her relationship with her family as "pretty healthy," though her siblings were all much older than her and in adult stages of their lives. This often left her to her own devices.

"My siblings are all quite older than me, by about seven to eight years," she explained. "They were further ahead of me in a lot of ways, and they hit their teens a lot earlier than I did, and they didn't necessarily want to be with me all the time. And they eventually moved out pretty soon. So, I grew up like an only child in a lot of ways.

"I was also struggling socially at school," she added. Chloe said she had trouble concentrating in class and keeping her grades up. She also found it hard to make and keep friends at school, and she didn't play any sports.

"I was often an outcast, especially from other girls."[13]

Young Chloe went through puberty much earlier than most of her peers and was frequently bullied and teased at school. This was compounded by the fact that she was struggling with her studies and had trouble with social interactions—because, she thinks now, she may have had a whole host of undiagnosed symptoms and concerns, including learning disabilities, anxiety, and autism-spectrum symptoms.[14]

Her troubles were only exacerbated by comments that her peers, and even some adults and authority figures, made about her body, Chloe told me.

She had been diagnosed with disruptive behavior disorder in 2012, at age eight, had an "encounter for school problem" in 2013 at age nine, and was diagnosed with ADHD in 2015, at age eleven. Though she had many indications of being on the autism spectrum, Chloe says she was never treated for autism spectrum disorder and never received counseling for her behavioral problems.

In hindsight, Chloe has pondered how being "on the spectrum" may have affected her struggle to make friends with other girls.

"I think this did play a role in that, and that in a lot of ways growing up I was a little more on the masculine side and I found that I related more to boys my age more than girls," she shared.[15]

The Centers for Disease Control and Prevention describes autism spectrum disorder (ASD) as a "developmental disability caused by differences in the brain," noting that "scientists believe there are multiple causes of ASD that act together to change the most common ways people develop" and that there is still much that we have to learn about the causes of impacts of ASD.

ASD can affect communications, social interactions, and behavior in a variety of ways that often present differently, depending on the person.

> People with ASD may behave, communicate, interact, and learn in ways that are different from most other people. There is often nothing about how they look that sets them apart from other people. The abilities of people with ASD can vary significantly. For example, some people with ASD may have advanced conversation skills whereas others may be nonverbal. Some people with ASD need a lot of help in their daily lives; others can work and live with little to no support.
>
> ASD begins before the age of 3 years and can last throughout a person's life, although symptoms may improve over time. Some children show ASD symptoms within the

first 12 months of life. In others, symptoms may not show up until 24 months of age or later. Some children with ASD gain new skills and meet developmental milestones until around 18 to 24 months of age, and then they stop gaining new skills or lose the skills they once had.

As children with ASD become adolescents and young adults, they may have difficulties developing and maintaining friendships, communicating with peers and adults, or understanding what behaviors are expected in school or on the job. They may come to the attention of healthcare providers because they also have conditions such as anxiety, depression, or attention-deficit/hyperactivity disorder, which occur more often in people with ASD than in people without ASD.[16]

Writer Christina Buttons emphasizes that both children and adolescents on the autism spectrum are "disproportionately represented among the large, newly emerging cohort of young people self-identifying as transgender."

Button's analysis of how autistic traits can be mistaken for gender dysphoria is informed by her own youthful struggle with mental illness and her eventual diagnosis with Asperger's. She argues that undiagnosed autism, particularly in girls, is contributing to the rise in transgender youth.

"During puberty, autistic girls often experience exacerbated social and sensory challenges due to hormonal changes affecting their bodies and brains," she explains. "These difficulties can be compounded by the pressure to navigate unfamiliar social situations and expectations, which can lead to the development of co-occurring conditions such as depression, anxiety, and body image issues. Unfortunately, the challenge of communicating their experiences may cause mental health professionals to overlook their underlying autism.

"Given that autism is greatly underdiagnosed in young girls," Buttons adds, "I do not believe it is a coincidence that we are seeing a significant surge in adolescent girls self-diagnosing with gender dysphoria. An incorrect early diagnosis can lead to inappropriate treatment, which can result in devastating effects to their mental health and well-being."

Buttons spoke with forty-eight detransitioners and found that forty-two of them (thirty-two females and ten males) had either confirmed or suspected autism, meaning that they identified with autistic traits. The last six were confident that they were not autistic, she says, but believed that their "perceived gender dysphoria was due to a variety of other reasons, including other psychiatric disorders."

And only five of these forty-two detransitioners who had confirmed or suspected autism had been diagnosed with ASD before or during their transition, according to Buttons.

"All 5 told me that if they had fully understood what being autistic entailed and how it could manifest in their lives, they probably would not have believed they had gender dysphoria. They also said that 'gender identity' and transgender issues became their 'special interest' for a period of time," she reports.[17] (As we will see, Chloe now sees her fixation with transitioning as a "hyperfixation" typical of ASD.)

Buttons's suggestion that autistic children are more likely to identify as transgender is confirmed by Dr. Kenneth Zucker, a prominent psychologist who was ousted from his thirty-year position as head of the gender-identity clinic at Toronto's Centre for Addiction and Mental Health.[18] Zucker has said that he was fired by the center for his views on children with gender dysphoria.[19]

"There is a general consensus that the percentage of patients with gender dysphoria who also have an autism spectrum disorder is higher than one would expect based on the base rate, so to speak, of the ASD," he told me in an April 2023 phone interview. "There is a general consensus that there is a co-occurrence."[20]

In a 2017 BBC Two documentary titled *Transgender Kids: Who Knows Best?*, Zucker suggested, "It is possible that kids who have a tendency to get obsessed or fixated on something may latch on to gender.

"Just because kids are saying something doesn't necessarily mean you accept it, or that it's true, or that it could be in the best interests of the child," he warned. "A four-year-old might say that he's a dog—do you go out and buy dog food?"[21]

Chloe shared with me some of the signs of ASD that she exhibited when she was younger: she was hypersensitive to certain smells, like yogurt, and couldn't wear certain fabrics because they irritated her so much.

"It sounds ridiculous," she laughed, "but every time one of my older siblings would open up a thing of yogurt, I would just start bawling on the spot. I would have to leave the room. Yogurt kicks my butt, apparently."

ASD mainly presented socially for her—even to this day, Chloe says she struggles to pick up on social cues. Growing up, she had a hard time reading people's intentions or trying to predict how they were feeling or what they wanted.

She believes she may also have had some attachment issues—she just really didn't like physical affection growing up, and she was pretty shy of her extended family.

"I guess it was too close to other people? I didn't like that very much. I don't know if it was a sensory thing or an emotional thing.... I didn't like hugs or cuddling or kisses or things like that, especially as a young, young kid. I was very touch-averse."

Chloe liked to wear boy clothes when she was a child, but she also liked to play with dolls.[22]

"I had interests that were typical of a girl my age," she shared in an October 2022 speech. "I loved pink, purple, and blue, skirts, dresses, necklaces, dolls, and I also liked drawings, video games, playing in the dirt, or with my older brother's Legos, or Nerf guns, or toy trucks."[23]

She loved, loved, loved to draw—and still does. Chloe says she has drawings at her parent's house from all the way back when she was three years old. "I would just draw all the time, every day during recess, on all my schoolwork, which I would also get in trouble for, and I would focus on it so much that other students would make fun of me for how focused I was," she said. "My face was just, in the notebook, working out all the little details on the page."

She recalls a few other hyperfixations from when she was growing up, mainly related to what she watched, and then eventually her attachment to the idea of transitioning and believing that she was actually a boy.

Chloe began struggling with her female identity when she was around nine years old—her body didn't match up to the ideas of "voluptuous" female attractiveness that she was being inundated with from modern culture.[24]

Spoiler alert: Chloe ultimately sued her medical providers. We will go into her lawsuit in depth down the line. But as the filings in her case explain, she was "exposed to many negative ideas both online and in her social sphere about being female"—including about menstrual cycles or periods, pregnancy, giving birth, male domination, and more.

"In Chloe's social sphere, there was never any discussion of the positive experiences of being female, such as the joy and intimacy that can be shared with a loving, caring spouse, and the joy and intimacy that can be shared between a mother and child," according to her lawsuit.[25]

Chloe told me that she was also very, very afraid of being sexually abused or raped.

"Growing up I knew a lot of girls and women who had been sexually assaulted or were victims of rape or abuse," Chloe said. "Hearing all the stories they had about that, I was terrified about that same thing eventually happening to me…and it did."

That sexual assault occurred when she was a few years down the road, in the process of transitioning: a classmate grabbed her breasts in the classroom. She was in eighth grade.[26]

Helena

Helena grew up in a two-parent household in an upper-middle-class family in the Midwest, where both her parents were working professionals. When she was really little, her family went to a Protestant church on Sundays.

"We eventually stopped because neither of my parents are actually religious," she told me. "When I went to Catholic school I went through a phase of being super Catholic around the ages of ten to twelve, but it's not something I got from my family, who are all secular."

Helena describes her family life as largely "stable": her parents were married her whole childhood until after she had moved out, and they were always financially secure. But emotionally, she says, her life was "pretty unhealthy."

As an adult, Helena has been devoting a lot of time and energy into healing symptoms that she believes are associated with emotional neglect and emotional trauma.

"I definitely feel that my childhood relationships and experiences have played a big role in why I have developed lifelong struggles with depression, body image, and self-esteem," she told me.

When she was very little, she was cared for by a Polish family friend she called her "aunt." That family friend had to return home to Poland suddenly when Helena was around seven years old.

"I took this as a huge loss because she and I were very close, and around that age is when I started having emotional issues," Helena said.

From preschool to ninth grade, she went to a private Catholic school. Then she attended a public high school—Indian Hill High School.

"From the beginning, I had an antagonistic relationship with school because it felt like I was coming to a place every day to be judged (on completing schoolwork, getting graded, and fitting in socially) by people who never had to earn my respect (teachers and administrators)," she shared. "I felt the whole thing was belittling and it was very difficult for me to be motivated to complete schoolwork."

Helena says she "skated by with average grades" until her freshman year of high school. That's when her "emotional life tanked," as she described it.

"Ninth grade was when a big influx of new students entered the mix for high school, and I found myself not scheduled for classes with any of my friends and surrounded by new people, and I didn't adjust to this well at all," she told me. "I was also more of a late bloomer socially, so I was completely overwhelmed by the way everyone else was starting to talk about dating and partying and stuff like that. I just started isolating, skipping school, and eating lunch in the bathroom."

This was when her social media use, self-harm, and eating disorder began. But the only thing that her parents and teachers appeared concerned about during this time period, Helena says, was her bad grades—leading to parent–teacher meetings, detentions, suspension, and angry conversations with her parents.

All this made her hate her school, her teachers, and her parents—and she threw herself more deeply than ever into social media. She switched schools in tenth grade, when her parents realized something needed to change on account of her severe emotional issues, and she did slightly better in public school. But her grades were so bad that she almost didn't graduate.

"I still have a lot of anger and disdain for the entire concept of school that I'm trying to work through to see if higher education is something I would like to pursue," she shared.

Sometime in middle school, Helena was exposed to online pornography. The first time she encountered this content, through some "weird videos on YouTube," she was deeply emotionally affected and "felt anxious for days."

In her teenage years, she would find that pornography was highly prevalent on the social media platform Tumblr—"both in the form of real-life videos and drawings."

"I got desensitized to highly sexualized and deviant topics like kinks and I just assumed that normal sexuality consisted of things that I now know most normal healthy adults would never want to engage in to have a fulfilling intimate relationship," she explained. "To be stewing in all of this gross content at a time when I had never even flirted with somebody or come anywhere close to a real relationship seriously confused me and my relationship to my body, sex, romance, and my self-image.

"I think optimally people should learn about sexuality through their own age-appropriate experiences that gradually build up to an adult sex life, but what I experienced was in many ways the inverse, where my adult romantic life was delayed but I was introduced to very obscure and intense sexual themes at an age when I barely knew what the basic sex act was," Helena added. "I think this can have a damaging, if not traumatic effect on children/teens and their development process."[27]

Helena has devoted some serious thought to this topic. She dives into the rapid changes in pornography—and the role it played in her transition—in an explosive February 2022 Substack piece she wrote on her transition experience. Pornography use, she notes, has rapidly snowballed from the days of young boys peeking at the stash of dirty magazines on the sly.

Hundreds of millions of users are watching daily pornography and building up a "tolerance," she explains, a tolerance that blocks them from feeling "sufficiently stimulated by scenarios that were once arousing."

That tolerance motivates them to seek even more extreme content.

Helena links the "ever-increasing normalization of pornography usage" by children and young people with an "unprecedented explosion in the number of children and teenagers identifying as transgender....

"As a young woman who both identified as transgender as a teen and grew up in a very online, pornography-influenced environment," Helena wrote, "I believe there is a profound connection between this new way of exploring sexuality and the identity confusion that we are seeing in so many young people today."[28]

Pretty much every detransitioner I spoke with was exposed to pornography at a very early age. It wasn't information they volunteered—in fact, they were surprised when I asked about it.

Prisha shared with me that she was exposed to pornography when she was around four or five years old at a friend's house, when her five-year-old friend discovered a pornographic DVD that her parents had stashed away and the girls watched the DVD together.

That DVD graphically depicted a woman performing oral sex on a man. In painfully childish terms, little Prisha would later describe the act to her mother as "a girl sucking on a penis like a pacifier."

I asked her how it affected her as a child.

"It fucked me up," she said, heavily.

As she continued to watch pornography throughout her formative years, Prisha saw women repeatedly, horribly mistreated.[29]

Much pornography depicts men spanking women, pulling their hair, slapping them, gagging them, choking them, and otherwise abusing them in sexual scenarios. Sometimes women are depicted being abused by multiple men. Hardcore and obscene pornography may show bestiality, women being raped, urinated on, or defecated on, multiple abusers hurting one woman, and much more.

A 2020 study found that 45 percent of Pornhub scenes included at least one act of physical aggression, that women were the target of that aggression in almost every single case, and that there were rarely repercussions for the aggression.[30]

And women are typically depicted as if they enjoy this treatment or are experiencing pleasure from it.[31]

Anti-pornography activists argue that this content promotes sexual violence and severely dehumanizes the consumer, who will desire more and more aggressive content to get the same rush as before. Leaders in the fight against sex trafficking have warned me that violence, obscenity, and child-related sexual fantasies in pornography prompt porn consumers to try to buy sex with sex-trafficking victims—and that these consumers may seek sexual experiences that are themselves dangerous and violent.[32]

There are also weighty concerns that the women who are being abused in these pornographic scenes may themselves be victims of sex trafficking or engaging in the scenes against their will.

It is important to note how many young people today are consuming pornography: 93 percent of boys and 62 percent of girls are exposed to pornography during their youth, according to a 2018 research summary on pornography and public health from the National Center on Sexual Exploitation. The summary found that 49 percent of college-aged males first encountered pornography before they reached their teens, and 64 percent of people between the ages of thirteen and twenty-four actively seek out porn at least once a week.[33]

The summary also found that pornography has significant negative effects on young people, including developmental impacts on the brain, poor emotional bonds with caregivers, viewing women as sex objects, sending sexually explicit images, risky sexual behavior, physical and sexual victimization, and the likelihood that they will go on to view animal and child porn (given that, if a young person begins viewing pornography at a young age and continues as they mature, they will continue to build up a tolerance and seek out more hardcore pornography).[34]

Prisha's consumption of pornography led her to stop "thinking women and sex were hot." She believes it messed with her understanding of womanhood, of sexuality, and of sex in general.[35]

Helena echoes that sentiment. "To girls who notice that this culture wants them to be sexual objects, who do not want to be sexually tortured but instead wish for loving intimate relationships, who do not want to rejoice in porn but are pressured into regurgitating how fantastic and progressive porn culture is, the very idea of being a 'woman' becomes repulsive," she reflects.

"Ideally, a girl should be able to explore sexual ideas in a safe way, when she's old enough to choose it herself, in ways and with people that are age appropriate for her," Helena added. "Today, that developmental pathway has been hijacked."[36]

In her middle teenage years, Prisha and her online girl friends would write fan fiction back and forth to one another (something that Prisha laughs at now, but that she said was fairly common in online circles). This included role-playing sexual scenarios in which Prisha and her friends wrote themselves as boys who had sex with one another. This was because, as she told me, the idea of having sex as a woman was too degrading.

"When you watch porn, they're so degraded, you know what I mean?" she said.

"Men seem to have sex for fun, or it seemed like that was the perspective, and women have sex happen to them," she added—similarly to how she was sexually harassed at school by her peers, and eventually raped.[37]

Chloe also believes porn played a role in leading her towards her transition. She was first exposed when she was around ten years old.

"I started using the internet at a pretty young age and because I had unrestricted access, I was involved in a lot of a lot of things online without being really monitored at all," she told me.

"It was only inevitable" that she was eventually exposed to sexual content.

"It did distort my view of my body and sex and how those things have to do with each other," according to Chloe. "And I feel like it did play a part in my body image issues."[38]

Most young girls have no desire to compete with pornography for male attention, Helena explains, not only because they are scared that violent intimacy might be demanded of them, but also because they feel inferior to the women who "seem to be thriving in the porn culture...

"Some end up feeling, as I did, that there is no way for a girl like them to be happy as a girl."[39]

CHAPTER 2

Encouragement

W hat happens if a young person feels discomfort in their body heading into puberty? Once upon a time, they might simply go through an uncomfortable period of life before maturing into their body and their emotions.

In the modern age, a young person who feels this way and seeks guidance on the internet (and then counseling in a therapist's office) is often told that there's a reason they don't fit in—they're gender dysphoric because they are in the wrong body.

Gender dysphoria is typically defined as the distress that a man or woman (or girl or boy) experiences when they have a disconnection between their internal sense of gender and their bodily or biological sex.[1] This distress used to be called gender identity disorder (GID), as Ryan Anderson notes in *When Harry Became Sally*, but was reclassified as gender dysphoria in 2013.[2]

Gender dysphoria is manifested in a "marked incongruence" between one's biological sex and one's sense of "expressed" or "experienced" "gender," a "strong desire" to get rid of "one's primary and/

or secondary sex characteristics" because of this incongruence, and to have the sex characteristics of the other gender, to be treated as the other gender, or to be the other gender (or else "some alternative gender").

That's according to the fifth edition of the *Diagnostic and Statistical Manual of Mental Disorders* (often referred to as the *DSM-5*), which notes that in order for a person to qualify for a gender dysphoria diagnosis, there must also be "clinically significant distress or impairment in social, occupational, or other important areas of functioning."

For children, the *DSM-5* defines gender dysphoria as marked incongruence between the child's "experienced/expressed gender" and their biological sex—or "assigned gender" as the *DSM-5* describes it—lasting at least six months.

That gender dysphoria may be manifested, under the *DSM-5* criteria, by, among other things, the child's expressing a strong desire to be another gender, saying that he or she is another gender, expressing a preference for toys or clothes of the opposite gender, or showing a "strong dislike" of his or her own sexual anatomy.[3]

Based upon stories that detransitioners are increasingly sharing, it would appear that a young person who is experiencing or is diagnosed with gender dysphoria and seeks help from professionals is almost always pushed towards transitioning. This typically begins with "social" transition (using the pronouns and names that match the sex they identify as) but may often lead to medical transition.

As you'll see from the true stories of the detransitioners interviewed in this book, these young people are typically told that they need to take action to treat their dysphoria. Medical professionals claim that transgender surgeries and hormones will drastically reduce the risk of depression and suicide for them.

Parents want what is best for their children. They will naturally shy away from the thought of dangerous or invasive surgeries, particularly for such an extraordinary purpose as attempting to change their child's biology. But if parents push back against this narrative, the inevitable response is a question that has only one right answer: "Would you rather have a dead daughter or a living son?"

Transition is presented to modern parents as the loving route, the affirming route, the route that provides a young person with "care"— and literally the only way to save their child's life.

And so, too many parents acquiesce.

There is a preliminary step here, however: the encouragement and affirmation the young person needs in order get to the point where they themselves are committed to transitioning and their parents are faced with the choice whether to "affirm" the transition. Where is this encouragement coming from?

Most often from social media, according to the detransitioners I spoke with. Snapchat, Instagram, Tumblr, Reddit—each platform offered a venue for them to connect with LGBTQ activists and trans-gender advocates eager to guide an impressionable young person towards transition.

This is exactly what happened to thirteen-year-old Prisha, who sought attention and solace online as she struggled to navigate her turbulent family situation and her lonely social life.

Social Media

Prisha

Prisha says she was mature for her age; she believes that the adult trials she was going through at home distanced her from her peers. So when she stumbled upon predatorial adults on the internet (who praised her and told her that her maturity made her fit to be intimate or share intimate information with an adult), their attention just "made sense" to her.

Her foray into the internet began with the pro-anorexia online community on Tumblr, largely filled with girls struggling with anorexia and centered on hating their bodies. At this point she was still struggling with her eating disorder.

That community pushed ideas like the "Ten Commandments of Anorexia," she said—ideas absurd to adults but attractive to susceptible troubled teens, who firmly believed that no one else understood what they were going through.

"If you aren't thin, you aren't attractive," reads one of these commandments. "Being thin is more important than being healthy," reads another. "Thou shalt not eat without feeling guilty," commands a third, and a fourth orders, "Thou shall not eat fattening food without punishing oneself afterwards."

Prisha sought community in these groups.

Desperately seeking to lose weight, she and other members of the pro-anorexia community would post naked "progress" pictures of themselves online to show each other how much weight they had lost. It wasn't until later on that Prisha realized she had been posting underage nudes on the internet.

"I didn't realize the magnitude of that," she told me sadly.

"I fell victim to two social contagions: I was at the tail end of the anorexia contagion," she explained, pointing to recent cultural shifts pushing back against anorexia and extreme dieting. "Anorexia is no longer popular and a social contagion because it is not being enabled by adults, shown in the media as a beautiful thing, etc. As anorexia died down, I went on to the transgender social contagion. I was just as impressionable.

"It was a social contagion," she said emphatically, almost emotionally, talking to me about her experience with anorexia. "And who is the demographic most victimized by social contagion? It's teenage girls. And of course there's a couple teenage boys and older people, but it's mostly teenage girls, the most impressionable, vulnerable demographic on earth. And how do we not see that with gender dysphoria and being trans?"[4]

The online transgender community wasn't too different from the pro-anorexia community, and in some ways they even overlapped, Prisha told me, so it wasn't long before Prisha found herself in this newly popular pro-trans online community—or rather, they "found me through the pro-anorexia community," as she said in her testimony before the South Carolina Senate in March 2023.[5]

"They encouraged me for every change I made and promised me that I was curing myself," she said.[6]

A lot of what they said really resonated with her. As she said to Kelsey Bolar of the Independent Women's Forum, they told her, "You're trans if…you hate your body, if you don't feel comfortable with it, if you want to be a different person."

"With everything I was going through," she told Bolar, "I thought that if I aligned my body with my brain or something like that, I would feel better."[7]

At this point she was around fifteen years old.

Just like the online pro-anorexia community, the pro-trans community had requirements and rules to follow. Members also posted photos to show each other how their bodies had changed—how much a girl's shoulders had grown and her body had masculinized from testosterone injections, for example.

When Prisha shared her mental struggles or physical ailments with her new online connections, she said they would insist, "These are symptoms that you are trans," or, "That's because you are trans."

Her Tumblr amassed followers pretty quickly. And those followers strongly affirmed her when she began asking about whether she was actually a boy.

We will mention "affirmation" a lot in this book. It goes far beyond just being emotionally supportive. In this context affirmation means, "YES, you are transgender. Anything that you need to do to transition is justifiable. Anyone who tells you otherwise hates you and wants you dead."

Prisha explains, "I started being love-bombed and worshiped and they started disconnecting me from my real-life community and family. They told me that anyone who didn't affirm me hated me and wanted me dead. And as a mentally ill person . . . you know, it all made sense."

Prisha was truly falling apart at this point: she describes herself as making everyone around her sad, being hardly able to walk around without blacking out because of her eating disorder, and being hospitalized for her inability to eat.

And both the medical professionals treating her and the trans community she was dabbling in were telling her that the root of all her problems was simple: she was born in the wrong body.

"They're like, if you're trans, you're going to be depressed and anorexic and suicidal," she explained. "They shoehorned all of my problems, the trans community and my doctors, into 'You're born in the wrong body.'"

Prisha began to believe it.

"I just wanted to be better, you know?" she told me. "And I thought, if I was just in the wrong body, of course, I wouldn't want to feed it. I thought that I wasn't being a girl right. So it meant I was a boy. I was being a girl wrong because I'm a boy."[8]

Helena

"The biggest influence on me was Tumblr."[9]

Helena also stumbled upon the world of social media at a young age. Sad and lonely, also struggling with an eating disorder, Helena says she was delighted to find a platform like Tumblr, filled with friendly "social outcasts" like herself.

"Finding a community of such like minded people felt amazing, and I quickly began spending nearly every waking moment on Tumblr or messaging some friend I had met on there," she says in the account of her transition and detransition published on Substack.[10]

For those of us who haven't spent time on Tumblr, the platform and its allure can be difficult to understand, particularly when it comes to the transgender and detransitioner communities.

Helena described it "as an all-day alternate reality escape from the real world," a culture or "a secluded island nation whose people rarely interact with the outside world, and thus have language, customs, hierarchy, and history that is entirely unique and at first incomprehensible to people from other nations visiting the island."

In what she titled "A Call-Out Post" on Tumblr, Helena wrote:

> We've all read *Lord of the Flies*, right? A bunch of tween boys get stranded on an island and all of their deepest, most repressed urges surface as they desperately attempt to organize and manage the tiny preteen society they've found themselves in. The novel ends in bloodshed, as the author theorizes that the immaturity, communication breakdown, and decision making difficulties one would find in a group of adolescent boys would create a chamber of destruction. How would it have ended differently, some have asked, if the story was one of a stranded group of girls? What would happen if every troubled, isolated, self-loathing, depressed, and emotionally overwrought teenage girl in the world wound up alone on an island?
>
> Tumblr. Tumblr would happen.[11]

As Helena encountered more and more woke content on Tumblr, she began to resent the characteristics that supposedly made her fall into the oppressor caste—"being white, 'cis', straight"—according to the hierarchy that her peers adhered to.

Gender ideology and a change of pronouns offered her an easy way out, she explains in her Substack piece: "Instantly you are transformed from an oppressing, entitled, evil, bigoted, selfish, disgusting cishet white scum into a valid trans person who deserves celebration and special coddling to make up for the marginalization and oppression you supposedly now face."

Helena had grown up playing with Barbies, using makeup, playing dress-up. She loved boys and described herself as "certified boy-crazy, but in the weird nerdy stalker way, not the actually dating boys way."

"I always had a crush on some boy I would never talk to, whether he was a celebrity, fictional character, or someone I just saw around at school," she says. "When I had a crush, it would utterly dominate my mind."

But real boys made Helena "painfully bashful." Like Prisha, she dove into intense fan fiction about boys, written by other young women, and she began to identify with these representations of men.

"The pairing being same sex seemed to give writers and readers the freedom to explore these characters and their relationships without being constricted by the norms that come with heterosexual dynamics," Helena explains.

This fan fiction about boys became a kind of "liminal space" where Helena felt she could explore the things that interested her about boys as well as "fantasies about relationships." And she could experience this all without the "pressure of interacting with real boys."[12]

Chloe

Chloe, struggling with understanding puberty, her femininity, and her rapidly maturing body, began searching for answers online. She was eleven years old when she made her first Instagram account.

"Little did I know that as soon as I made my first Instagram account at eleven, I would immediately be recommended, no, bombarded, with trans-identifying kids, unachievable body standards, and even softcore porn. I never stood a chance, because that was just the beginning."[13]

Chloe isn't the only young girl to be so negatively influenced by Instagram. For years Facebook, which owns Instagram, has been studying the effects that Instagram has on its users. The *Wall Street Journal* obtained a March 2020 slide presentation that let the cat out of the bag: Instagram and Facebook were aware they were harming young girls, but expanding their young base was vital to the company's growth.

"Thirty-two percent of teen girls said that when they felt bad about their bodies, Instagram made them feel worse," the researchers inside Instagram said in the slideshow. "Comparisons on Instagram can change how young women view and describe themselves...."

"We make body image issues worse for one in three teen girls," said one slide from 2019 that summarized research about teen girls experiencing body image issues. Another reported, "Teens blame Instagram for increases in the rate of anxiety and depression. This reaction was unprompted and consistent across all groups."

Worse: some teens were blaming their suicidal thoughts on Instagram, and the social media platform was aware of this. According to the *Wall Street Journal*, "13% of British users and 6% of American users traced the desire to kill themselves to Instagram."

Why is Instagram so harmful to young women? For starters, it offers users a million carefully curated, picture-perfect moments that give snapshots of only the highlights of other people's lives. But for a naïve, vulnerable young girl scrolling Instagram, those snapshots are what *she is supposed to be*. She's supposed to be that skinny, that charming, doted on by friends, with boys at her fingertips, a wardrobe full of designer clothes, and the ability to jet off to an envy-inducing vacation or concert at a moment's notice.

She doesn't take into account, or even begin to fathom, that each perfectly curated video or picture is merely one moment in another person's life full of struggles and challenges. But she is acutely aware that she wants what she sees. And that desire oftentimes leads to eating disorders, more scandalous ways of dressing, riskier photographs posted online, depression, unhealthy body image, and more.

Instagram's algorithms present a dangerous slippery slope for users who are on this path. The "Explore page," as the *Wall Street Journal* noted, "can send users deep into content that can be harmful." And Instagram caters that content to users—when you view one photo or video or Reel, Instagram is instantly ready to offer you many more in the exact same category.[14]

And that's not all: a *Wall Street Journal* investigation published in June 2023 found that Instagram "helps connect and promote a vast network of accounts openly devoted to the commission and purchase of underage-sex content"—a.k.a. pedophilia. The *Journal* found that Instagram enables searches of hashtags like #pedowhore and #preteensex that connect people with accounts that use these terms to advertise the sale of child-sex material (which violates federal law and Instagram owner Meta's rules).

Instagram assured the *Wall Street Journal* that it is taking steps to fight this pedophilic activity (the report in the *Journal*, which is well worth the read, suggests that Instagram has done an abysmal job at this, leaving many questions unanswered).[15]

There is a ton of content on Instagram promoting gender ideology and more and more transgender-promoting accounts that push transitioning, and it appears that algorithms on that platform may be pushing transgender material on users (as Instagram has been documented to be doing in the case of pedophilic content).[16] Apparently gender ideology isn't considered something that needs to be fought, at least not by Instagram. My press inquiries on this subject went unanswered.

Chloe was young. She was lonely. Confronted by online images of voluptuous adult women, she was confused and frightened. She didn't think she could ever be the kind of woman she was seeing online—confident, beautiful, perfectly sculpted, demure, and yet also sexually aggressive. After all, she was a kid, a kid going through an awkward but pivotal stage of life.

She was beginning to think that becoming a woman was not only undesirable but also unachievable. And she had never learned that the changes brought about by puberty are hard for everyone, boys and girls alike.

So Chloe began exploring transgenderism online, and she quickly found a variety of LGBTQ groups and transgender influencers. These people were praising and glorifying individuals who were going through gender transition in order to become the opposite sex. They were so brave! So courageous! They weren't afraid to be themselves!

And Chloe, lonely and craving this type of praise and social approbation, began to wonder if she herself was a boy.

She was still attracted to males and didn't have a significant interest in romantic relationships with girls. But Chloe was heavily influenced by these ideas she was finding online, and she began to abandon the idea that she could become the "voluptuous female" ideal she was seeing there, as her legal filings say.

"She perceived that she could never meet this voluptuous female standard, and she was strongly influenced by all the imagined negative connotations of being female. Consequently, this idea that she was a boy became very attractive to her."

She began engaging with the online LGBT groups and "came out" to some of her peers: she told them that she was actually a boy.

And, as she had hoped, Chloe received the support and praise that she was craving. This all happened before she was even twelve years old.[17]

I asked Chloe if there was anyone at her central California schools who was experimenting with transgender ideology when she first began to explore these ideas. She said no, and that none of her peers seemed interested in transitioning until about the time that she entered high school, a year or two into her medical-surgical transition.

"When I was in middle school, there wasn't anybody who identified as transgender," she said. "There was a girl I knew who was lesbian, who unfortunately has since transitioned in her sophomore year."

When Chloe began cutting her hair, dressing like a boy, sounding different, and just generally looking different, she said she got bullied a little bit.

"I mostly attribute this to having been in middle school," she said. "Kids between the ages of eleven and fourteen, they're not very nice...they're like, 'Well this kid's being weird. Gotta bully them in the trenches, right?' That's just how it goes."[18]

Chloe was twelve years old when, in May 2017, she wrote a letter to her parents saying that she wanted them to treat her as if she were a boy. She also wanted her parents to call her "Ky" or "Chi," she said.[19]

During an interview with my Daily Signal colleague Virginia Allen, Chloe shared what it was like to tell her parents that she wanted to undergo surgery to medically transition—a.k.a. remove her breasts.

"They were pretty surprised," she said. "They knew I was a tomboy, but I don't think any parent could really foresee that kind of thing, their kid saying that kind of thing. They wanted to support me, but they were also pretty cautious. They didn't understand why I was pushing so much for medically transitioning until after I got the gender dysphoria diagnosis when somebody on my medical team had told them that," she added.

Her parents were concerned. They were not convinced that treating Chloe as a boy was the best thing for her, and ultimately decided that they would seek the advice and guidance of medical professionals. So on June 2, 2017, Chloe's parents contacted her pediatric care provider and asked about counseling for their daughter.

The doctors never gave her parents any other options besides transitioning, Chloe said.

"When my dad asked, he asked what the regret rate looked like, and they gave him a figure of around 1% to 2%, if not less," she told Allen. "And they never talked about what would happen if I were to regret my transition and go back on that decision. They told them that if I wasn't affirmed in my identity and allowed to transition as I wanted, then I would be at risk of suicide," she added.

"So they were pretty much coerced into allowing this to happen."[20]

Chloe and her family are far from the only ones impacted by this claim—that youth identifying as trans are at a high risk of suicide if they don't get gender-affirming care.

This frequently made claim is based on research such as the 2014 study by the American Foundation for Suicide Prevention and the Williams Institute, which analyzed results from the National Transgender Discrimination Survey and found a 41 percent suicide rate among those who identify as transgender and gender-nonconforming.[21]

But some psychologists and psychiatrists have argued that the statistic is exaggerated and also that its dissemination might even encourage suicides, as The Daily Caller News Foundation's Laurel Duggan reported.

"Every suicide is a terrible tragedy, and we're all on the same page when it comes to protecting young people from any sort of suicidal thoughts or behavior," psychiatrist Dr. Miriam Grossman told Duggan. "But the transgender suicide rate is nowhere near what those other statistics are suggesting. Those are exaggerated, and there is such a thing as social contagion."

"There's an effect on people, especially on kids," Grossman added. "It makes an impression on you, and it can then influence your own thinking and your own behaviors. If you are questioning your gender, or you identify as transgender, and you keep hearing over and over and over again, 'These kids are killing themselves, these kids are thinking of killing themselves,' you're being placed in that category."[22]

And according to Dr. Alison Clayton, an Australian psychiatrist, the exaggeration of the suicide risk by activists and the media may literally be increasing the suicide risk for teens struggling with gender dysphoria.

"Excessive focus on an exaggerated suicide risk narrative by clinicians and the media may create a damaging…'self-fulfilling prophecy' effect," Clayton explains, "whereby suicidality in these vulnerable youths may be further exacerbated."[23]

Therapists

Luka

Luka, who had been placed in a partial hospitalization program because of her struggles with mental health, said she had quite a few meetings with a therapist during that time period.

"I had expressed to her that I was uncomfortable with my body and I had seen stuff about questioning my gender," Luka explained.

The therapist encouraged Luka to communicate this to her parents, Luka told me, since the program wasn't equipped to handle this type of situation. So in a meeting with that same therapist, Luka told her parents that she had been questioning her gender.

Luka's family spoke with a number of medical professionals and therapists in the following weeks and years, and those professionals continually cited suicide statistics for transgender youth and warned her parents that failing to affirm Luka's gender dysphoria would lead to dire consequences.

As Luka told me, about her parents, "They couldn't really question anything." They were terrified. The predominant attitude from the therapists and medical professionals, according to Luka, was, "Would you rather have a dead daughter or a living son?"

That first therapist they talked to brought up suicide statistics merely as a cautionary note, the young woman believes. But further down the line into her transition, Luka told me, gender clinic workers clamored to urge her family to affirm her or face her untimely death.

"The gender-specific therapist and the people at the gender clinic, they were definitely the ones that used it," she said. "Almost an emotional blackmail thing."

Luka said she did three different sessions in the partial hospitalization program throughout her freshman year of high school. After that, she started going to a therapist that specialized in "gender-diverse children."

"She worked directly with the gender clinic," Luka explained.

After a long period of talking to therapists, Luka began to believe that the most effective options to make her feel better all involved medical interventions. She had been offered puberty blockers at one point, she said, but she had declined them since she was already fifteen or sixteen and didn't feel she needed them.

Her chest was the number one issue. Luka became convinced that if she no longer had breasts, she would feel better and be happy. And her therapist agreed that rather than follow normal protocol for so-called gender transitions, in which the person seeking a transition takes hormones for a period of time before surgery, Luka could just skip that step and get her breasts removed.

"So from there, she wrote the letter for that," Luka said.

"I was just very uncomfortable, in a normal, teenage way, with my body at the time," Luka shared thoughtfully. "I didn't like going bra shopping. I didn't feel all that comfortable with how I was growing. And then there was definitely an aspect of just not wanting to have to deal with the sexualization that comes with that."

And having been preyed upon earlier in her life, Luka believed that if she didn't have breasts, she would no longer have to worry about that happening again.

"There was definitely evidence of me truly believing I wanted this because it was the option I was given, like, 'this will help,' and I wasn't really given any other path to go down," Luka explained. "But I also had several other mental health issues going on. I had really bad depression and anxiety. I was dealing with ADHD, I was medicated at the time for depression and anxiety. Throughout this whole time, I was on several different medications, switching around."

Her surgery had to be rescheduled so that it wouldn't interfere with her spring break, Luka said. She had one meeting with the gender clinic, to get her in the system, and then she had one meeting with the surgeon before the actual surgery.[24]

Prisha

As soon as Prisha decided she was trans, she was incredibly relieved. She had been told that she had solved every problem—that she had the cure.

"I was like OK, that's it. I was born in the wrong body. I just need to align my mind and my body and I won't want to die anymore," she said. "Step one is hormones, step two is top surgery, step three is hysterectomy, step four is bottom surgery. I was ready."

And the online trans community told her everything she needed to do: letters of recommendation, a therapist, how to legally change her name.

Her parents were understandably opposed to Prisha's plans to become a man. But Prisha wasn't too anxious to follow her mother's advice on this. And her father just wasn't quite sure what to do or make of the situation, so he told Prisha to see what professionals said.[25]

"Looking back," IWF's Bolar writes, "both parents say they were emotionally manipulated by therapists and doctors into supporting their daughter's medical transition—a position they now regret."[26]

She had already been going to therapy, and at her father's instructions, she Googled around and made an appointment with the first gender-affirming therapist that she came across. In an interview with Project Veritas, Prisha revealed that this therapist was Shana Gordon-Cole, a therapist who was working for Tree of Life Counseling in North Carolina at the time.[27]

Prisha told me: "That's what the trans people told me to do: If you get a WPATH-certified, affirmation-only therapist, you're good. You're set."[28]

Gordon-Cole did not respond to my requests for comment. She appears to have been scrubbed from Tree of Life Counseling's web pages,[29] and the organization similarly did not get back to me. Her name comes up on multiple different lists of recommended U.S. "gender therapists" who will assist biological women seeking testosterone, such as a Tumblr blog page titled "FTM Help Desk" where users post questions about transitioning.

"I am a Transgender Specialist/Therapist that serves the North Carolina Triad area since 2009," her description on that blog page reads. "I'm a Licensed Professional Counselor, Certified Rehabilitation Counselor, and a Certified Forensic Screener Evaluator. I provide therapy, referral letters for transgender CSH treatment and SRS, advocacy, training, supervision, consultation, and conference presentations on transgender issues/needs. I am a member of WPATH, GLBTIC, ACA, CRCC, NCBLPC, LPCANC, the International Foundation for Gender Education (IFGE), and the National Center for Transgender Equality (NCTE). I helped to bring a chapter of Transforming Family to the Triad area which I co-facilitate and help co-facilitate the Triad Gender Association meetings."[30]

According to Prisha's lawsuit, "As of some point in 2023, Gordon appeared to be no longer listed on the Tree of Life Counseling, PLLC website, but she was listed as that entity's registered agent on the North Carolina Secretary of State's website." Gordon-Cole is named (as "Shana Gordon") as a defendant in Prisha's lawsuit.[31]

As Prisha's legal Complaint explains, "The session was brief—lasting only minutes—but that was somehow long enough for Defendant Gordon to determine and tell Prisha that she was actually a boy and that changing her body to look more like a boy's body would solve her many psychological and mental health problems."

Gordon "provided a letter recommending Prisha for cross-sex hormones (i.e., testosterone injections) in furtherance of the deception that Prisha was a boy. Instead of showing an evaluation of Prisha's long-standing mental health and psychological issues, and the role gender dysphoria might play, the letter, which appears to be a boilerplate form letter, shows that Defendant Gordon assessed Prisha based solely on 'the requirements for cross-sex hormone therapy, under the guidelines of the "WPATH Standards of Care, 7 Edition."'"[32]

"On that very first appointment with Shana Gordon, she told me my projected path," Prisha explained to the Project Veritas team. "She said, 'You are going to get top surgery and bottom surgery because you need it to be aligned, and I will write you your letters of recommendation when you need them for the next one. Here's yours for hormones.'"[33]

Project Veritas published Prisha's surgery referral letter from the clinic, Tree of Life Counseling, in which the therapist refers to Prisha as "Charlie." This is the full text:

I am the outpatient mental health therapist currently working with Charlie (Abigail) Mosley (DOB 2/14/98). Charlie has been receiving weekly outpatient visits since October 14, 2014 to address his diagnosis of Gender Dysphoria, as well as Anorexia Nervosa and self injurious behavior linked to the primary diagnosis. He has regularly attended all weekly sessions with me, as well as with his previous counselor at Family Solutions, who left in August 2015, to pursue another job opportunity. During the sessions client has made significant progress, ceasing all restrictive eating behavior and self injury, as he has embarked on the gender transition process. It was found that these behaviors were a result of feeling that his physical body was incongruent with his mental self identification. He shared that he has felt like a boy since the age of 3 and began identifying as "Charlie" instead of "Abigail" at the age of 12. He began hormone therapy with his PCP on July 17, 2015, and has reported significant improvement in mood and functioning since then.

In preparation for a surgical transition, Charlie has researched his options extensively, both in medical journals and with peers in the transgender community. He has demonstrated an extensive knowledge of the process and I am confident that he is making this decision from a well informed place. I have also observed no undue influence or coercion from any one; indeed he is working hard against adversity from extended family to continue down the path he feels is best for him. With the help and support from his immediate family he has made a plan for his recovery, establishing a network of people that will be able to care for him as he recovers, and ensuring that his job will be waiting for him when he is back on his feet. I am hopeful that he will be able to continue forward on his path to self realization with the help of this procedure.[34]

Helena

Helena was spending all of her time online, in fantasy dreamlands. She reflects that this probably confused her young brain about what realities she was actually living in: "spending so much time in fantasy without building much of an identity through real social and life experiences can lead to the identity and fantasy elements becoming indistinguishable."[35]

And somewhere during this time period, she wrote, she began to perceive herself as transgender.

"My perception of myself as trans formed in the intersection between overwhelming emotional struggles, heavy fantasy, emotional and intellectual infatuation with males (real people, fictional characters, and the idea of males generally), fanfiction, social and ideological incentives to be trans, and insulation from experiences and perspectives that might have challenged the views I was developing about myself and the world," she explains.

She kept this newfound identity secret for a while, except in online spaces like Tumblr. She told a few of her school friends—"also avid Tumblr users, and all but one also identified as trans."

Helena cut her hair. She began wearing a breast binder that someone on Tumblr had gifted her. She began wearing baggy clothes that hid her body's feminine shape.

She didn't share any of this with her parents until she was a senior in high school.

"By this time, I fully identified as a 'trans boy,' wished I had a male body, and wanted to medically transition," she writes.

She had it all planned out, how she would tell her mother: she was planning on handing her a packet of transgender-promoting resources and information on why she needed to transition and what words and language her mother should begin using.

But one day Helena just blurted it out. "For some reason I still don't quite understand, on one gloomy day we were driving back from the grocery store and I just blurted it out mid conversation, telling her that I was going by a male name, male pronouns, and was going to transition," she says. "I immediately wanted to stuff my foot into my mouth, but it was too late, and the dead awkward silence was setting in. For what seemed like eternity, she drove in silence."

"No," Helena's mother finally responded. She added, staring straight at the road ahead of them: "No, I am not going to call you that. You are Helena and you are a girl."

They finished the drive in silence, Helena says. She didn't say anything in response to her mother other than a short comment to the effect of, "If you feel that way, I guess."

She still wanted her mother to read all the transgender-promoting resources that she had saved, so at school the next day she printed them all out. She stapled her "coming out" letter to the top of the packet, and after her mom had gone to bed, she slid the packet under her mother's door.

"The following day, I anxiously awaited speaking to her, wondering what she thought of all the articles," Helena writes. "Had they convinced her? They had to, right? I was showing her that experts clearly agreed that trans people like me are valid."

The packet was in the trash can when Helena got home from school. Helena describes herself as "distraught" at this, and incredibly anxious about how her mother would react when she got home.

"Would she yell at me?" Helena pondered. "What did she think of the packet? I wondered if she had already read 'transphobic' material that countered the articles I sent her. Hopefully she read my letter and could see past any transphobia and realize that this was the real me."

But her mother didn't yell. The two just avoided one another for several days, acting like nothing had happened. Several days blended into several months, until a "fateful confrontation" between the mother and daughter in the dairy aisle at Kroger.

Somehow they began arguing, Helena says, and the argument turned to whether Helena was actually transgender. Looking back, Helena believes her mother didn't understand that the underlying issue was that Helena believed she was part of the transgender identity group, not that Helena was suffering from repressed masculinity. "I don't understand why you can't just be a masculine woman," Helena's mother insisted.

"Because I'm not a masculine woman! I'm a trans boy!" she told her mother.

"Yelling and crying between us ensued, very classy for the middle of the dairy aisle at Kroger," Helena recalls. "She told me I had lost my mind and needed to see a psychiatrist. I told her she was a hateful person who wanted trans people to die. We went back to not talking much after that."

Her mom's reaction left Helena "heartbroken" and distraught that her mother wouldn't cooperate with what she wanted.

Helena, who was attending high school at the time, writes that she went to her school guidance counselor and said that she was incredibly depressed because her parents were not accepting her as transgender (though Helena had not yet spoken to her father about the matter).[36]

She can't remember this guidance counselor's name, though she recalls it as a "very unusual name."

"Honestly, I was so emotionally unstable and out of it at this time that I don't remember many details like that at all," she told me.[37]

That school guidance counselor "completely affirmed" Helena's perceptions of herself, Helena writes. What is more, the counselor began prepping Helena to begin a gender transition without her parents' knowledge or consent.

"She looked online with me at the local children's hospital gender clinic and said she would call to see how long their waiting list was," Helena explained. "We also came up with a budget plan for how I would pay for testosterone using an informed consent clinic if I waited until I turned eighteen."

"In the meantime, she said I should talk to the school psychologist to help me deal with my family being so transphobic," Helena continued. "I asked my mom if I could stop seeing the therapist I had been seeing occasionally and switch to the school psychologist. My mom, having no idea that the school was affirming me and helping me put together plans to transition behind her back, agreed."

The school psychologist that Helena began seeing was also very affirming of Helena's new ideas about herself.

And Helena was grateful to suddenly have adults taking an interest in her mental struggles: "It was just further proof to me that being trans was my ticket to happiness, anybody who urged caution only wanted to hurt me and hold me back."

Confident that the psychologist was on her side, Helena agreed to a family counseling session with her mother. During that session, the "therapist and I all but ganged up on my mom, telling her that I needed to transition to be happy, and that trans youth are at a high risk of suicide if they are not given 'access' to hormones and surgeries."

"Predictably," adds Helena, "my mom did not respond well and we both left the session feeling bitter."

Soon after this, Helena's father communicated to her that though he did not think she was a boy, he would not fight her on the matter. He then offered to help her learn to drive stick shift.

Helena muses that her father may have been trying to show her that she did not need to be trans to be masculine or manly, but his efforts fell short.

"It was this weird belief system I found on the internet that made me want to be trans, not a repressed yearning to do 'guy things,'" Helena said. "I had never been all that interested in 'guy things.' My dad and I didn't talk about it much other than that."

She began dressing like a boy in preparation to begin taking testosterone, and in July of that year, Helena turned eighteen years old. As a legal adult, she no longer needed her parents' permission to get testosterone.[38]

Chloe

On June 13, 2017, Chloe and her parents had a preliminary consultation with a psychologist.

That psychologist, according to the complaint in Chloe's lawsuit, immediately affirmed Chloe's diagnosis—that she was a boy born into a girl's body.

So Chloe began her social transition—presenting as a boy in public.

She had a variety of visits with mental health providers following this first meeting, according to her lawsuit. In these she described feeling anxious, depressed, socially anxious, shy, lonely with limited friends, and more. She also expressed that she was feeling disgusted with her hips, her thin arms, and her chest, and had "a desire to bind her breasts that were growing larger."[39]

For those unfamiliar with chest binding, it is a process in which a biological female compresses her breast tissue to make herself look more flat-chested, more like a man.

Even transgender-promoting sites are open about the fact that chest binding is risky. "Binding using ace bandages, duct tape, or plastic wrap can be dangerous and harmful to your body," FOLX Health warns. "These materials are meant to constrict and constrain, which can restrict both movement and breathing or even cut into your skin and break ribs."[40]

According to the McLean Clinic, which describes itself as "one of the leading providers of gender-affirming surgery,"[41] chest binding can result in compressed and broken ribs (permanently damaging small blood vessels, causing blood flow problems and increasing the risk of blood clots), collapsed lungs, back problems, and further problems from these complications down the line.

The clinic cautions those binding their chests to be on the lookout for loss of breath, pain throughout the back or shoulders, increased pain or pressure with deep breaths, and more—particularly since these things "may stop you from being able to move forward with surgery."[42]

In spite of these risks, these transgender-promoting sites still frame chest binding as helpful and affirming to women or girls with gender dysphoria.[43]

And according to Chloe's lawsuit, her mental health providers agreed that binding could be helpful to her—without warning her that the practice has health risks.

Her serious comorbidities were also not discussed, Chloe's legal complaint says. But they didn't go away. Her symptoms "persisted and intensified."

"It was as though her providers believed that once the criteria for gender dysphoria were met, there was nothing to do but put her on the chemical/surgical path," her filings say.

"Thus, they failed to afford her the opportunity that any other child with psychiatric symptoms would be given: thorough evaluation, appreciation of her developmental history, and an opportunity to treat the symptoms through understanding within a trusted extensive relationship with one qualified psychotherapist."

On November 30, 2017, Chloe first met with an endocrinologist. That endocrinologist advised Chloe against beginning hormone treatment (taking testosterone) because of Chloe's age.[44]

She was, after all, a little girl.

But Chloe and her parents sought a second opinion.

CHAPTER 3

Getting the Hormones

The now prevalent "informed consent" model allows patients seeking hormones to merely go over the physical and psychological benefits, limitations, and risks to taking hormones. The patient then signs a consent form and can move forward.

According to Johns Hopkins physician Jill Crank, the informed consent model "moves away from the need for a qualified mental health care provider to 'verify' someone's gender dysphoria" before that person begins hormone treatment. It's a "less burdensome experience for patients," she says, warning that delaying hormone treatment may worsen a person's gender dysphoria.[1]

Helena, who obtained her testosterone prescriptions through such an informed consent model, says that there is no "therapy, psychological screening," or in her case, "even physical health screening involved in the informed consent model."

"At most, a provider could decline a candidate for some reason at their personal discretion," she has written.

"Informed consent is now the most popular method of distributing cross sex hormones and surgeries to people old enough to give medical consent in their state of the US today," Helena adds. "There are even online telehealth services that will ship you hormones so you don't even have to leave your house to get them. Don't you love innovation?"[2]

It used to be much harder to get hormones—at least, hormones intended to change your sex.

Dr. Crank explains that when she began her career as a nurse practitioner in 2007, "the process for an adult to access gender affirming hormones was more involved than it is now. First, a person would meet with a mental health care provider and receive a referral letter." According to the Johns Hopkins physician, "The letter would indicate that the provider had interviewed the patient and determined that they met diagnostic criteria and understood the risks and benefits of hormone therapy."

After this, Crank says, the patient would take the letter from the mental health care provider to a prescribing provider to begin getting their hormones. But that letter-review process might present "financial and logistical challenges," she points out.

"It was also seen as an unnecessary hoop to jump through to prove someone identified as a different gender than their sex assigned at birth," says Crank. "As a result of this requirement, many patients had to delay a crucial step in their transition process, which often worsened their gender dysphoria."

It is this claim—that slowing down the transition process worsens gender dysphoria—that appears to have led to the informed consent model.

Activists like "transfeminine" University of Toronto Faculty of Law doctoral student Florence Ashley, who has authored a number of academic pieces on the topic, claim that slowing down the process with the former cumbersome requirements is "dehumanising."

According to Ashley, simply telling a physician that one has gender dysphoria, combined with an informed consent process, "should suffice to obtain a prescription since gender dysphoria is distress or discomfort towards those very features that people seeking HRT want to change."[3]

But it would seem that speeding up the process with the informed consent model enables many people, often young people, to access hormonal treatments far too easily. Many detransitioners have publicly shared, often emotionally, that medical health professionals skimmed over their severe mental health issues and suggested that hormones and surgery would fix it all.

It is worth noting that I repeatedly sought to speak with Johns Hopkins medical professionals for this book. I specifically asked to discuss the institution's informed consent model in order to provide the most accurate information possible. Johns Hopkins staff repeatedly told me that they would not, or were unwilling to, speak with me on this topic. "Sorry we're not able to help with this request," I was told.

I reached out to a number of other institutions, widely regarded as prestigious, asking about their informed consent models for "gender affirmation procedures." Vanderbilt University Medical Center, the University of Oklahoma's OU Health, the University of Minnesota's Sexual and Gender Health Clinic, and the Transgender Health Program at University of Utah Health did not even dignify my press inquiries with a response.

Why? They did not specify. Perhaps it was because they distrust me or the news outlet that I write for. That is certainly their prerogative. But the medical professionals performing and pushing these surgeries should have to answer to someone.

Helena

Helena drove herself from Cincinnati to a Chicago-area Planned Parenthood, the Elizabeth Cohn Morris Health Center. It was August 15, 2016.

Her goal: go home with testosterone.

"I decided that what I needed to do for myself was to go on testosterone and start transitioning," Helena told me. "I had kind of this fantasy in my head that I was going to transform into this cute boy and be really popular. Very not realistic."[4]

Since there didn't seem to be any "informed consent" clinics in her area, Helena had taken the advice of her Tumblr friends and looked into which Planned Parenthood clinics offered hormones.

"The closest location to me offering informed consent HRT (hormone replacement therapy) was all the way in Chicago, a six-hour drive from my home town," she wrote in her Substack piece. "I figured I could tell my parents I was out with friends and would make the drives to and from Chicago in one day. I had only gotten my driver's license a few months before, and had never attempted such a long drive," Helena added. "On the drive back, I got caught in a terrifying thunderstorm so bad that I couldn't see 10 feet in front of me and the winds were shaking my car. Now that I'm older and have done many long drives, I recognize this was a stupid thing to do. But I was doing a lot of stupid things."[5]

During the summer of 2022, I wrote about Helena's experience getting testosterone.[6] I repeatedly asked that particular Chicago-area Planned Parenthood and the umbrella organization Planned Parenthood of Illinois to discuss Helena's experience with me.

Neither would address Helena's story specifically, but Planned Parenthood of Illinois assured me that it "provides high-quality health care and adheres to all local, state and federal regulations for our sexual and reproductive health services, including gender-affirming care."

Planned Parenthood, commonly known for the large number of abortions it performs (it has long been "the nation's largest" provider),[7] began offering "transgender hormone therapy" as far back as 2013. That's according to remarks made by former Planned Parenthood director of health media Elizabeth Clark.[8]

Planned Parenthood offers estrogen and "anti-androgen hormone therapy," testosterone hormone therapy, and puberty blockers throughout the country.[9]

According to the abortion giant's local affiliates, it is not hard to obtain these hormone drugs from Planned Parenthood. Planned Parenthood of Illinois promises that staff "want to affirm you at every step of the process,"[10] while the California-based Planned Parenthood Mar Monte notes that "most people are able to get a hormone prescription at the end of their first visit with us."[11]

As NPR reported in August 2022, "Over 35,000 of Planned Parenthood's patients nationwide" sought estrogen or testosterone in 2021.[12] That report was based on an interview with Dr. Bhavik Kumar, the medical director of primary and transgender care at Planned Parenthood Gulf Coast. Kumar revealed the statistics in an attempt to explain how the overturn of *Roe v. Wade* would adversely affect people who identify as transgender.

But aside from that information, Planned Parenthood would appear to be playing these numbers close to the chest.

The website of Planned Parenthood of Central and Western New York formerly stated that "nationally, Planned Parenthood is the second largest provider of Gender Affirming Hormone Care."[13] That language has since been removed (and Planned Parenthood did not respond to my requests for clarification on this point).

In its 2019–2020 annual report, as Heritage Foundation scholar Melanie Israel notes, Planned Parenthood stated that it operates "more than 200 health centers in 31 states providing hormone therapy for transgender patients."[14]

"It's possible they're the largest provider of trans health in the country," Mara Keisling, executive director of the National Center for Transgender Equality, told The Daily Beast in February of 2022, at which point she estimated that about sixty-five Planned Parenthood locations were offering transgender treatments.

"We don't know for sure," she added. "But it's certainly among the biggest, if not *the* biggest."[15]

Planned Parenthood's 2021–2022 annual report (the most recent, as of this writing), released in 2023, says that forty-one Planned Parenthood affiliates provide "gender-affirming hormone therapy." Interestingly, that report only mentions "gender-affirming" services twice, and it lists transgender services under "other procedures."[16]

It is not immediately clear how much money Planned Parenthood makes from offering hormones, or how many patients the abortion giant has prescribed hormones to. I asked repeatedly, but Planned Parenthood did not reveal this information.

Regardless, the vast number of Planned Parenthood locations throughout the country means that the hormonal side of "gender-affirming care" is much more readily available than one might guess. Advocates of transgender hormone treatments have considered this fact and regard it as a net positive.

"The thing about Planned Parenthood is that there are clinics all over the place," the National Center for Transgender Equality's Keisling told The Daily Beast. "There are clinics in lots of less urban places. So having a nationwide network of these clinics is extremely helpful. It means there's a Planned Parenthood near you."[17]

Helena has thoroughly discussed and documented her journey through transition. Screenshots of the social work intake form that she filled out at the Chicago-area Planned Parenthood paint a very stark picture of an isolated young girl, just days before she leaves for college to study biochemistry, preparing to make a life-altering decision.

"Any young person, teenager, or young adult who maybe doesn't fit in or just feels insecure is really vulnerable to getting caught up in this gender ideology," Helena told me. "Pretty much any safeguard or selection process or screening process or anything like that, it's all kind of been taken down in the last couple of years.

"There's really nothing protecting a young person who decides they're trans and then two weeks later wants to go on hormones or wants to get a surgery or something like that," she added. "I think most people who aren't familiar with this topic really don't understand how urgent it's becoming."[18]

The Planned Parenthood social worker who filled out the form referred to Helena using male pronouns, as Helena preferred at the time.

"Patient was well versed and knowledgeable about hormone therapy," wrote a staffer (Helena does not remember who this staffer was). "Patient reports that he has thought about using hormones for some time, especially the last 2 years. Patient states that turning 18 is why he was unable to start the process."

As the staffer noted, "Patient states that he is 'out to everyone' and identifies as trans. Patient states that he has told one friend about starting hormones and is also connected to online communities for support."

The intake forms reflect the fact that Helena's family did not support her desire to transition and refused to call her by her preferred name or pronouns at home. But Helena, according to the form, told the Planned Parenthood staffer that she thought her family would come around once they saw how happy she was with a transition.

"Patient states that he is 100% confident that he will get top surgery in the future," the form continues. "Patient states that he has considered some facial masculinization work as well, but states that he wants to see what the hormones will do first. Patient states that he would consider bottom surgery if the options that he would like for a penis became available, but he is not interested with the current options."[19]

The form also states that a general screening found Helena capable of making informed consent for the treatment—at least according to the standards set by the clinic at the time.

The record of her general screening is stunning: the form contains the information that Helena had experienced suicidal thoughts only two weeks before. But the clinic nevertheless found her capable of giving her informed consent, noting that her depression was "significantly improving" since she had started to transition.

"Patient expects that his whole life will be quite different and he will be very happy when he starts to change," the consent form says.

According to Helena, the entire conversation with the social worker took about twenty minutes. She got her prescription for a three-month supply of testosterone from Planned Parenthood that very day, went to CVS and picked it up, then went back to the clinic. The staff at the Planned Parenthood clinic guided her through her first testosterone injection, she said.

She believes she paid around $200 or $250 for a three-month supply.

"The whole thing from the time I arrived at the clinic to the time I left to begin my drive back to Cincinnati took about an hour," she said.[20]

Both CVS and Walgreens will fill prescriptions for "gender affirming" hormones. Neither corporation would tell me how often or how many prescriptions they fill, or whether they are also filling prescriptions for puberty blockers like Lupron Depot.

"Thanks for reaching out, but we do not share prescription sales data," a CVS spokesman told me in June 2023.

But for years, both companies have received perfect scores on the Human Rights Campaign Foundation's Corporate Equality Index. CVS Pharmacy is owned by CVS Health, which also owns Aetna, a healthcare company that provides medical insurance. Aetna covers transgender surgeries, including breast augmentation for biological men, which it considers "medically necessary rather than cosmetic for transgender members."[21] And CVS Health openly promotes and implements gender ideology when it comes to its own employees.[22]

And in 2018, when an employee at a CVS pharmacy in Arizona refused to fill a hormone prescription for a biological male who identified as a transgender woman, CVS condemned the pharmacist's actions, saying the incident "does not reflect our values or our commitment to inclusion, nondiscrimination and the delivery of outstanding patient care"—despite the fact that CVS allows pharmacists to refuse to fill prescriptions for specific medications if doing so would violate their religious beliefs.[23]

Walgreens even went so far as to allow an LGBTQ clinic to begin operating inside one of its Dallas locations in June 2022. Kind Clinic, which is quietly tucked away in the back of the Oak Lawn Walgreens, offers free "gender-affirming care" to transgender patients as young as sixteen years old, as well as financial assistance for individuals seeking hormone treatment.

Clinic administrator Michael Carrillo told a local outlet that Kind Clinic hoped to take some of the attention "off of the type of clinic that it is" by putting it in a Walgreens.[24]

Hiding a transgender clinic in the back of a Walgreens drugstore is an interesting move, particularly since the individuals who go to that clinic looking for testosterone can likely get their prescriptions filled at that very same Walgreens.

When I called the Oak Lawn Walgreens and asked if they filled prescriptions from Kind Clinic, I was told that yes, they most certainly do. When I inquired if I could get a prescription for testosterone from Kind Clinic filled, the pharmacist I spoke with repeatedly said that they could likely get me testosterone within fifteen minutes of the Kind Clinic sending them the request. Walgreens would not address whether it sees a conflict of interest.

Since those who are seeking "gender-affirming" hormone treatment often have to get their prescription filled at a pharmacy, it would make sense that pharmaceutical corporations would have a vested interest in not ruffling any feathers on that front.

A study published in *Transgender Health* in 2019 notes: "Pharmacists play a key role in the health care needs of [transgender] persons," and adds, "the pharmacy's physical environment, staff training, and policies and procedures can offer unique services to [transgender] persons."[25]

Pharmacies are not the only places to get hormones, however. Websites like FOLX Health and Plume offer to help customers do it all virtually. Plume boasts of being "the largest virtual clinic for transgender, nonbinary, and gender non-conforming people in the world."[26] FOLX promises virtual consultations and gender-affirming care to all patients.

FOLX promises to discreetly ship hormones to your door, as well as send automated prescription refills and lab reminders. As of September 2023, FOLX's website states that biologically female patients can get testosterone shipped to their homes every ninety days for $94 (they'll pay more if they want testosterone gel as well).[27] Biologically male patients can get oral estradiol shipped to them every ninety days for between $45 and $90. These men will pay more if they want injectable estrogen (between $214 and $372 every ninety days) and even more if they want an estrogen patch ($175 to $582).[28]

How long does FOLX expect users to use their products? They wouldn't tell me. But considering that trans-identifying individuals need to continue taking hormones for the duration of their lives,[29] it may be that FOLX figures on maintaining customers until they are in the grave.

In June 2023, a former producer for *Tucker Carlson Tonight* went undercover for The Daily Wire. Gregg Re says he used the fake legal name "Chelsea Bussey" on his intake form with Plume. And without even attempting to pass as a woman, according to The Daily Wire, Gregg obtained a letter of approval from Plume necessary for insurance companies to cover the medical expenses for a surgical sex-change procedure.

Matt Walsh, who led and publicized the exposé, slammed the standards of care employed by "gender-affirming care" practitioners as well as the insurance approval process. Walsh warned that there's "big money" behind the processes for obtaining trans surgeries.

Video footage that the Daily Wire host posted shows Gregg in an apparent FaceTime video interview with an alleged nurse practitioner who worked for Plume, whose name and face were blurred out for privacy reasons. Though Gregg stated that he had never experienced gender dysphoria for six months or more (meaning, under the current version of the *Diagnostic and Statistical Manual of Mental Disorders*, that he doesn't have gender dysphoria), Plume allegedly scheduled him for a video interview anyway.[30]

Plume hasn't answered my requests for comment.

"He didn't even attempt to pass," Walsh said. "He badly mispronounced the name of the surgery he wanted. He made it clear he didn't know what effect the surgery would have. Nevertheless, Plume's nurse practitioner said she wanted to write the most 'solid' letter possible to justify surgery. Gregg tells her that he once wrote an essay in school about being a woman, which everyone thought was ridiculous."

Walsh continued, "Gregg also tells Plume's nurse practitioner that his father has been prescribing him hormones for years. The nurse doesn't question this in any way. Instead, she says that arrangement is 'perfect.'"

Three days later, Gregg got a letter addressed to Chelsea Bussey from Plume. That letter said that Chelsea Bussey was experiencing "significant, ongoing gender dysphoria"—and it recommended him for testicle removal. The letter also notes that since Plume operates on a virtual basis, Gregg would need to first see his "primary care provider or surgeon" for a "pre-operative risk assessment or for post-operative care."

That same Daily Wire exposé highlighted something else concerning about FOLX, the transgender organization providing "gender-affirming care" over the internet.[31]

FOLX explains that they may write you a referral letter including information that "may not be specific to you. For example, they may use a gender dysphoria diagnosis, but you really do not have dysphoria, even if you want top surgery," the website says.[32]

Why? So that insurers will pay up, as FOLX explains: "Even if some of the details are not as specific to you and your situation as you would like, it may be more helpful to understand some of the 'whys' behind including such information for coding and or payment requirements. Be aware providers can use different versions of letter templates to meet these requirements."

It's hard to read this as anything but a scheme to get insurance companies to pay for surgeries that don't meet their criteria.

Walsh scathingly critiqued the process in a now viral thread, calling FOLX's operations a "scam" that "is the cutting-edge of 'trans healthcare.'" As he noted, "After launching just a couple of years ago, Plume now operates in 41 states. Folx is in 47 states. How is it possible they've expanded so quickly?"[33]

FOLX also has not responded to my requests for comment.

Helena didn't know any of this, of course. She just knew she could get hormones through Planned Parenthood, and she did. When she later refilled her prescriptions, she switched to a new clinic—Chicago Women's Health Center, which she described as "another place like Planned Parenthood where they do a bunch of abortions and then give girls testosterone."

Most of the Chicago Women's Health Center nurses were transgender themselves, Helena noted. She says she liked that clinic because it was even more "woke" than the Planned Parenthood one, and she had made a trans-identifying friend who was also using it.[34]

This center, which did not respond to my requests for comment, offers hormones to individuals aged eighteen or over (for patients younger than eighteen, Chicago Women's Health Center recommends Lurie Children's Hospital of Chicago's gender program).[35]

Chloe

According to Chloe's lawsuit, when she and her parents sought a second opinion, hoping to find a doctor that would prescribe Chloe the hormones and puberty blockers she thought she needed, California pediatric endocrinologist Lisa Taylor proved the woman for the job. (Taylor has not responded to my requests for comment.)

"Remarkably," Chloe's complaint says, "Dr. Taylor was willing to begin puberty blockers and testosterone treatment immediately, and with no proper evaluation or treatment of Choe's constellation of other symptoms."

Taylor allegedly prescribed Chloe both the puberty blocker Lupron Depot and testosterone, chemicals intended to stop the natural progression of Chloe's puberty and to medically induce other changes in her body that her lawsuit describes as "various endocrine disorders, including among others, hypogonadotropic hypogonadism."[36] (That's a condition in which the female ovaries or the male testes produce very little to no sex hormones, caused in Chloe's case by the lack of the normal hormones that stimulate the ovaries.)[37]

The puberty blocker that Chloe was prescribed, Lupron Depot or leuprolide acetate, is a gonadotropin-releasing hormone, also known as a GnRH agonist. Lupron has not been approved by the Food and Drug Administration (FDA) to treat gender dysphoria, FDA press officer Chanapa Tantibanchachai confirmed to me on March 21, 2023.

It *has* been approved for treating "precocious puberty, prostate and breast cancer, endometriosis, for use in in vitro fertilization, and to perform chemical castration on sex offenders," according to a FOIA request filed by American First Legal (AFL) in September 2022.[38] When the FDA refused to comply with the request, AFL sued, accusing the Biden administration of "illegally concealing records related to the off-label use of puberty blockers and cross-sex hormones on children."[39]

In July 2022, the FDA had added a warning to the labeling for these puberty blockers or GnRH agonists, warning that patients must be monitored for symptoms of pseudotumor cerebri, "including headache, papilledema, blurred or loss of vision, diplopia, pain behind the eye or pain with eye movement, tinnitus, dizziness and nausea."

Disturbingly, the FDA said it had identified six cases showing a link between GnRH agonist use and pseudotumor cerebri. All of these cases were biological females (the FDA called them "birth-assigned females") between the ages of five and twelve years old. One of these girls was undergoing treatment for "transgender care," the FDA said, while the other five were undergoing treatment for precocious puberty.

"The onset of pseudotumor cerebri symptoms ranged from three to 240 days after GnRH agonist initiation," the FDA warning said, describing symptoms such as visual disturbances, headaches or vomiting, and blood pressure increases.

But, the FDA said, there is not enough information available for the FDA to properly study this danger: "The incidence rate of pseudotumor cerebri associated with GnRH agonist use in pediatric patients could not be reliably established due to the small number of cases and data limitations."[40]

Chloe's lawyers allege that Dr. Taylor didn't obtain any informed consent form for Chloe's puberty blockers. And while Chloe was given an informed consent form for the testosterone treatment, her lawsuit alleges that that form failed to identify any of the risks that Chloe would face. Her lawsuit also contends that the limited informed consent discussions that took place "fell grossly short of properly advising Chloe and her parents of the relevant serious risks and perceived benefits."

But even if everything had been minutely explained to her, Chloe still doesn't think she would have been able to understand the full implications of what she was agreeing to—to go through menopausal symptoms, to have her reproductive organs atrophy as a teenager, and to risk losing the ability to ever carry her own child.

Chloe had never had sex. It was not until she was a junior in high school that she first imagined that she might want to have a romantic relationship with a man that could blossom into a family. She had never imagined raising children or considered whether she would want to breastfeed her own babies someday.

And the doctors and other medical health professionals that she dealt with hadn't tried to explain the significance of these things to Chloe, her lawsuit alleges. They didn't try to impress on her "the gravity of the life-long and devastating decision that she was making" as a minor, and they "falsely represented to Chloe that her symptoms would never resolve unless she transitioned and that she was at a high risk of suicide."

Chloe's parents were given an ultimatum: "Would you rather have a live son, or a dead daughter?"[41]

Prisha

When Prisha made that appointment with Shana Gordon-Cole, the Tree of Life therapist who billed herself as a transgender therapist, she attended the first session with her parents, who shared their experiences with Kelsey Bolar of the Independent Women's Forum.[42]

Gordon-Cole, a WPATH-certified gender specialist, quickly approved Prisha to see a doctor for testosterone hormones and affirmed to her that she was on the right path: Prisha was a transgender man and needed to begin her medical transition.

"The minute I said the word gender, they were all over me," Prisha told Bolar. "I was being medicalized so fast."[43]

She's not the first one to articulate this same experience, and she won't be the last.

Dr. Joseph Burgo, a clinical psychologist and the head of the Beyond Transition program at Genspect, said in an interview last year, "The moment you mention trans identity, everything else is forgotten."

"So, you could be suicidal," he said. "And if you announce you're trans, then all of a sudden transition becomes the focus of treatment and addressing all the other things that were going on before then just falls into the background. You see [this] all the time. Everything goes out the window once you identify as trans."[44]

"They often use this threat of suicidality or self-harm as an argument in favor of encouraging transition," he added. "The argument being that if you don't, this will, as you said, encourage their stress and will increase the likelihood that they'll commit suicide."

"That is not true," Burgo insisted. "There's no evidence to support that belief. And if you look at the actual data, this cohort has a high suicidality rate, and it starts beforehand, during and after transition. There's no evidence that gender-affirming transition actually reduces suicidality."

Prisha's mother Christine also spoke with Bolar about that short, ten- or twelve-minute meeting in which the therapist convinced her that her daughter needed to transition.

"Are you telling me that you believe my daughter is transgender?" Christine said she asked the therapist. "And she said, 'yes.'"

"We were emotionally manipulated," Christine said. "We weren't asked questions. We weren't referred to therapy. We weren't told anything other than, 'Here's a solution because she self-identifies as a boy, so go ahead and do it.'"

Prisha took the recommendation that she received from this therapist, for cross-sex hormones, to a doctor who just so happened to work in the very same clinic helping Prisha with her eating disorder, as Bolar reported. The doctor didn't seem to be interested in any correlation between Prisha's eating disorder and her gender dysphoria.

"You would think that they would maybe put two and two [together], that if the kid has body image [issues], that maybe testosterone's not the way to go," Christine told Bolar. "They didn't."

Prisha had begun to gain a little bit of weight back, and that caused her to get her period again. The weight gain made her upset.

"I thought that meant I was fat," she told Bolar. "And I told my [doctor] that I was uncomfortable with my periods, and that was the point in which I was put on testosterone."

Christine cried when the doctor prescribed her daughter testosterone. She told Bolar that she had a gut feeling that this wasn't the answer, and she asked the doctor whether she was positive that this was the right move for Prisha.

"Yes. Christine. Yes," the doctor allegedly told the distraught mother.[45]

Prisha had personally saved up some money for her transition by working at Panera and Teavana. Half of the cost of the mastectomy she put on CareCredit, which she tells me is like a medical credit card.[46]

CHAPTER 4

The Hormones Set In

Prisha

P risha began taking testosterone at age seventeen. She hadn't really finished puberty because of her eating disorder, she says, so the testosterone had "pretty extreme" effects on her bones, her muscles, and her frame.

And the effects were quick.

When Prisha shared her story with me, she warned that some of it was "TMI"—too much information. And it is true that many aspects of detransitioners' stories are neither for the faint of heart nor for family dinner table conversation. But it is important to hear them in their entirety to fully understand what these individuals have gone through.

One disturbing effect of testosterone is what trans activists call "bottom growth."

Guidance from the University of California at Los Angeles describes this as an ultimately permanent increase in the size of the clitoris that may take from one month to six months to fully kick in.[1]

Prisha experienced the effects within days.

"I felt pain in my genitals within three days," Prisha explained to me. The pain was so persistent that she couldn't "wear panties anymore."

She had known ahead of time that this would happen, but she had been told that it would be something that was "affirming." Prisha says the process had been presented to her as if her clitoris would be slowly turning into a penis. And she wanted to present as a male![2] (An infographic on the FOLX website, which makes it appear as if bottom growth will turn a woman's clitoris into a biological man's penis[3]—something it will not do—is a good example of the hopes that Prisha was buying into.)

"I was told it was a good thing," Prisha added. "And they told me, used language like it was my penis growing...."

"It's not like I have a penis or anything," she told me, trying to give an accurate idea of how the testosterone had ultimately changed her body. "It's just...a little bit bigger.... It's not in the head anymore...so there's nothing to protect it. It's very sensitive and painful."

The large online transgender clinic Plume acknowledges in a blog post that bottom growth may be disturbing for some people taking testosterone, admitting that it might even worsen their gender dysphoria. But Plume wants those scared of bottom growth to know that "you don't have to give up using gender-affirming hormone therapy. While not everyone needs or wants to take testosterone, those of us who do know that T is a life-saving medication," the post says. "Every person deserves to feel safe, comfortable, and affirmed. Testosterone can create the sensation of gender euphoria, which is the overwhelming joy that people experience when their gender expression matches their gender identity."

The post also emphasizes that "every medication has side effects, including testosterone," and that "some of these effects may be more desirable than others.... Unfortunately, it's not possible to pick and choose which of the side effects of T you will experience. That includes bottom growth," Plume admits. "Hormones work over a period of time, not overnight. Taking a higher dose of T will make your hormone levels higher and result in more pronounced changes."[4]

And FOLX, which recognizes that the many side effects of T may be scary and startling to gender-dysphoric individuals who are preparing to take it, promises, "Many people have the fear that they won't be attractive or that by transitioning, other people will no longer find them attractive or worthy. We are here to tell you that transgender and non-binary people are some of the hottest people we know."[5]

Now that she has detransitioned, Prisha doesn't have as much pain related to bottom growth. But she still endures discomfort from it, and she said that the testosterone's effects on her genitalia have made it difficult for her to have sex.[6]

In blog articles on bottom growth, FOLX acknowledges this side effect of taking testosterone for biological women can be painful, and more important, that this type of growth is largely not reversible. The transgender group also acknowledges, "Here's the hard truth. We don't have much clinical info about bottom growth for [those] on T."

According to FOLX, "Typical bottom growth on testosterone therapy is approximately 1 to 4 cm. One small study about bottom surgery reported the average length of bottom growth measured from 2.5 cm to 4 cm in the study participants who eventually underwent surgery. Another study found that at one year, the average growth was 4.6 cm....

"Whether or not bottom growth reverses after stopping testosterone depends on the person," FOLX claims, alongside an infographic of a biological woman's genitals growing from testosterone into what appears to be a male penis. "The standard advice is that bottom growth is not reversible once it starts. However, anecdotally, we have heard from people who weren't on T for a long time, were on low doses, or didn't have a large amount of growth, that bottom growth reverted completely (or almost entirely) after stopping T."[7]

Detransitioners who were formerly on testosterone describe a variety of other side effects that accompany the hormones. Some of the permanent ones, according to the UCLA guidance on testosterone for "gender affirmation," include the deepening of the voice, increased growth and thickness of body and facial hair, and hair loss on the scalp.[8]

Prisha formerly had a very high, operatic voice. Her favorite movie was *The Phantom of the Opera*, and she loved to sing the songs sometimes at "old folks' homes and hospitals." She used her voice, she told me, to bring joy to others.

But when she began taking the testosterone, Prisha became unable to hit high notes. Realizing this made her incredibly sad, but she was in heavy denial.

She continued to push forward with her transition.

Her voice started getting quieter and quieter. "I couldn't raise it anymore," she said. "It just kept changing the entire time I was on testosterone, which was about five years."

She has been off testosterone for about two years now, Prisha told me, and she has since done some voice training that has helped her slightly recover her voice. "I've gotten by really lucky but I can't sing anymore and I can't scream, which is a little scary because…God forbid I go travel somewhere or something and I get mugged, I can't scream."[9]

When she told me this, my heart sank for her. Most people have experienced nightmares where they are being chased or attacked, they open their mouths to scream, and nothing comes out. That is Prisha's reality.

The UCLA guidance also describes changes from testosterone that are likely not permanent. A biological woman who uses testosterone may find that her skin becomes more oily and coarse, for example, or that she has an increase in muscle mass and strength (depending on diet and exercise). Her body shape may change, with a decrease in fat around the hips and pelvis. She could have genital dryness, and her periods may stop.

"Depression and anxiety typically improve," the guidance says. "People often report fewer mood swings, and a feeling of being more 'removed' from emotions. Some people notice more irritability and are more easily annoyed. Occasionally people find these changes bothersome. Overall, most people have an improvement in mood as a result of the treatment."

The guidance doesn't mention the feelings of rage which multiple biologically female detransitioners described to me.[10] And the pro-trans organization FOLX Health claims it is a "myth" that testosterone makes you "angry or violent."[11]

It wasn't a myth for Prisha.

"My dad was having me chop wood outside, with an ax and everything, to get my anger out," Prisha told me. "Yeah, it was really bad."

But, believing that she was truly becoming a man, Prisha also initially got more confidence. She said she walked with her head higher and her shoulders straighter. "This is going to surprise you maybe, my sense of direction was better," Prisha told me. "And since I've been off it, I've lost it again. . . .

"It was nice," she admitted. "There were a lot of things that were affirming, you know? I thought that was because I was aligning myself in the right body."

Mentally, Prisha said, she was still suffering from the eating disorder. But suddenly she could eat. "The increase in appetite made me think I was cured of my eating disorder."

As she moved forward with her transition and continued taking testosterone, Prisha noticed that she was still suicidal and struggling with her mental health. But she attributed that to the fact that she hadn't had top surgery yet, or that she hadn't been on hormones long enough, or that she hadn't had a hysterectomy yet.

"I was like, I have to keep chasing, and chasing, and chasing, and then I'll be happy and then I'll be aligned, and then I'll be in the right body," she said.

She believed that getting a double mastectomy would make her less suicidal. "I was like, if I don't do this, I'm going to stay suicidal forever, or until I don't have the energy to fight it off anymore. That's what every day was like, I used to sleep twelve to sixteen hours a day because I needed to have the energy to not kill myself."

And, still struggling with her eating disorder, Prisha also realized with excitement that a mastectomy would mean that she would lose more weight.

She was eighteen when the surgeon removed her breasts forever.[12]

Helena

"When they tell you about testosterone, they mostly frame it as a cosmetic thing," Helena explains. "Sure, you might feel more irritable, you'll probably have a higher sex drive, and there is that whole thing about increased risk for heart disease and cancer, but for the most part it's all about fat redistribution and getting a deep, commanding voice."

Helena's "informed consent" document warned her about mood changes. "But," she wrote, "I don't know if anything would have prepared me for what it actually felt like."[13] Almost immediately she felt what others have described as a weird type of energy. Helena told me that she herself wouldn't describe it as energy as much as it was "kind of like restlessness."

She felt intensely different.

"My sex drive was incomparable to anything I'd ever experienced before," she said, with a rueful laugh. "It was really uncomfortable for me."[14]

During the first few months of taking testosterone, Helena says that she felt a "general feeling of suffocating numbness and inability to identify my emotions" accompanied by easily triggered "bouts of anger" and rage. "Something that before would have made me mostly sad, or even frustrated, made every cell in my body overflow with rage," she wrote on Substack. "The anger was also of a different quality than the kind of anger I experienced before. Previously, I might have gotten so angry that I cried, or yelled, or very occasionally slammed a door, but I rarely if ever felt much more of an urge to externalize it physically beyond that."

But on testosterone, Helena's anger "demanded to be externalized." "I felt like my body would explode if I couldn't hit or throw something, and this scared me," she explains. "Crying was no longer an option, at least at first, as crying was nearly impossible to achieve. When I was emotionally overwhelmed, instead of easily crying like before I would start to feel extremely angry, and instead of hitting others or anything in my surroundings, I resorted to hitting myself."[15]

Rather than cast blame on testosterone for such negative effects, FOLX Health instead suggests that increased anger may stem from "hangry"-ness.

And regarding what they call the "myth" that transitioners on testosterone often lose their ability to cry, FOLX says, "We all have a wide variety of emotions and processing styles that may or may not intersect with our gender expression. You might find it easier or harder to cry at various moments in your life depending on your emotional circumstances, your healing journey, or the world we live in."[16]

Helena reports that she would struggle against the anger by punching herself until she could cry from the pain, and then she would cry for hours. Often she'd fall asleep while crying and not remember much when she woke up.

She also believes that her testosterone injections caused her to experience huge emotional attacks: "I had these kinds of meltdowns about once a week or so, and regularly had bruises on my head and body from where I would hit myself."

In one of these episodes, in the summer of 2017, Helena hurt herself very seriously with a kitchen knife, prompting her roommate to persuade her to go to the emergency room at AMITA Health Saint Joseph Hospital Chicago. She was identifying as a transgender man at the time, and she believes she used the name Vincent Jaszczak (her mother's maiden name).

"I still, at this point, made no connection to the testosterone," she wrote on Substack, adding, of her roommate, "We both just thought I was a severely mentally ill person; even though I had never experienced anything remotely like this before testosterone (and never again since!)."[17]

AMITA Health Saint Joseph Hospital Chicago is a Catholic hospital that is supposed to abide by the United States Conference of Catholic Bishops' (USCCB) *Ethical and Religious Directives for Catholic Healthcare Services.*[18]

It is worth noting here that the Catholic Church is very black-and-white on gender and sexuality, teaching that God created only two genders, male and female, and that only men and women can and should get married since only between a man and woman can the sexual act be both unitive and procreative—producing children.

But until 2023, the bishops had not formulated moral and ethical guidelines for Catholic hospitals on what types of transgender affirmations and procedures the Catholic Church would condone. While the bishops stressed that every human person deserves to be treated with love and dignity, they also recognized that the times called for more specific instruction. And if Catholic hospitals were performing surgeries and dispensing "gender affirming" hormones, particularly to kids, this was a grave contradiction of Catholic teaching.

In March 2023, as the number of transitioning and detransitioning individuals became more and more high-profile, the bishops updated their directives for Catholic health care services to clarify that "Catholic health care services must not perform interventions, whether surgical or chemical, that aim to transform the sexual characteristics of a human body into those of the opposite sex or take part in the development of such procedures."[19]

And in June 2023, a Catholic organization named the Lepanto Institute released a report that found "the largest Catholic health system in the United States, CommonSpirit Health, is acting directly against Catholic moral teaching in direct defiance of its Catholic identity."[20]

It remains to be seen what will be done about such revelations—on June 16, 2023, the bishops voted to move forward with significant revisions that would make the Church's ethical position on Catholic hospitals facilitating sex-change attempts even more explicit.[21] By the time this book is published, it is likely that more steps will have been taken.

During the summer of 2022, I wrote about Helena's experience at AMITA Health Saint Joseph Hospital Chicago, and I repeatedly reached out to both AMITA Health Saint Joseph Hospital Chicago and the USCCB about the matter. Neither of them would acknowledge Helena's situation, and they still will not.[22]

As a nonmedical observer I assumed that *of course* the medical professionals at the hospital would routinely question Helena about her dosage and how it was affecting her when they found out she was taking testosterone.

Distressed girl gets checked into a hospital and there is a foreign substance in her body that she is regularly injecting? Seems like a no-brainer that they would ask her about whether the high dosage that she had started taking relatively recently was related to her extreme mental suffering.

According to Helena, they did no such thing.

She said the medical professionals at AMITA Health Saint Joseph Hospital Chicago who treated her not only didn't seem to care about the underlying cause of her distress (the testosterone), they also began medically treating her as though she were a biological man in emotional distress. All even though Helena says she listed on her intake form that she had been taking 100 milligrams of testosterone per week!

That decision to favor her stated gender over her actual biology is not surprising in light of the "very complex psychological" debate on gender identity that has permeated the medical world, Helena told me last summer. "It's an incredibly politically charged issue and you're at risk of being accused of discrimination or harassment or conversion therapy," she said. "I think it should be different. Gender identity stuff might be incredibly complex, but an 18-year-old girl on 100 milligrams of testosterone having meltdowns, that's not very complex."

Helena speculated that doctors and nurses may think "it's just not worth the risk" to broach these topics in a way that could harm their standing within the medical community. "It's just too dangerous for these providers who are really only going to be talking to these people for a week or so until they leave the hospital and they never see them again or don't see them until they come back to the hospital," she said. "I think it's more of an issue with psychiatry as a field and the way that these hospitals work."[23]

David Gortler, a former senior advisor to the Food and Drug Administration commissioner and current Ethics and Public Policy Center scholar, gave me a similar answer when I questioned him in the spring of 2023 as to why hospitals across the country are implementing gender ideology principles and diversity, equity, and inclusion recommendations from far-left organizations like the Human Rights Campaign.[24]

"Hospitals are no longer run by physicians following scientific evidence anymore," he told me. "Non-physician administrators outrank medical doctors in leadership hierarchy.... Hospitals are also too administrator heavy, affecting the practice of medicine."

Academia has the same problem, Gortler noted. Many of the people in academia and hospitals nowadays have irrelevant degrees, he suggested, and gain their positions through "H.R. departments, which are also fully saturated with leftists" that "keep hiring DEI people in order to force through unscientific policies."

And the new generation of physicians coming into hospitals are "fully pre-indoctrinated by the aforementioned medical school administrators," Gortler added. "It's a very pernicious way of altering the practice of medicine."

"These are the next generation of pharmacists, physicians, and nurses, and they're being taught to specifically ignore fundamentals of biology and data-driven findings," he emphasized. "They're not following what science is trying to tell us. That's a really bad problem."[25]

So instead of acknowledging the root cause of her problem—that she was a biological woman pumping herself full of testosterone—Helena says the medical professionals diagnosed her with borderline personality disorder, depression, and acute psychosis.

She also says they prescribed her four separate psychiatric medications.

"I was checked into the hospital psychiatric ward that night and remained for seven days," Helena wrote in her Substack piece. "There, no inquiry was made into my high testosterone dosage or whether it might have been having an impact on my behavior.... Upon my discharge, I dutifully took my prescribed medications and even felt validated by my being prescribed an 'anti-psychotic.' I was thankful that I had finally been diagnosed as severely mentally ill and given strong medications that would fix my faulty brain chemistry and allow me to live a better life."

Helena attended an outpatient group therapy program three times a week for the next few weeks, discussing "mindfulness" and how to manage mental illness. "But deeper psychological work was absent," she writes, "and once again the fact that I was a young biological female on a supraphysiological dosage of synthetic testosterone remained completely unaddressed."

Over and over again, Helena believes, medical professionals failed her by turning a blind eye to the root cause of her struggles. "Throughout every experience in any mental health treatment during my trans identification, my testosterone treatment was never identified as a potential source of mental health symptoms, and my desire to be a 'boy' was never questioned as possibly a result of pre-existing emotional issues," she wrote. "My 'preferred name and pronouns' were always used without hesitation or question, and I was 'affirmed' by every professional I saw during this time."

But Helena wasn't improving in the outpatient program. "I was still unemployed, using substances (including some of my prescribed medications), unable to get out of bed most days, talking about suicide in group, and having 'episodes,'" she says.

The psychiatrists and therapists in the outpatient program finally sat her down and told her she needed to go back to inpatient—partially because Helena had been sharing about her rage attacks (testosterone-induced rage attacks that she thought were psychotic episodes) and how she felt suicidal and hopeless.

"I did, and this time stayed for about half a week," she wrote. "When I got out, I decided these programs were not helping me and that once I unenrolled from them, I was going to get a different therapist (at the local LGBT center), get a job, and try making some friends...."

Sadly, she didn't really make friends until after she detransitioned, Helena said.

For the next six months, she worked in a cookie shop. The job involved long hours and late shifts, and she often didn't get home until the wee hours of the morning. But those late-night shifts gave her plenty of time to reflect. "Needless to say, this wasn't fantastic for my mental wellbeing either, but it's where some changes started to take place," she writes. "I started interacting with people regularly, and though I didn't make any long-term friends, it was helpful just to know some names and faces and be a fly on the wall listening to the drama in the lives of my coworkers."

One of her coworkers, who identified as transgender, told her about an organization that helped pay for transgender surgeries. That coworker even told Helena how to apply, but Helena kept putting it off. "Strange, considering I would publicly talk about how badly I wanted the surgery," she muses. "So I never got any surgeries, something for which I am extremely grateful."[26]

Luka

Luka's situation was a little different from that of the other girls in that she began hormone treatment *after* her surgery.

Luka had initially been very happy about the results of the surgery. And she was determined to continue her transition, taking testosterone injections because she believed they would help with it. At first her mom had to help her administer the testosterone shots in her stomach, but eventually she got to the point where she could do it herself.

"I just was not OK with needles," she explained. "I still don't like them, but eventually I got to the point where I was able to do it."

Her dosage varied over the four years that she was on testosterone, from around .25 milliliters to about 0.4 milliliters.

On the shots, Luka quickly noticed that her skin began to feel different. And then from there, more of the "typical testosterone changes" began to take place: her voice dropped, she grew more body hair, her weight began to redistribute around her body. "Since I took it young enough, I feel like I grew a little bit more, and my jawline broadened out a little bit," Luka said.

"I grew an Adam's apple, hairline pattern changed a little bit, it was easier to build muscle, just stuff like that for the most part."

Her shoulders also grew and widened some, she added, but she isn't 100 percent sure how much of that was the testosterone, since she hadn't stopped growing when she started taking it.

"So it's not like I have a good baseline to compare it to of what would have happened if I didn't," she shared.

The biggest emotional change was that, like Prisha and Helena, she was unable to cry.

"I just couldn't," Luka said. She didn't cry super easily before the hormones, she explained. "But when I was really sad or got hurt or something, I still would. Or if my dog died or something. But when I was on T that just did NOT happen."

Luka said that her sex drive was higher on the testosterone, though until recently she was also on SSRIs, which she thinks may have slightly canceled out this effect.

She also felt and expressed anger differently than she had before.

Her doctor and her parents had made the decision to put her on birth control when she was about thirteen years old. The thinking behind this decision, she said, was that birth control would get rid of her period. She was having panic attacks and trouble getting out of bed, and stopping her period would give her one less thing to worry about.

So before she began hormones, she didn't have a period. "Once I started [testosterone] I didn't have to take [birth control] anymore to stop it," she said. "In general, my reproductive organs just shut down.... I didn't get a period anymore."

A fundamental part of her reproductive system just stopped functioning.

"Ultimately, I still think it wasn't a great idea to give such a young teenager birth control to skip periods, but that's neither here nor there at this point," she told me.[27]

Luka is right—the latest research on the topic from Sweden's Uppsala University suggests that women who take birth control as teens may face much higher rates of depression compared to their peers who do not take birth control. Researchers also found that teenage users of contraceptive pills had an increased incidence of depression even after they stopped using the Pill.

Therese Johansson, one of the study's leading researchers and a Ph.D. student in the Department of Immunology, Genetics, and Pathology at Uppsala University, suggested in a June 2023 press release that "the powerful influence of contraceptive pills on teenagers can be ascribed to the hormonal changes caused by puberty."[28]

In the past, if you questioned birth control health risks, you were typically portrayed as a radical religious objector who didn't support women in the workforce. But now—perhaps as a result of the amount of time that some women had to consider and better understand their health as they spent time alone during the coronavirus pandemic—it has actually become trendy for girls on TikTok and Instagram to share how birth control was ruining their lives.

Many of these girls claim that birth control made them "ugly, fat and depressed,"[29] and say that the Pill changed their sexual preferences when it came to men and that they broke up with their boyfriends when they got off birth control.[30] (There's some basis for these viral claims—studies have found that birth control does affect your "partner preferences" in various ways.)[31]

But given the very recent overturn of *Roe v. Wade*, the topic is still highly political. And the medical community does not seem too concerned: in spring 2023, a panel of FDA advisors voted unanimously that the benefits of allowing women to obtain birth control without a prescription far outweigh the risks.[32]

The trend to question the effects of birth control aligns with a similar social media interest in "clean" food and non-toxic products like makeup and house cleaning supplies, as well as in natural methods of charting your monthly cycle. But so far, that trend to prefer the natural doesn't seem to be provoking people to ask questions about the pharmaceutical and surgical interventions involved in gender transition.

Chloe

When Chloe was thirteen years old, she began a puberty blocker and testosterone treatment. This was around January 2018, under the supervision of Dr. Lisa Taylor, according to her lawsuit.

But these chemical treatments didn't help her—if anything, they made her comorbidities worsen. Her mental health began to decline after several months of this chemical treatment, her legal filings state, causing her to experience "increasing anxiety, depression, and related issues."[33]

As she explained to me, "When I started the blockers, once all the hormones cleared out of my body, I started to feel kind of depressed. I was pretty low on energy a lot of the time. I was very lethargic, and I found it a little more difficult to focus in school."

"And I also started to experience hot flashes because it basically induced an artificial menopause," Chloe said. "Menopause is usually something that women start experiencing at around fifty to sixty, and I was going through this when I was thirteen."

When she got her first testosterone shot, she felt amazing.

"I finally had all my energy back. To me, it was a big milestone. I felt like I was becoming closer to this idea of myself that I had in my head. You could say that it was almost euphoric."

She had what she described as a "honeymoon period" for a bit, but then the testosterone began causing her some problems, both physically and emotionally.

"I started experiencing a lot more anxiety and just a lot more negative emotions in general, which I could attribute both to medically transitioning and socially transitioning," she said.

Then her appearance started to change. "My hair got thicker, my eyebrows got thicker, my jawline got sharper," Chloe said. "And I started to develop a lot more muscle. I started to become more squarish in my build, and I felt good about this."

In fact, Chloe didn't just feel good about her decision. "I felt great about this," she emphasized. "I felt like I looked great."

But even as she was starting to appear more and more like she was a young man, Chloe was still attracted to boys. This was confusing, and it really limited her dating pool, she told me.

Meanwhile, many of her friends were starting to date. "I was completely missing out on this, and this caused me a great deal of distress," Chloe said. She feels like she didn't get to develop socially by dating much. "I was really hard on myself about this. It was one of many factors, I would say, that contributed to my developing depression."

Socializing in general was becoming problematic for Chloe. People were beginning to view her as a guy and to treat her differently. And she started realizing how vastly different male relationships were from female ones.

"While it was nice to fit in with the boys, it was also considerably lonelier," she said. "I wasn't nearly as close with my friends as I used to be. Friendships between two males are a lot less intimate, a lot less comforting than the friendships between two females. And I learned that the hard way."

It became a lot more difficult for Chloe to regulate herself emotionally. And she began to develop some markedly negative physical side effects from the testosterone: urinary tract issues, including clots in her urine.

These were issues that would require her to go see a doctor who could treat a biological woman, and young Chloe found the situation baffling and frustrating.

"It was alarming, but I felt like I couldn't speak up because I was supposed to be a boy, but I would have to go to a women's gynecologist or a urologist for this issue because I was biologically female. And so I felt stifled in a lot of ways."[34]

As she was taking the cross-sex hormones, Chloe also "experienced a host of other significant and severe physical and mental sufferings" that her lawsuit describes, such as hot flashes and severe itching in random places on her body preventing her from wearing warm clothes in the winter. Sometimes when she was merely breathing, she would hear loud cracks in her neck and her back.

During this time period, Chloe also experienced an incident that deeply traumatized her: a boy at school, who Chloe says would often tease her and harass her, sexually assaulted her.[35]

That boy groped her breast in a classroom full of students, Chloe told me, and no one seemed to notice—or care. "That was the final straw," she said. "I was afraid of being sexually assaulted again...."

"I wanted this part of my body GONE," she told me. "And now it is. And it will be that way for the rest of my life, because I was allowed to make an adult decision as a traumatized fifteen-year-old."[36]

The experience was "earth-shattering" for Chloe, as her lawsuit says.[37] She was afraid to report the incident to the school administrators out of concern that the boy would just come back to school after a short suspension and continue to bother her.

"Growing up, I knew a lot of girls and women who had been sexually assaulted, or they were victims of rape or abuse. And hearing all the stories they had about that, I was terrified about that same thing eventually happening to me, and it did," she shared with me.

The groping incident "kind of just hit the nail in the coffin."

"That taught me that this part of me would only bring me pain and attention that I didn't want and I didn't want it on me," Chloe said sadly. "I didn't realize at the time just how much of a role it played in me eventually deciding to get a mastectomy, but by the time I did, it was far too late."[38]

Chloe was already transitioning at this point, and as her lawsuit details, it took her a couple of years to fully unpack the impact that this sexual assault had on her and on her decisions following the incident.

"She thought that she was already a 'boy' and that she just needed to 'man up,'" her legal complaint says. "But the truth is she was not a boy, and this was a deeply traumatic event that constituted a sexual assault. This exacerbated her fears, and further propelled her into the belief that she did not want to be female and that she needed to get rid of her breasts to protect herself from further such abuse."[39]

So the young girl started binding her breasts every day, trying to hide them from the world and from anyone else who might want to treat her in such a way. That painful practice, combined with the weekly testosterone injections, began to deform her breasts.

"It was tiring," she told my Daily Signal colleague Virginia Allen about the chest binder. "I got really sick of it quick. I would wear this thing for about 8 to 12 hours a day sometimes," she continued. "I would wear it basically whenever I was out of the house or whenever we had guests over. I'd wear it while I was on a run or working out or swimming. Sometimes I'd be walking home from school in 110 degrees."[40]

As Chloe said at the October 2022 End Child Mutilation rally in Nashville, "I wanted a way out. I wanted to stop wearing this binder, while going on runs, swimming, or walking home from school in 100-degree weather. I wanted to look more like boys my age, and most importantly, I wanted to avoid the sexual attention that came from having a visibly feminine chest."[41]

Chloe realized that her breasts were beginning to lose their form, and they disgusted her. As long as they were on her body, she thought no one would ever be attracted to her. So she told Dr. Taylor that she wanted to continue transitioning and get a double mastectomy. She was "naively thinking," as her lawsuit says, "that it would solve all her problems."

Taylor didn't ask Chloe about her underlying feelings about her breasts or why she wanted to proceed with the surgery, according to Chloe's lawsuit. The doctor "instead blithely affirmed this tragic decision" and provided fourteen-year-old Chloe with a referral for a plastic surgeon.

She was fifteen years old, in her sophomore year of high school, when she went under the knife.[42]

CHAPTER 5

Surgery

Luka

Luka shared with me that she had been seeing a therapist specializing in gender-diverse children, and that that therapist affirmed all of her thoughts that she might be transgender. And from there, Luka said, the logical next step seemed to be to get medical intervention. "I was offered puberty blockers, but I said no because I was already fifteen at that point, almost sixteen. So the first medical intervention I had was surgery on my chest, the mastectomy....

"My chest was the biggest thing I had issues with," Luka explained. "So instead of, I guess what would be considered the normal procedure (you have to be on hormones and have lived that way a certain amount of time) my therapist was okay with doing surgery first." Luka says her therapist wrote her a letter of recommendation. And, according to Luka, in between that and the actual surgery, she had two meetings: one with the gender clinic, to get her into the system, and one with the surgeon.

She was sixteen at the time, which meant that she needed her parents' permission to get the surgery. "My mom was hesitant about it and had a lot of concerns," Luka explained. "But she was also just kind of…bullied into going along with it, for lack of a better term." Like so many other parents, her mother was told that if she blocked Luka's transition, she would be endangering her daughter's life. Luka's father was trying to be very supportive of her decision, she said, and he also pressured her mother to support her.

When we talked about how the doctors pressured her mother to allow Luka to medically transition, Luka didn't place blame on her mother. It was the medical professionals who, she felt, had betrayed them. "A doctor doesn't say 'Do this or your kid's going to kill themselves,'" Luka said with a sad laugh. "That's not what a doctor should be saying. That's what an activist says."

Her surgery was scheduled in the afternoon, and she couldn't eat or drink anything for twenty-four hours beforehand. It took place at an outpatient plastic surgery center rather than a hospital.[1]

This is a common theme among the detransitioners who have undergone double mastectomies. For those unfamiliar with outpatient procedures, it means that the patient typically goes home to recover on the same day the surgery takes place. It appears that a good number of mastectomies take place at outpatient facilities—one 2020 study found that 64 percent of mastectomies were outpatient procedures, though the mean age for those patients was 58.5 years, and that study was not specifically about transgender sex-change procedures.[2]

"We drove out there, they got me all prepped for surgery, they had me change into the hospital gown," Luka said. "And then the anesthesiologist came and put the IV in my arm. I really don't like needles….I was already really stressed and anxious about it, just because it's in a hospital setting.

"The surgeon came in, and he was like, 'Can you stand up?' And so I stood up, I felt the needle in the IV move slightly under my skin, and I blacked out. A nurse had to hold me up, and I came to with a wet washcloth on my head before the surgery even started." The staff was nice to her, Luka said, but she described the situation as more of an "in-and-out" vibe rather than supportive.

Luka can't remember much about coming out of the surgery. I asked if she looked down at her chest in the moments after she woke up, to see what it looked like. She said that by the time she was awake and gathered enough to be aware, she already had the compression vest on. "My surgeon wasn't one of them that does the pose-for-a-picture-right-after-surgery thing," she said, somewhat wryly.[3]

Transgender-promoting surgeons like Sidhbh Gallagher have gained prominence by taking pictures with the people they operate on and posting the pictures on social media.

This public visibility has helped Gallagher to build "a thriving top surgery specialty," as the *New York Times* reported: most of her patients find her on TikTok.[4] Dr. Gallagher's fast-growing social media presence prompted a slew of watchdog groups to report her to the Federal Trade Commission in October 2022 for using her TikTok to "unfairly and deceptively" sway teens into getting sex-change operations.[5]

Gallagher posts graphic before-and-after pictures of her patients, including biologically female patients who get double mastectomies. Her captions are peppy and excited, and she congratulates the patients for their transformations. "This is Masculoplasty plus—a technique we developed—where we combine a reverse tummy tuck at the same time as top surgery to smooth out the upper belly," she explains in one graphic post. "In some folks the scars tend to ride too high—this technique also allows me to get the scars down underneath the pecs."[6]

Another one of her pictures depicts her surgically crafting a fake vagina on a biological man—apparently after the first one failed—using the man's intestines. She matter-of-factly explains the process in the Instagram post. "Intestinal vaginoplasty is often considered a backup option for patients who have lost a previously created vagina," Gallagher explains. "While it may sound like an easy fix, there are a few things you should know before considering this procedure.

"The appearance of the vagina created from intestine can look unnatural and may not blend well with the surrounding genitalia," she explains. "Plus, discharge can be a problem, and there is no guarantee that the new vagina will auto-lubricate as desired. Additionally, this procedure involves working inside the patient's abdomen, which can lengthen recovery time and require a longer hospital stay."[7]

Gallagher has started advertising that many of her biologically female patients are "choosing to add in torso masculinization," whereby she uses liposuction at the same time as top surgery to remove their curves. This gives these biologically female patients a straighter, less feminine torso shape, Gallagher says, claiming that it doesn't add much time to patient recovery.[8]

Neither Gallagher nor her sister, who works for her at Gallagher Plastic Surgery in Miami, Florida,[9] would respond to my requests for comment.

Luka told me that much of her recovery was spent at her mother's house. She can barely remember the first week after the surgery. But she did share that she had surgical drains in her sides and wore a kind of compression vest.

"Throughout that week, all I remember really is the fact that the antibiotics and pain medication made me feel so nauseous that I couldn't really sit up," she explained. "I had bruising but not too bad of swelling," Luka added. "I also had the drains in my side, each side, which I think are supposed to help with swelling because they drain out the excess fluid.…

"After a week, we went back out to the doctor, and they took the drains out, which was *the* most painful process," Luka explained with a shudder. "It felt so weird, and I hated it so much."

And after that, Luka fell into the routine of consistently fixing her bandages, cleaning her wounds, keeping them moisturized, and being careful not to stretch her arms too much. "I definitely had limited mobility for a while, just in terms of if I could carry heavy things or raise my arms all the way up and stretch like that," she explained. "But I was pretty fortunate that I did not have any complications really."[10]

For those who have not seen photographs of a young woman whose breasts have been removed for "gender affirmation" purposes, it is important to understand that the surgery leaves women with dark, thick scars across their chests and under their arms.[11] These scars will never fully go away, though they may flatten and lighten over time. And for some patients, like Chloe, as we shall see, they may take years to heal—to stop being wounds.

Some surgeons attempt to recreate or re-install nipples or the areola region through nipple grafts or nipple and areola resizing, and even say that the point of this is to maintain some sort of erotic sensation in the nipple. Dr. Scott Mosser at the Gender Confirmation Center in San Francisco, California, posts a slew of before-and-after photos on his website. A simple look at one of these photographs will quickly inform you that attempts to create nipples hardly look like a human nipple—they carry more the appearance of a dark spot of skin, sometimes dried or shriveled-up-looking skin, and other times just a big dark circle.[12]

These pictures are both upsetting and powerful. On the one hand, your average American who sees a photo of someone's chest after "top surgery" is horrified and appalled that our medical system even allows this type of gender transition procedure to be performed, especially if the photo depicts a young person or a minor.

It's easy to believe the activist talking point that denying "gender affirming care" to minors is cruel. It's another thing to be confronted with visual representations of what that nebulous "gender affirming care" actually is—so the photos can be instrumental in changing hearts and minds on whether these surgeries are *actually* "care" and *actually* affirming.

But it is vital to remember that each photo depicts an individual. And each individual depicted is a human being who has endured great mental (and often physical) suffering and anguish over who they are and why they were created male or female. These photos are incredibly intimate and often upsetting reminders of decisions that people will very likely deeply regret, if they do not already. And so the people pictured are naturally sensitive about their photos. Sensitive about descriptions that call them mutilated, mangled, or disfigured. Nervous that they and their scars will be used politically. Scared they will be ostracized from the social circles they clung to throughout their turbulent attempted transition process.

Your breasts, your ability to nurse: these things don't grow or come back once they are gone. But not every young woman seeking "top surgery" is aware of that reality. In fact, a whole slew of gender clinics address confusion on this very topic.

Gallagher addresses this question in a "Pride Month" post on her Instagram: "Will the chest grow back after top surgery?" Though her post ends with a cautionary note stating that she is not giving medical advice and that patients should consult with their own doctor, Gallagher proceeds to tell her prospective patients that she gets this question quite frequently and that chest tissue doesn't "naturally regenerate" after top surgery. "It's important to note that the remaining chest contour can change due to factors like weird fluctuations and hormonal changes," she says. "Nevertheless, the transformative power of top surgery is truly remarkable! By removing excess breast tissue, we create an appearance that aligns with one's gender identity, fostering confidence and self-expression."[13]

Prisha

Prisha's double mastectomy wasn't performed by a trans specialist, she told me, but by a regular plastic surgeon she was recommended to.

Years after everything occurred, he excused his actions to the Independent Women's Forum by saying that Prisha "had been in therapy for over two years prior to surgery" and that she had "full family support," saying, "I will not operate on a patient who has not been fully evaluated by a therapist or therapists."[14]

"How much do you think he made from that surgery?" I asked Prisha.

"$7,100," she told me.

She paid half of it up front and put the rest on a healthcare credit card. (Prisha had trouble making the payments later on when she lost her job at Panera Bread because she couldn't lift her arms from the surgery, but she told me she did ultimately pay it off.)[15]

Her medical records from the plastic surgeon's office, according to Kelsey Bolar of the Independent Women's Forum, show that Prisha had been seeing a licensed counselor in North Carolina for just over a year "to address issues related to gender dysphoria."

And according to a letter from that counselor, Prisha was "quite stable" and had a "strong support system that includes his parents and his sister." Those records also say that Prisha did not present with any "apparent residual psychiatric symptoms" and that the counselor had "no hesitation recommending him [Prisha] for the procedure he has requested."

Prisha's parents, Christine and Mark Mosley, pushed back on these claims in a statement to Bolar and the Independent Women's Forum. They said that in fact the only specialty evaluation that Prisha had received for her gender confusion was a meeting with a gender specialist who wasn't even mentioned in the surgeon's medical records.

> Our daughter was seeing [Gordon-Cole] for multiple very serious mental health issues that required multiple interventions that included institutionalizing her.
>
> She was extremely depressed, causing her not to come out of her dark room for days. She was suicidal, had severe OCD, very anxious and was struggling with many mental health issues. She required a variety of services. These services consisted of private and state counseling, trips to medical doctors and trips to the emergency rooms.
>
> The woman who wrote that letter was very aware of all of this because we saw multiple therapists within her organization who dealt with our whole family and shared notes. The person who wrote that letter was fully aware of all the details going on in my daughter's life and our lives at the time. We do not understand how a compassionate professional could write this letter in good conscience knowing all of these facts and the background of her client.[16]

The morning of her surgery, Prisha was excited. Her eagerness was slightly dampened when she arrived for her procedure and found out that hers was one of three surgeries that day...this somehow seemed to lessen the import of her own surgery, which she was convinced would change her life.

But she was getting the attention she so desperately craved from both her parents, who drove her to the appointment, and from the medical staff. And she believed things were about to change. "It was an exciting day," she told me. "I wanted to feel different. I wanted to feel closer to who I was supposed to be," she told me. "I wanted to be able to go out shirtless and not be sexualized. That was a big deal, and not have people look at or touch my chest."

Her parents drove her to the appointment, but her mother was extremely against the mastectomy. Her dad still had that "prove it" attitude about it—Prisha described it as, "I guess if you are trans, you'll start acting like it, so make your appointments."

They didn't talk on the way to the appointment. Prisha found their silence a little scary. "I knew they didn't want [me] to, but I was just like... do you want me to do this or die? I really thought that too."[17]

Her parents told Bolar that they felt that the doctors and therapists gave them no other choice.

"We were told what to do or our child will die," Christine said. "You can't be more psychologically abused than that. We didn't want our kid to die."

Mark, Prisha's father, compared their experience to a "hostage situation where you look at the gunman and then nod your head."

As he told Bolar, "We had no power or authority. They took it from us."[18]

Like Luka's mastectomy, Prisha's took place in a little private plastic surgery building rather than in a hospital.

"Did that alarm you at all?" I asked her.

"I mean, kind of," she said. "I was just really trusting. I thought of categories of people as either all good or all bad, and doctors were in the good category. So I blindly trusted them all."

Prisha was a little scared as she headed into the plastic surgery building for her surgery appointment. She was also stressed about having to take off work for a while, since her bosses often pressured her to pick up shifts (and Prisha said she did end up going back to work too early after her surgery and hurting herself).

The doctors put her under for the surgery. "The anesthesiologist was really nice," she said. "The doctor was kind of...serious, I guess, and seemed like he wanted to get on with it. But the anesthesiologist was great."[19]

It's a wild thought, to put yourself in the shoes of a young person who closes her eyes with a healthy body and then opens them again to find a prominent body part is just...gone.

Prisha told me that when she first opened her eyes after the surgery, she initially thought she was at work at Panera. "I can't get soup like this," she thought groggily. It took her a minute to figure out where she was, and she momentarily freaked out. Her chest was so swollen that it didn't even seem that her breasts were actually gone—and she said it stayed that way for several weeks.

She was given pain medication. And then it was time to go. "Within five minutes they were wheeling me to my car and being like, 'Bye.' They had a deal with a local hotel where, if you got surgery with them, you could pay the hotel for however much cheaper or something. We went to that cheaper hotel and I stayed there overnight."

Her parents got her Chick-fil-A that night, she recalled with a laugh. Her dad spilled it in the car, but he still gave her a milkshake that wasn't completely ruined.

When we talked, Prisha hadn't spoken with her parents in some time. But I could tell from the emotion in her voice just how much she had appreciated her parents' attentions, even though she now regrets that day and its events.

Prisha's mother washed her daughter's wounds the next day. Prisha described this experience as "really emotional."

"She was really sad," Prisha explained in a low voice. "And she had to look at me."

What mother would not be distraught at seeing her child like this? Her daughter's breasts were gone. Two long scars laced the girl's swollen, discolored chest, all green and blue, and covered in gunk.

It took about four or five months for Prisha's new wounds to heal, she said. She couldn't even lift up her arms for two or three months.

But her work kept calling her and calling her, Prisha said. In the end, she went back to work a week or two earlier than she was supposed to because she didn't want to tell them the real reason that she had been gone or the real reason that she needed to rest and recuperate. "I had a guilt complex," she said. "I didn't tell anyone at work what [the surgery] was. I was trying to be completely stealthy."

Part of this was that she didn't want to be thought of as someone who had her breasts removed to become a transgender man, Prisha told me. She just wanted to be thought of as a man. "That's another thing that has kind of changed," she told me. "I never wanted to be a trans man. I always wanted to be a man. And now everybody is identifying as trans. And that's different than when I was doing this. I wanted to be in the right body and not suicidal."

Prisha had what she calls "surgery euphoria" following her operation. And, as someone who had struggled with mental health for so long, she thought that her high spirits were a good sign.[20]

She even bragged to her friends that she had lost eight pounds in one day. As she told Bolar, about the double mastectomy, "That was the best part for me. I was just happy to have some fat lopped off of my body."[21]

It's worth noting here that Prisha had also tried to convince her team to let her get liposuction. But they had refused, Prisha told me, claiming that Prisha wasn't able to consent to this type of surgery because of her anorexia. Her desire for liposuction was attached to her body dysmorphia and eating disorder.[22] Perhaps if she had articulated a desire for "torso masculinization" liposuction, such as

Gallagher performs, her request would have been looked on more favorably.

In a post on this torso masculinization, Gallagher notes that many of her patients experience dysphoria because of their feminine body shape. One user whose profile contains "he/him" pronouns commented in reply, "The curves that I have are the #1 reason I have so much dysphoria."[23]

"Apparently when you have a mental disorder, fixing your body, changing your body isn't the answer," Prisha reflected to Bolar. "Liposuction is not a treatment for anorexia, but surgery is a treatment for gender dysphoria."[24]

Things didn't get better. Eventually Prisha found herself realizing, "Damn. I'm still suicidal."

But rather than deciding she had made a mistake, she pushed forward. "I guess it's my uterus," she told herself. "I need that gone. Or my vagina. I need a penis.

"Eventually, I was just back where I started."

Thankfully, Prisha couldn't get any more surgeries. She didn't have the money.[25]

Chloe

Chloe woke up really early on the day of her double mastectomy.

"I was pretty sleepy on the way there," she told me. "It was about an hour drive or so. My mom and dad were driving me.

"And as I got closer, and they were preparing me for the surgery and checking all my vitals and eventually rolling me into the operation room, I got more and more nervous." But she was sure about her decision—she wanted her breasts removed.[26]

Chloe's legal filings emphasize that the medical professionals responsible for Chloe's hormone treatments and surgery never asked about or treated Chloe's underlying psychological traumas. They never "elicited information related to the assault, and never elicited or evaluated Chloe's complex, conflicting, and confused feelings regarding her thinking that she would be safer being a boy.

"Any competent provider should have easily discovered this information and recognized the need for an extended period of psychotherapy and further evaluation," her lawsuit insists. "A competent provider would also have discovered this decline in her mental health condition and recognized it as a failure to respond to the 'treatment.'"

This did not happen. Rather than stopping treatment, Dr. Taylor provided Chloe with a referral for a plastic surgeon, according to the lawsuit. The complaint alleges that Chloe also consulted with plastic surgeon Dr. Hop Nguyen Le several months later, and that Dr. Le also affirmed Chloe in this decision to have the double mastectomy, without evaluating whether this was the right move for a fourteen-year-old girl to make.

He didn't inquire into the assault or go into any of the emotional or psychological reasons why she wanted to remove her breasts, according to her complaint[27]—even though the American Society of Plastic Surgeons' policy statement on aesthetic breast surgery for teenagers specifically says candidates should be at least eighteen years of age.[28] (The American Society of Plastic Surgeons confirmed to me in June 2023 that this policy is still applicable.)

"The FDA has not approved breast augmentation in patients younger than 18 for the following reasons," the American Society of Plastic Surgeons' policy statement says. "Teens and their parents may not realize the risks associated with breast implants. The teen's body may not have finished developing. The teen needs to be psychologically ready to handle the outcome of surgery."[29]

Instead of evaluating such factors, Dr. Le "perfunctorily affirmed that a double mastectomy was an effective way to treat her gender dysphoria and proceeded with the consultation and with scheduling the surgery," Chloe's lawsuit says.[30]

Who was the next person to walk Chloe down the path to her surgery? That would be Susanne E. Watson, Ph.D., according to the lawsuit. Dr. Watson, whose LinkedIn account claims she has worked for Kaiser for the past twenty-seven years, is the clinical director of Kaiser Permanente Oakland Medical Center's transgender clinic. Watson recommended Chloe for a double mastectomy during a two-hour visit, the lawyers allege.

That was it.

Chloe's complaint states that Watson never performed a long-term regular evaluation or assessment or scheduled any kind of follow-up evaluation of Chloe's psychological condition; instead, Watson met with a fourteen-year-old girl for two hours and O.K.'d her to have her breasts removed.

> Like Drs. Taylor and Le, Dr. Watson engaged in a very limited and perfunctory informed consent discussion that occurred in this single visit, as a part of the more general evaluation, and which glossed over the significant health and psychological risks of permanent breast removal surgery and continuing hormone treatment.
>
> Dr. Watson's informed consent discussion was fatally flawed by the failure to evaluate properly the full scope of Chloe's psychological condition and underlying trauma, negative emotions, and mental suffering. Dr. Watson neglected to discuss and evaluate her co-morbidities, related diagnoses, treatment options for these varying co-morbidities and for gender dysphoria itself, and entirely failed to present a truthful and complete risk/benefit analysis for Chloe and her parents.[31]

It is important to note that, as her lawsuit details, Chloe and her parents had been told that if Chloe did not receive treatment "resolving her internal conflict," she would likely commit suicide. Her lawyers repeatedly emphasize how the medical professionals failed to discuss the fact that only "very low quality studies" on treating gender dysphoric children exist. Nor did Chloe and her parents hear that there was a significant probability that Chloe's dysphoria would resolve on its own without hormones or surgery.

Chloe now believes that these doctors lied to her and her family and pushed, or coerced, her into getting her breasts removed by implying that she would commit suicide if she didn't. Ironically, as her lawsuit points out, "She had a complex and multi-faceted presentation of mental health symptoms, but she was never evaluated to be at a significant risk of suicide.

"Representing that Chloe's suicide risk would increase without transition was unwarranted, false, and manipulative," her legal filings say. "Presented concurrently, this emotionally supercharged suicide threat and this false decision-making dichotomy backed Chloe and her parents into a corner. They felt they had no option but to continue moving forward with transition and surgery."[32]

After the evaluation by Dr. Watson, Chloe's mental health issues (depression, anxiety, fears, and "passive suicidal ideation") became even worse. None of the medical professionals were aware of this, according to her lawsuit, because they did not conduct any further review of her mental health.

And Chloe was convinced that these negative feelings would go away when she completed her surgery—she thought they were all stemming from her dysphoria and her discomfort with her body. Her mental health issues became so distressing that Chloe's mom had to work with her pediatric care center to prove to Chloe's school that she needed to be excused for a bit.[33]

She had a few more visits with Dr. Le. Chloe's legal filings say that Le "obtained a so-called 'informed consent' document" addressing the normal risks of a breast-cancer-type mastectomy unrelated to gender dysphoria. "Additionally, even as to the surgery itself, the informed consent discussions were woefully inadequate," her lawsuit says. "Dr. Le never showed Chloe any pictures of poor results of the surgery and never showed her any pictures of what the surgery looks post-op prior to healing. Dr. Le only showed her pictures of 'successful' results."[34]

"A critical part of any informed consent discussion for an elective breast removal surgery includes showing unsuccessful results and showing pictures of the healing process," the lawsuit continues. "This discussion and presentation did not occur for Chloe. Complications of mastectomies for adolescent trans-identified patients are well known to plastic surgeons."[35]

On June 3, 2020, Chloe went in for surgery. And according to her complaint, it was Dr. Le who removed both of Chloe's breasts.[36]

Chloe recalled to me that in her last moments before they put her under for the surgery, she locked eyes with a young male nurse in the back of the room. "While everybody else was preparing me, he was just standing back there. And he was staring at me with this look of concern on his face," she said. "I didn't really understand why at the time. Now that I've actually gone through the process of transitioning, and then going through the surgery, and then regretting it, and stopping my transition, I think he must have been feeling some sort of guilt.

"I mean, now that I've seen it all, I just can't imagine operating on a kid like that in good conscience."

After she woke up from the surgery, Chloe says she felt great. The pain wasn't that bad, she told me. In fact, the pain from the constipation caused by the medicine they had prescribed her was much worse than the pain in the actual surgical site. "In my chest, it was like a deep muscle soreness, like I had worked out my chest really hard or something," she explained. "But it wasn't too bad. I went off the medication within, like, two days."

Once the medication wore off and she realized that her breasts had been removed, she felt that this was a big milestone. "I was proud of myself and I was happy that these things were finally off my body," she said. "Up until a few months after, I felt like I was excited, if anything."

For the first few weeks or month, her mom helped her around the house with cooking meals or performing small tasks. Chloe couldn't lift anything heavy or do yard work...she was "practically disabled" from the surgery, as she said. "It was a major surgery in the upper area of my body, in my chest, where a lot of muscles are. So I didn't really have much of a range in terms of range of motion for a while. I think I was only able to lift up my arms after about the two- or three-month mark."

Chloe also told me that she had to keep wearing the compression binder and bandages for about five to seven days, to preserve the integrity of the skin grafts and her new scars. And then after a few days, they took the stitches out. It was the first time she would see her chest post-operation.

She emphasized to me that her surgery took place in an outpatient facility. As soon as she was able to walk and was fully conscious after the surgery, she went home. "It's kind of crazy," she told me, "I guess double mastectomies in general, for the most part, are [performed] at an outpatient surgery. But I was born with a cleft palate and I got my first repair when I was about two or three years old, and I had to get a revision for that when I was about thirteen, because it wasn't growing with the rest of my skull as I went through puberty...after that surgery, I was in the hospital for three or four days."

But after getting her breasts removed, while she still wasn't able to move most of her body, Chloe was immediately sent home.[37]

CHAPTER 6

Realization

Luka

Like Chloe, Luka was initially thrilled with the results of her surgery.

She describes having a kind of "post-surgery" high. "This is great," she thought to herself. "I don't have to wear a binder anymore, I can just wear a T-shirt." As she told me, "The realization of how significant of a surgery that actually was for a sixteen-year-old to be having didn't really set in until much later."

It was about three years later, when she was around nineteen years old, that Luka slowly began to wonder if she had made a mistake. And then, when she was around twenty years old, it "really hit."

As we have seen, unlike in the cases of the other destransitioners whose stories we have explored so far, Luka began taking hormones after she got surgery, rather than before. And at first she was happy about taking "T" and determined to continue it because she believed it would help her transition.

But as we have also seen, Luka hates needles. And the testosterone required that she give herself a shot in the stomach once a week. She struggled so much with the injections initially that her mom had to help her.

The changes that Luka experienced on the testosterone—to her skin, to the shape of her body, to her hairline, to her sex drive, and to her emotions, as she detailed to me in the interview quoted at length in chapter 4 above—were drastic.

When she was almost eighteen, Luka began to ponder whether the next step in her journey was to get a hysterectomy. That ultimately didn't happen—"thank God," she said—but when Luka went to talk to her doctor at the gender clinic, that doctor made it sound like "the easiest thing in the world."

Her doctor also implied there were no "real, long-term complications with removing an organ like that," and that as long as Luka still had ovaries, her body might be able to produce hormones again if she were to stop taking testosterone. Luka emphasized to me that her doctor was "very OK" with Luka getting a hysterectomy.

But on this point, Luka's parents stood firm. "That is one of the surgeries that both my parents know a lot about and know a lot about what the long-term complications of that will be," Luka said. "So they were like absolutely not."

Luka was briefly frustrated. "But then I got over it. I was like yeah, that's probably for the best."[1]

Hysterectomies are used to treat a range of conditions besides gender dysphoria—such as uterine fibroid tumors and uterine or cervical cancer. Hysterectomy has become the second most common surgery for American women, after the caesarean section, according to Yale Medicine, and though it was once considered highly invasive, modern medicine has brought about minimally invasive techniques that ensure a quicker recovery.

Yale Medicine defines the procedure as "the surgical removal of the uterus," intended for women with conditions including "fibroids, uterine prolapse, and endometriosis," and warns, "After a hysterectomy, a woman will no longer be able to have children," noting, "Depending on the severity of the condition, it might be possible to delay surgery until after a woman has had all the children she plans to have."

In a total hysterectomy, surgeons remove the entire uterus including the cervix. In a supracervical hysterectomy, surgeons remove the body of the uterus and leave the cervix intact. And in a radical hysterectomy, usually to remove cancer, all of the uterus and some of the surrounding tissues are removed.

There are a couple of different ways the surgery can be performed: In a vaginal hysterectomy, the surgeon removes the uterus through the vagina. This is considered safer and requires less hospital recovery, according to Yale Medicine. In a laparoscopic hysterectomy, the surgeon makes three or four abdominal incisions, inserts a tiny camera into one of them and surgical instruments into the other ones, and then performs the surgery, ultimately removing the uterus through the vagina or through the abdominal incisions. And occasionally physicians may perform abdominal hysterectomies requiring larger incisions.

"Many women also have emotional responses to surgery because they can no longer bear children," according to Yale Medicine.[2]

That's all outside of "gender affirming care." When it comes to "gender affirming bottom surgery," FOLX explains, there are "a variety of reasons" for deciding to get a hysterectomy. "One common reason is that a person's uterus simply doesn't belong to them," the transgender-promoting website explains. "For many trans and gender non-conforming people, removing body parts that don't align with your gender is an important way to affirm their identity."

FOLX goes on to justify hysterectomies for women who don't
want to have periods anymore, women who want to lower their testosterone dose "with more ease knowing their bodies won't be con-
tinuing to produce estrogen and progesterone," women who want their
cervix removed so they don't have to worry about pap smears, and
women who don't want to have babies. "There isn't one right reason
to get a hysterectomy," FOLX assures readers. "Like other medical
decisions, it's up to the individual person to choose which pelvic parts
to keep when thinking about bottom surgeries such as a hysterectomy.
It's important to note that if you're interested in family building and
want to maintain the ability to carry a pregnancy or use their eggs,
you'll need to keep both ovaries and the uterus (as well as cervix and
fallopian tubes)."

FOLX warns against doctors who "make assumptions" such as
thinking that "everyone must or might want to carry a pregnancy,"
or that young women "cannot decide their future (in)fertility for
themselves." The transgender-promoting group goes so far as to say
that some women (or as FOLX says, "certain people assigned female
at birth") have health conditions that make a "stronger case for a
hysterectomy"—in other words, health conditions for which a hysterectomy is the appropriate treatment. "Those pursuing a gender
affirming hysterectomy with these conditions may have an easier
time navigating the procedure as well as interactions with insurance," FOLX shares. "Remember, both cis and trans identified
people who can consent to care can have these organs removed for
problems with menstrual periods, abnormal bleeding, and problems
with pain."

After getting a hysterectomy, trans-identifying patients may be
interested in pursuing "other gender-affirming bottom surgeries," as
FOLX suggests.[3]

These could include phalloplasty, in which surgeons construct a fake penis on a biological woman with skin flaps from her wrist and forearm, her leg, or the side of her back. Those skin flaps are "reshaped, contoured and reattached to the groin to create the penis," according to Johns Hopkins Medicine.[4]

The operation can also include an attempt to create a penis tip and scrotum, the removal of the vagina, the placing of erectile and testicular implants, and the lengthening of the urethra to help the biologically female patient "stand to pee," as FOLX notes.[5]

"Penis size depends on patient preferences and the skin flap harvested from your body," Johns Hopkins Medicine says. "Thinner patients with less fat on the skin flap will have a penis with less girth. Alternatively, patients with a greater amount of fat will have a thicker penis.

"The length of the penis depends on the patient's donor site, but typically it is about 5–6 inches. After the first stage, the penis may decrease in size as postoperative swelling decreases and the tissue settles into its new location." Johns Hopkins Medicine suggests that biological women get a hysterectomy before the phalloplasty, if they are interested in both.

"Penis function is determined by what you and your surgery team agree on for your surgical plan," they advise. "If it is important for you to urinate out of the tip of your penis, then urethral lengthening may be a good choice for you. If sensation is most important, your team will focus on a donor site with good nerve innervation. If penetrative sex is most important, and you would like to maintain an erection, then implanting an erectile prosthetic can be part of your surgery plan."

Incredibly, Johns Hopkins Medicine has to warn its biologically female patients, "It is important to note that your penis will not ejaculate with semen at the time of orgasm."[6]

Prisha

Prisha had gotten her long-awaited surgery.

Things were supposed to be better. But they weren't. "I figured I should try therapy again, therapy that my parents weren't involved with or orchestrating," she explained. "So I did find a trauma therapist who specializes in dialectical behavioral therapy (DBT) and trauma therapy."[7] (DBT therapy is typically thought of as therapy for borderline personality disorder, though it has also been shown to be helpful for other mental health conditions.)[8]

And from here, she began to "figure it out," she told me. Prisha says she began resolving many of her family trauma issues, as well as her personal trauma, including her distress surrounding her rape. She found the "healing" that she had so desperately sought through transition, she shared with me.

"Did you have a moment of realization there, when you just knew?" I asked her.

"I did," she said. "I kept it secret for like a year, a year and a half, because I felt ashamed and like I had invested so much in being trans and I couldn't go back, and like...my family wouldn't accept it."

She quit taking testosterone "cold turkey."

About a year after the mastectomy, when she was nineteen, Prisha had moved out of her parent's house and into a place with a trans-identifying friend she described as "a stranger from the internet." Prisha "fell in love" with that individual and moved out of her parents' home to be with that friend.

But this person pushed Prisha to become even more unhealthy. She described the individual as "the kind of person that wanted someone to 'doctor.'"

"So eventually, when I wanted to detransition and started getting healthier, [that individual] was really discouraging and trying to make me sicker, to have someone to doctor," Prisha recalled.

So, Prisha says, she left that relationship, and moved to Big Rapids, Michigan, where she sought a job at a local dispensary and ultimately started going to college. Things were still incredibly difficult for her, however: she was still figuring things out, still very emotional, and she says she was fired from her job for crying. She took only online courses because she didn't want anyone to see her.[9]

"I truly hate myself," Prisha told Kelsey Bolar of the Independent Women's Forum. "I'm not trying to sound piteous or anything, but it's hard to think of anyone else thinking differently than I do. I'm very wounded and vulnerable so I take everything personally. I just kind of isolate a lot."[10]

Helena

Helena's lonely late-night shifts working at the cookie shop were giving her plenty of time to think about the choices she had made. "In some ways, it was a bit maddening, but dispersed within the general neuroticism were moments of clarity," she writes.

"I remember deciding to take my chest binder off at work for the first time, because it was just me and one other worker who always sat in the back, and that fucking thing hurt. It felt so much more natural not to have anything constricting my chest underneath my work shirt."

And she started skipping testosterone injections, mostly because of how anxious they made her. At this point, she says, she was only injecting herself with testosterone once or twice a month.

And as a result, the frequency of her "episodes" dramatically decreased.

She started wondering what this meant. Why was she feeling better, not worse, when she took less "T"? And what if transitioning wasn't, in fact, helping her mental health?

That's a forbidden question in transgender circles, she quickly found. "I remember browsing trans subreddits in hopes I would get some answers for what to do if transitioning wasn't improving my mental health," Helena said. "There were many posts asking this question, and by far the most common answer was to 'just keep going' and that one day, when you passed well enough, it would all be worth it."

Helena began questioning her life choices up to this point. All these things she had done thinking they would "save" her had not done anything of the sort. "The only thing I didn't outright question was my choice to be transgender," she writes. "That would require a more up-front reality check."

Helena started thinking about the comfortable clothing she used to wear before she started her transition process, back when she didn't have to worry about whether or not her feminine clothes would make people doubt whether she was transgender. She thought about how much she hated the way she looked in men's clothing (and "the way masculine styles looked on me in general").

"I also wished I 'wasn't trans,' and even recall making a reddit post to this effect, lamenting how even though 'being trans' was making me miserable, I knew it was who I really was and after I got surgeries it would be right for me," she wrote. "This kind of thinking, I now realize after talking to so many detransitioners, is common in the weeks or months leading up to detransition," she shared.

Helena's "a-ha" moment happened in February of 2018. Her friend Jamie, a biological woman who also identified as transgender at the time and with whom Helena was then in a romantic relationship, made a video montage with pictures of Jamie and Helena showing the progression of their relationship since the day they had met—which was two days after Helena started testosterone.

"As I watched the video, I saw the way my face changed from so young, hopeful, and most of all, recognizable, to weary, deadpan, and foreign," Helena said. "I began to sob uncontrollably," she recounts. "At first, Jamie thought I was crying because I loved the video so much, but I quickly informed her it was something else, but I wouldn't say what. I cried, and cried, and cried. Every memory those photos evoked was flashing before my eyes, all the pain I knew was behind my eyes was emerging vividly. I saw innocence turn to anguish and I knew I had been on the wrong path for a long, long time. I didn't know. I didn't know it would be this way. I was just a kid," she wrote. "How could I have been so stupid?"[11]

Chloe

Initially, Chloe had thought jubilantly that she would be able to hang out with boys without wearing a T-shirt. She could swim with ease. She wouldn't have to wear the chest binders anymore! She would finally be happy.

Her regrets began to creep in little by little.

It started when she went in to get her stitches removed. That experience was both disturbing and unsettling for her, she told me as we chatted over the phone in the spring of 2023. It was the first time that she had actually seen what her chest looked like after the operation.

And the sight shocked her. Her skin grafts were all black and grisly-looking…the outside layer of skin had died, since it had been separated from the tissue beneath it and then reattached. Her chest was all "cut up."

But what bothered her more than the appearance of her chest was the sensation she felt in it.

"Stuff had been rearranged, they removed some nerve endings and some tissue, so it was kind of numb," she explained. "Especially with the tightness of the skin."

And even though she was so numb, she could still feel everything—including the doctors removing the stitches from her chest. That sensation made her sick. She made the doctors stop taking the stitches out halfway through the process because she just found herself too overwhelmed. "I need to stop, take a breather for a moment," she vaguely recalls saying. "I'm getting sick." They stopped and gave her a juice box. Then they finished taking out her stitches.

Chloe used to look forward to showers at the end of a long day—she loved being alone, after being around everyone, and processing her day on her own. But now, with every shower and bath, she had to take off all her bandages and do the aftercare for her wounds.

"It was just hard to look at myself being in that state," she reflected, "with the markings of the surgical marker, and the scars, and the changed shape, and the skin grafts…it was just rough to look at."[12]

Chloe had to look at her body every single day and see what had been done to her. The confusing sensation in her chest was strange and uncomfortable. Her lawsuit says she was "appalled" at how she looked: "She felt like she had been turned into a monster."[13]

Chloe explained to me that she had to put Vaseline on the grafts to keep them moist, to encourage the old skin to fall off and the new skin to develop. "It was just kind of a gross process," she said. "And then I had to be careful with my grafts while showering, and basically do a reverse of the process after [showering], putting the stuff back on.

"It took up a bigger chunk of my days and nights," Chloe said. "And it was just a reminder that things had changed permanently.

"At first I saw it as battle scars, and something to embrace and be proud of," she added. "But after a while it became really monotonous."

OK, she thought. *I want it to look normal now. I want to be able to go swimming and have my shirt off, like any other boy.* But that never happened.

Chloe had thought that she would be fully healed from her surgery after a few months. She most certainly thought that she would be fully healed within a year. But now, over two years since her surgery, she told me she's still dealing with significant complications and problems that she had never discussed with her doctors as possible complications, as her lawsuit notes.[14]

To this day, her chest is not healed. "Would you say you had open wounds for years?" I asked her.

"Oh, yeah," she responded emphatically.

For a while she thought the grafts were healing normally, except that the skin grafts that they had taken (that included her areolas) were slightly dry on the surfaces. Then the grafts started leaking fluid. And she is still wearing bandages to deal with that. She has no idea why the wounds haven't healed. She's not sure if it is an infection or some other complication from the surgery. And she can't find medical professionals to help her figure it out. "I'm not sure whether it'll even go away or if I'll have to live like this for the rest of my life," she said in a February 2023 interview with Fox News.[15]

Her lawsuit describes how her mental health issues continued to worsen to the point where Chloe developed suicidal ideation—she began to think about and even to plan how to commit suicide.[16] And she began to wonder if everything that she had put herself through, and that others had done to her, was a huge mistake.

But Chloe didn't truly regret her surgery until about a year afterwards. Her moment of realization came during school, in her psychology class, when she began to learn more about breastfeeding and the bond between a mother and child.

In that class, for the first time, the fifteen-year-old began to desire to be a mother. "I realized that I had taken so much more from myself than my breasts," she explained.

Her surgeons had told her that she would no longer be able to breastfeed after the operation, Chloe said. She had listened and said she understood, but at the time she had not had any conception of what that would actually mean to her. "Obviously it didn't really affect me to hear that at the time," she told me. "I realized that what had been taken away from me was so much more than I had realized, and that I had made this decision, I was allowed to make this decision, at far too young of an age," she said sadly.[17]

Her lawsuit explains that Chloe was and is heartbroken that she will never be able to "nourish and nurture" her future babies through breast-feeding, and that she will never "experience the physical touch, bonding, and intimacy that a mother and child can share" in this intimate way.

Processing all this, Chloe began to have "severe distress" about the hormonal drugs she was taking as she began to fully realize the impact that her potential loss of fertility—and any other side effects from the hormones—would have on her future. Her lawyers argue that Chloe, a mere child when this began, could not possibly have comprehended the tragic consequences that would result from such powerful drugs.[18]

And by this point in time, Chloe's body image was getting worse and worse. "I started to miss being feminine, being pretty, and being able to present myself in a more feminine manner, using makeup or hairstyles or dressing in a certain way," she told me. "I would secretly wear some of my old girl clothes or I would buy skirts or dresses online that I would just wear in the comfort of my room."[19]

How much things had changed in such a short period of time! Here she was, hiding in her room as she sought to see herself as a woman.

"I never went out like that because it was shameful to me," Chloe added. "By that point in time, I had already been about three or so years on testosterone, and I no longer looked like a girl.

"I felt like I looked ridiculous in that I couldn't really talk to any-body about it, but there just came a point when I couldn't take it anymore," she said. "And I had to stop."[20]

She was sixteen years old.

CHAPTER 7

Detransition

Luka

Luka is a sophomore in college now. She dealt with some incredibly heavy life struggles before even becoming a legal adult. And interestingly, it was the COVID-19 pandemic that slowed down her life enough to allow her to ponder whether she regretted transitioning.

"My high school class was the class of 2020, when everything shut down suddenly. I went on spring break and never went back to high school," she explained. "And so after that, I was like, OK, I'm not going to pay out-of-state tuition to sit in my bedroom on Zoom. I'm taking a gap year right during COVID. And that just gave me a lot of time to really think about everything. And I think that's when the first little inklings of whether that was right for me or not popped up."

During the spring semester of her freshman year, she stopped taking the SSRI drugs she was on for her depression, and she was amazed by how much better she felt.

August and September rolled around, and she stopped taking testosterone.

When Luka stopped taking "T," she was having quite a bit of joint pain. But her decision to stop was compounded by another factor: she realized that if she continued to take testosterone, she was looking at spending the rest of her life as a patient.

And that prospect was not only expensive. It was exhausting. "I got to a point where I was just very tired of having to do the shot each week," Luka said. She said she realized that even if the shot was only once a week, it was still affecting her mood, giving her brain fog, and affecting her ability to go out and do things spontaneously. She began thinking about whether she might be a "permanent patient of the medical industry," taking testosterone every week for the rest of her life, and how that would impact her freedom.

"I can't do it," she finally resolved. "I can't continue to live like this." So she began to slowly lower her dosage over the course of a couple weeks. "That way it wasn't cold turkey," she explained. "I didn't want to leave my body without any functioning hormones and find out what happens."

Since stopping, her brain feels "less foggy," in a way. "On testosterone, I definitely had more energy during those first few days after my shot," she said thoughtfully. "Just because it is basically a steroid." But since she stopped taking it so recently, Luka still feels that this is a waiting game—she doesn't know what will "bounce back" and what is "here to stay."

The moment when she realized that she regretted her mastectomy, Luka was thinking about her future and whether she wanted to have kids and a family someday. "And that is where that moment really hit for both the testosterone and the top surgery...kind of like a 'holy shit' moment."

"I messed up," she realized. "I messed up and I would have been better off if someone had just helped me through this another way." She was twenty at this point—her realization came in late August 2022.

Luka had experienced moments of regret before this, but this was the first time she had allowed herself to come to grips with her reality. In the past, she hadn't allowed herself to get there. "I had brief moments of thinking about that throughout different periods of time," she said. "But then I would get busy with something and it would go on the back burner."

Luka was alarmed at how her friends reacted when she began questioning gender ideology, particularly the transitioning process. She posted something about the dangers of puberty blockers and how the National Health Service in England was rethinking how to handle the matter, she told me, and one of her friends sent her a very long text accusing her of being hateful and causing children to kill themselves.

Luka couldn't believe it. It didn't matter that she had transitioned as a minor, lived the very experience in question, and wanted to point out problems with the system. Heck, this—using the threat of suicide to shut down any doubts—was literally how the doctors had swayed her family into letting her get the double mastectomy!

Her lived experience, she realized, only counted if she agreed with "them"—the pro-trans voices that were drowning everyone else out. "What mattered at that moment was I was pushing back against something that, at least according to him, could not be questioned," she said.

"At that point I was like, OK, I'm in a cult, I need to leave," she told me.

I asked Luka how she is doing now. When we spoke, it had really not been that long since her moment of realization.

"I've been pretty good at this point," she said. "I've been trying to focus on school and stuff." There are stressful moments when she thinks about the leftover aspects of her transition, she told me—like, for example, how all her legal paperwork says "male" on it. That's a stumbling block she is still dealing with.

The first way she ended up telling people that she was detransitioning was through some videos that she posted on Twitter in the fall of 2022, Luka told me. She put them out there thinking that maybe twenty people would see them. After all, her pro-trans friends and the online community had made her think that there weren't that many people like herself out there.

The videos blew up online. And Luka began to learn how many others had been duped like herself.[1]

Prisha

When Prisha stopped taking testosterone, the anger and rage that she had been feeling largely receded. She felt like she was able to "think more clearly," to connect with her emotions again. "I was able to cry," she told me. Huge.

"I really feel like the testosterone just kind of made me dumber," she insisted. When I asked her to clarify this a little more, she explained that she felt "emotionally dumber," and "not as emotionally intelligent," unable to articulate the deep, consuming emotions she was feeling.

Now she is back to normal, Prisha told me, and she feels in touch with her emotions again. She elaborated that testosterone hadn't stripped away her empathy, but it had made it harder for her to identify the emotions that she was feeling. She recalled moments where she struggled to put a finger on the cause of her inner turmoil, asking herself in bewilderment, "Am I angry? Am I sad? Am I hungry? I have no idea what's going on, I just feel bad...."

"I'm more cognitive, more clearheaded, more calm, soothed, I guess. Just generally better.

"And I can cry," she said again.

She used to be so proud of her ability to sing. Now she can't. "I believed that my voice would even out," Prisha told me, "because I was told over and over I would have just as good of a voice, but in a male range. Instead, I have a crushed larynx. I have no volume, it hurts to sing, and it hurts to talk for long periods."

The testosterone also affected her sexuality and preferences in a potential mate, she came to realize. "It made me bisexual," Prisha said. "Which I feel weird about...it just made me like...horny all the time. And just care less about who my partner was.

"That sounds awful," she added. "I'm a very emotional person and I think that sex is for intimacy. But my body was not on the same page, you know what I mean?"

"So it was more like the person mattered less and the physicality mattered more?" I asked her, to which she agreed, "Yeah."

"I just wanted it more often. I lost genital preference. I just wanted it to feel good."

Throughout our conversations, Prisha often apologized for being frank. "I'm sorry for being vulgar," she told me at this point. And as I had before, I told her that her openness would help others understand the truth of what she had been through.

As she weaned herself off the testosterone, she told me, all the negative side effects that she had experienced were decreasing. "My body temperature has changed. I don't feel like I'm on fire anymore, which is pleasant.

"I was hot all the time on the testosterone," she added. "Unfortunately my shoulders grew a lot and I lost some of my hair and I gained hair on my face and my body. And my feet grew. None of that was going to change." But now her hair is shinier, she told me with relief. Her skin is softer. Little things like that, she said, are more feminine.

Prisha's eating disorder was so severe that it kept her from finishing puberty before she began taking testosterone and undergoing her surgery. She thinks that because of this, her experience may be similar to that of a child who is put on puberty blockers—"I had big changes," she reflects.

She's had chronic, burning pain in her neck and her shoulders since being on and especially since stopping the testosterone. Prisha told me she's pretty sure this pain is linked to the fact that her body had not finished going through puberty when it was pumped full of hormones. "I've heard that from other women who have been on testosterone and transitioned," she told. "My neck and my shoulders literally burn all the time, like I can't hold them up or something, like they're too big for my frame, they literally always burn."

She described the sensation as similar to the burn that comes from working out. "It's like that. All the time." And she isn't sure how to fix it other than going to the chiropractor or getting massages. "I can't make the rest of my body grow bigger to fix it," she said. "I'm out of puberty.

"There's no cure," she said. "I can kind of...fix the symptoms."

And there are no doctors brave enough to offer her their help—but we will get into that more later.

I asked Prisha if there was a point where she suddenly regretted her mastectomy. She didn't recall an exact moment, but she said that she began having "phantom breast syndrome" about eight months to a year after the surgery. "And that's when it started setting in really hard," she said. "I was in really deep denial. I was just like, 'This is the price I have to pay to not be suicidal.' The feeling of [the phantom breasts] was less severe than the suicidal feelings so I was like, 'I can take it,' you know?"

Multiple detransitioners have told me that they aggressively used drugs and alcohol when they were beginning to detransition. Prisha told me that she was "stone-cold sober" when she was detransitioning, at first in secret. But she smoked a lot of weed and meditated in attempts to slow down and "not be frantic."

She added, "I'm being actively cautious to not overdrink or overuse."

Prisha did share that she has cut herself a few times since detransitioning, to the point where she needed stitches.

But she is a lot more at peace now. "I feel like I'm not really fighting as hard anymore to try and be something that I'm not and try to 'be in the right body' anymore," she shared. "I'm trying to accept my body and appreciate it rather than change it.

"Changing it is like anguish. I was really actively putting energy into hating myself and my body," she said. "And not doing that is saving me and bringing me peace."

She has struggled with her relationship with her parents. When I first spoke to her, Prisha had not seen them in a long time, and she was upset that her mother was receiving hate online from Prisha's old transgender-promoting support group.[2]

"I've already put my mom through so much," an emotional Prisha tweeted in April 2023, "she bathed me when I couldn't move my arms after my mastectomy...she was told if I killed myself it would be her fault...she didn't deserve it. Now she's being harassed by my old trans support group and it is more pain for her...."[3]

In June 2023, Prisha finally made the decision to go see her parents again. She hadn't seen them in seven years, she said. And she shared a little bit of her journey on social media: "I've arrived. My mom picked me up. She brought me to their house and we ate. I got to talk alone with my dad after he dropped me off at the hotel. I'm here now, and my parents are at their house to take a nap. A lot of emotions, and I'm exhausted too."[4]

But the main thing that has helped Prisha to ground herself, focus on the future, and accept her femininity is the daughter of the man that she loves.

She told me that she grieves over her miscarried baby, June, to this very day. "I've even struggled with phantom pregnancies," she said. "I just wish that I could get pregnant now," she told me tearfully, "and have a body for that soul to go into."

Her boyfriend's daughter is the reason for her social detransition, Prisha shared. "He has a three-year-old daughter, and she calls me mom," Prisha said. "She clocks me as a woman, and I fall into that role with her, and everything is very motherly and feminine, and I'm not a father at all, not like the big protector, I'm the nurturer and the carer...."

"It's amazing," she said simply.

Though she initially "medically detransitioned" by stopping her testosterone injections ("I stopped poisoning myself," she said somewhat sarcastically), she continued to live, act, and dress like a man for a while. She also had a bit of a beard at this point, and she wasn't shaving. "I was too deep in the shame and the lie," she said. "I was like, well, I've uprooted my entire life and everybody else's for this. I have to live with it."

She had poured all her resources, mental and physical, into this transition attempt. And at that point, she didn't know what to do. *Do I cut my losses and take zero?* she thought to herself. *Or do I continue to hemorrhage everything I own for the rest of my life until I die?*

She began dating her boyfriend, Prisha says, and he eventually trusted her enough to bring his daughter around her. "She was about two at the time," Prisha reminisced. "And despite all that stuff I said about living as a man and literally having a beard, she started to call me 'Mommy.' And then I was like, 'That's it. I know exactly what I want. Anything is worth getting that which I have just had a taste of.'"

"Do you remember the first time she called you 'Mommy'?" I asked.

"Yeah, yeah, I remember it clearly," Prisha said eagerly. "I was sitting on the couch and she was standing up and she looked at me and she said it with her arms extended towards me."

When I asked her what she felt in that moment, she responded: "Disbelief. Shock. Wonder. Amazement. A little bit of terror, maybe of responsibility. And the weight of love. But mostly love.…

"And it's been like that ever since."[5]

Helena

The decision to stop taking testosterone was extremely difficult for Helena. "My mindset was, 'I'm so desperate, I've invested so much time and thought into this identity,'" she shared with me in the summer of 2022. It felt too embarrassing to back out of it. So she kept telling herself, "No, you can't doubt this, you gotta keep going."

She's not the only one who was convinced that pushing forward with her transition was the right thing to do, she said—on Reddit forums, all of the responses that she read urged her to "keep going." She was told that she just needed to push through her concerns, ignore the hesitations holding her back.

But Helena was developing an "intense aversion" to the massive needle that she used for injecting herself in the leg with testosterone. After her second time in the hospital, she said, she slowly stopped taking testosterone until she had quit completely.

She doesn't remember much about coming off the testosterone, describing that next period as a "very low point" in her life when she was on a ton of medication, her hormones were "screwed up," and she was drinking heavily and smoking copious amounts of weed. So she didn't remember specific withdrawal feelings beyond bewilderment and regret.[6]

But to rewind a little, to the moment when Helena saw Jamie's slideshow of their relationship: As she watched it, she couldn't believe that she had allowed herself to stray down this path. And she couldn't bring herself to explain what she was feeling to Jamie, thinking Jamie would try to make her "rationalize away these feelings."

"But it was too late for that now," she wrote. "The dam had broken. Instead, I silently berated myself and catastrophized internally until I mustered the courage to tell my very pro-LGBT therapist: being trans had been a massive mistake."

Her therapist was no help. "But you always tell me about your terrible dysphoria!" Helena says her therapist told her.

"I know," Helena says she told her therapist. "But I...I don't think that's what it is." Helena started to explain to her therapist all her thoughts on her experience thus far: "how I had developed the 'dysphoria' after finding out about gender identities online as a teenager, when I had been struggling with so many other emotional issues for a long time, and that in retrospect I must have gotten carried away, thinking that being trans was the explanation and solution for all of my problems. She wasn't really hearing me, and questioned the things I said from the angle of 'you're trying to talk yourself out of being trans because transphobia is making you hate yourself,'" Helena wrote.

"Ironic that nobody ever questioned my desire to be trans that way."

That therapist's response made Helena wonder for the first time whether something was wrong with the transgender movement. "I had experienced this massive realization, and it was agonizing but at least it was finally something real, and here I was being met with all these rationalizations for why this of all things was a psychological symptom," she said. "Not the effects of the testosterone, not my belief that all of my problems would be solved by transitioning, not my aversion to being female, but the fact that I now knew transitioning had been a mistake."

Helena said she didn't go back to that therapist again.

She wrote in her Substack piece about how she left the session frustrated and, as she sat in the car outside the building, told Jamie that she was questioning her transgender identity and regretted her transition. Jamie was the person closest to Helena in the world at the time, but even she accused Helena of "having these thoughts due to some underlying psychological issue, like only an insane person would ever regret being trans."

Helena emphasizes that Jamie wasn't being "uniquely harsh" here—this type of response is a "common occurrence in the trans community. In one direction, there's a desire to encourage gender questioning in others who have not questioned their gender yet (some people call this 'cracking an egg'). In the other direction, there is an intense fear of others changing their minds about being trans or wanting to transition," she explains. "Once someone is questioning their gender, there's a push to encourage them to take steps towards social and medical transition, which, once initiated, makes changing one's mind more complicated and going back to living as they did before more difficult."

Helena says that in the past she herself got "angry and desperate" when her friends expressed doubts about being transgender. She also said that she encouraged her friends who didn't identify as trans to question whether maybe they actually were.

"I regret this very much now, as some of these friends have gone on to medically transition, and I no longer believe this was remotely in their best interest," she says. "But in the trans community, people cope with the inherent doubts and cognitive dissonance of pretending to be someone they are not by encouraging others to do the same. This is also why so many adult trans people advocate for child transition," she explains. "If an innocent, pure child can 'be trans,' that validates their identity and belief system too. An enormous amount of mental energy is devoted to the crowdsourcing of validation and firefighting of anything that triggers internal conflict, which is always nagging in the back of the mind.

"When a person is at peace with themselves and expressing themselves naturally, they don't desperately micromanage everything and everyone around them."

Jamie and Helena had long, long conversations with each other, reflecting on their lives up to that point, and during these conversations Jamie admitted that she, too, "didn't want to be trans anymore."

Now they had to decide what their next steps would be, and they were afraid to share what they were thinking with their families. "There's an enormous amount of shame in realizing how much hurt and chaos has been inflicted on others in your pursuit of ideas you now think were ridiculous and destructive," Helena wrote. "You think of all the decisions you made that weren't directly related to your transition, but were made in the effort of chasing the fantasy more broadly, and you feel like you've just woken up in a pit of your own digging, too deep to climb out of. You feel trapped, cornered, panicked, and deeply ashamed. Regret comes with a lot of self-flagellation, and at the time, there wasn't the big detransitioner community there is today to let us know that we weren't alone."

Helena, who briefly began calling herself nonbinary and had picked a gender-neutral name to go by, struggled to find online resources on transition regret. She finally stumbled on a detransitioner essay by an older woman who identified as lesbian, but Helena couldn't see herself in the story. "I felt an incredible emotional whiplash, like I had just woken up from a five-year spell and was suffering amnesia about how I'd gotten to where I was," she wrote. "I was hungry for clues that would help me make sense of my position."

She finally stumbled on the Reddit r/detrans forum.[7]

This forum has become hugely influential in helping detransitioners connect with one another and discover just how many detransitioners there actually are. Here are a few sample posts from r/detrans:

- "Anyone else know/speculate that their hormones were off before transitioning?" asks a user. "While taking a low dose of T I became aware of how quickly my body reacted to hormones and that made me start wondering if perhaps my body's hormones were out of whack to begin with...."[8]
- Another user asks for advice on dealing with "testicular implants." "I stopped T after a few years and look as I did before, as an androgynous female," she writes. "I would like to ask a doctor to take the implants out, but I feel lost as to where to start, and scared. Do I contact surgeons who do metiodioplasties? The doctor I went to before? A different doctor? Is it as involved as typical surgeries, hospital stay?"[9]
- Another apparently biologically male user posts about his desire to achieve an athletic body post-detransition: "So I was a couple of months on estrogen and now I am off since a few weeks, I lost a lot of my muscle mass. Has anyone here managed to regain an athletic and healthy physique? I'm doing some push ups, pull ups, dips at the moment, and the body aches are horrible. I feel like an old man at 25. It's depressing."[10]

- "I genuinely don't know how to cope with this kind of grief," reflects another user. "I try so hard to get over it and move on but every now and then it will hit me and i start freaking out and crying uncontrollably. i get so jealous of all the other girls at college who are so beautiful and can feel free enough to wear what they want. i want nothing more than to just be a normal girl. my face still looks like my dads and it freaks me out every time i look in the mirror, i dont know what to do i just want my old body back i just want to have a normal life, this one decision i made when i was 17 is fucking up every aspect of my life."[11]

The forum includes FAQs about legal options that detransitioners have, including advice from an allegedly anonymous lawyer who posted in the r/detrans forum in July 2019. Its head moderator is a biologically female detransitioner named Alex. I reached out to Alex for this book, hoping to include her story, but she was not open to interviews. She did encourage me to speak with Chloe.

According to some online detransitioners, the Reddit forum has saved their lives.

"One year ago this month I had a noose tied in my closet and had done research on the best way to hang myself, tested the strength of the rope, wrote a note, and went to bed with full intention of killing myself the next day," said Twitter user "naro," who goes by Jesse. "Until God intervened and I found r/detrans."[12]

As of June 2023, r/detrans has almost fifty thousand members. Helena thinks that the now massive forum had only about one hundred subscribers at the time she found it, but it helped her realize that there were other people out there feeling the same way she was.

"When I had my detransition realization, I immediately wanted to go back to looking like a girl," she said. "The men's clothes, short hair, and my wispy little testosterone mustache made me sick to look at." Helena bought some basic feminine clothing, some cheap makeup, and a wig. These items helped her a little bit but she still "felt kind of like a man in drag. It was a really gross, uncomfortable feeling," she reflected. "I didn't know if I would ever feel normal. The realization that my escapist fantasy I had hoped would save me from my teenage misery was a fraud sucked me right back into that old misery. The consequences of my decisions compounded it further. I felt utterly, hopelessly trapped."

Working more solitary hours at other jobs, Helena stumbled on another subreddit called r/GenderCritical (one of the most prolific forums questioning gender ideology, which was banned from Reddit in 2020 for promoting "hate speech" by saying transgender women are not women).[13] It was the first time that she had been exposed to a countercultural perspective on transgender ideology, and she "couldn't look away."

As Helena explains on Substack, "I searched the subreddit for topics of detransition and regret, and I saw other young women posting similar stories to mine. I made a post, and was met with a surge of positive, encouraging comments. Somebody recommended me the book *Female Erasure* by Ruth Barrett, which presented me with both illuminating facts that contradicted the trans narrative and an alternative, positive image of womanhood. I still remember the exact moment, standing crouched over the work iPad alone in my smoothie store, when I had the mind-bending realization that not only was I not the only one going through this, but it was a full-fledged phenomenon. I had been manipulated, taken advantage of, and involved in a cult-like community."

Helena dove deeper into online discussions of gender. She dabbled in radical feminism and examined the work of the group 4thWaveNow (pediatric transition skeptics), activist Lily Maynard, and researcher Lisa Littman. From Littman, Helena learned about rapid-onset gender dysphoria (ROGD), which Littman discusses in her 2018 study, "Parent Reports of Adolescents and Young Adults Perceived to Show Signs of a Rapid Onset of Gender Dysphoria."[14] ROGD, Helena explains, "describes certain patterns parents have reported that preceded the sudden declaration by their adolescent children that they are transgender, most notably in adolescents who showed no pronounced gender incongruence in childhood."

Reading Dr. Littman's study made Helena realize she ticked just about every single box: she had the preexisting mental health issues, the decline in mental health and in her relationships with her parents, and the increased social media use; had been spending less time around her non-transgender friends; was isolating herself from her family and only trusting transgender-promoting sources; and more. "I was in shock," she wrote. "This was…me! Perhaps more importantly, this was…EVERYONE! All of those young biological females I had been friends with online and offline who identified as trans also fit this exact description."

Helena also saw that Littman had received heavy backlash from transgender activists for her research.

"I was pissed," she said.

"I was angry about having this kind of information kept from me by the community, which I now understood exhibits information control dynamics similar to that of cults or extreme religious sects. I was angry that clinicians either didn't understand or didn't make the effort to read this information about demographics and gender dysphoria. I was angry that I had been affirmed every step of the way, and only questioned when I was starting to express regret. I was angry that people who seemed to be making a genuine attempt to understand this new phenomenon were being targeted, and I was angry that I would have targeted them too if I had known about this not long ago."

Her fury prompted her to get back on Twitter (she says her account had about twenty-five followers at the time) and describe her own experiences. "I didn't know if anybody would see my post, but I wanted to get these thoughts out," Helena explained.

Her account grew—and quickly. Before she knew it, she was being quoted in major media outlets and invited on television. "People did see it though, and I began to interact with other detransitioners, parents, and gender-critical people," she explains. "Hearing how deeply so many people were being affected by this phenomenon that had been so damaging to me too was invigorating, and I became passionate about understanding it (and my experiences) as thoroughly as I could and exchanging ideas with others who were lost in the confusion with me."[15]

Chloe

When Chloe stopped taking testosterone, she didn't have some magic reversal moment.

But she did become intensely suicidal and severely depressed. She also began having emotional outbursts and had a very hard time focusing on anything in school or anywhere else. Consequently, as her lawsuit lays out, she failed her senior year of high school and was forced to get a California High School Proficiency Exam Certificate.[16]

Chloe had missed out on a several-year period of socialization while she was focused on transitioning. It's hard to fully grasp all the developmental milestones that she had skipped—even just spending time with other girls her age, learning to read their facial expressions, likes and dislikes, social cues, what is "cool" and not cool, group dynamics, and more.[17]

And the testosterone permanently changed Chloe's body. Her bone structure is altered. Her shoulders are wider. She has an Adam's apple. She has a stronger jaw, forehead, and nose. Her ribcage is bigger. Her hips are underdeveloped. Even though she has stopped taking the testosterone, her voice is still deeper, more masculine, and also weaker, with a "greater tendency to crack and lose power."

The testosterone also caused her to suffer "loss of sensation and severe atrophy of her reproductive organs," as her legal complaint explains. She suffers from frequent urinary tract infections and related discomfort. Her UTI symptoms are ongoing and, as her lawsuit notes, she had clotting issues, incontinence issues, and digestive tract issues in the first few months after stopping hormones.

These are far from the only repercussions Chloe faces from taking testosterone. She developed joint pain in her knees that somehow has spread; sometimes she has unpredictable pains that shoot across her back.

She has to deal with extra facial and body hair.

Chloe's lawyers also allege that the testosterone cut several inches off Chloe's potential full adult height. Her lawsuit suggests that, because of her hormone treatment, she is at higher risk of facing bone density problems and bone fractures, particularly at an elderly age.

And her "top surgery" is still causing her a huge amount of pain and distress. "Chloe has ongoing complications with her grafts for the mastectomy, which require regular care to address and that make showering and swimming problematic," her lawsuit says. "The damaged area of her skin on her right nipple graft has also spread off the graft and is moving downwards. She has lost erogenous sensation in her chest area. The nerves are not connected properly, and she will feel sensations in her arm pit instead of her chest."

That is far from the end of Chloe's problems. She's at a "significant increased risk" of facing fertility issues, making her potentially unable to have children. And if she is able to have children, her lawsuit emphasizes, "she may be unable to deliver them naturally due to inadequate development of her pelvic bones."

Further, Chloe's lawyers expressed concerns that the hormones may have stunted her neurological development. They argue that she should have been treated for autism spectrum disorder, but she has lost the ability to receive this treatment and "related neurocognitive development" that may have benefited her as an adult.[18]

And because of her massive increase in libido, brought on by the testosterone, Chloe's lawsuit alleges that she "suffered from and developed a pornography addiction."

Her complaint also explains, "Chloe has suffered severe anxiety, depression, and suicidal ideation as a result of this so-called treatment. She now has deep emotional wounds, severe regrets, and a deep distrust for the medical system. She continues to struggle with depression. It is very difficult for her to cope with the possibility of being unable to have biological children, and her inability to breastfeed them if she is able to have children. She also struggles considerably with her body image, which she describes as having 'taken a major hit from all of this.'"

"The full extent of Chloe's damages are being investigated and are not fully known at the time of filing this complaint," the filing continues. "The allegations herein are intended to be only a partial summary of the relevant facts and medical records, and Chloe's medical issues and damages resulting from the gross negligence, coercion, and fraud Defendants committed in this case."[19]

I asked Chloe if she ever talked to her surgeons or doctors again after her procedures. She said that immediately after her detransition, she consulted with Dr. Taylor, basically to tell her that she was going off hormones and that she regretted transitioning. "I didn't really get any help with that," she said, "no guidance on how to stop it, I just went totally cold turkey off of that and I don't know if that was the best way to do it because it caused me a lot of issues with my health, both physically and psychologically.

"Although, I did get my period back pretty soon afterward," she pointed out, "just two months after stopping. Which is a total miracle, especially because it's so regular now. It wasn't like that when I started because I was so young."

Can you imagine that? Chloe hadn't even had regular periods before she went on puberty blockers.

Dr. Watson retired the year that Chloe detransitioned, Chloe told me. But before Watson retired, Chloe spoke with her that one time, over the phone, about her detransition. She wanted to ask Dr. Watson how to deal with the mental and physical pain she was experiencing, whether she could fix what they had done to her, whether her chest could be reconstructed.

She wanted help.

Instead, Chloe says that Dr. Watson asked her, "Don't you think that this is just another part of your gender journey?" Chloe's young voice was almost bitter as she told me this. "Failure of a treatment. It's just the journey, right? Since when are children supposed to have a gender journey? What does that mean?"

"What did you say?" I asked.

She couldn't remember exactly. "I think I said, 'No…?'" Chloe said. Then she laughed, asking, "What else am I supposed to say to that?"

She became more serious, adamant: "It's not just a journey. That really de-emphasized all the pain, regret, and everything that came from going through what I have. And all of it was unnecessary. It's *not* a journey," Chloe emphasized firmly. "It's a nightmare."

Dr. Watson even suggested that her detransition was actually just another transition, Chloe told me.

"Nooo, it is *NOT* another transition," Chloe said, with some of the most marked firmness I have heard in her voice. "Not a retransition. This is a detransition. I'm not transitioning to anything, I'm just living as myself."

She explained, "It was frustrating hearing things like that. It was kind of like she was trying to spin things around, about this horrible experience I had, to match her idea of what this all is. Almost very ideologically led."

Chloe said that Dr. Watson even told her, "I've never had a patient like you before! I've never had anybody tell me that they regretted their transition."

Some people might have doubted themselves at this point. But Chloe says she was immediately skeptical.

"When I heard that, I was just like...it can't be. It just can't be," she said. "There's no way. Even if nobody's reported that to her, even if that were true...it's hard to go back to your doctors and tell them that. Because they're the people who got you to that situation in the first place. And you don't know if you are going to get any care from them.

"I mean, I tried my best," she said. "I thought that they were going to care for me, just the way that they did while I was taking these treatments."

Chloe had gone to her doctor begging for help and understanding— trusting that the doctors who had forever altered her life would have her best interests at heart. And now she was being made to feel like her experience was not only unusual, but unknown. The enormity of that overwhelmed me.

I asked Chloe if she found it discouraging to be told that she was Watson's first patient to regret her transition.

"A little bit," said Chloe. "But I still knew, there must be some other kid out there like me. There has to be. I had spoken to a few adults in the detrans online communities who detransitioned. I didn't know of anybody who had transitioned as a kid, really, not medically.

"I just knew intuitively that it wasn't just me," she said. "There is no way. No way."

She also grew more and more convinced that it wasn't just her because of how many adults were talking about detransitioning in the r/detrans subreddit (the same one that Helena had dived into) and in private and public Discord servers.

The way that her doctors and the transgender community treated her also strengthened her belief that she wasn't alone. "They tried to silence me just for talking about the pain and regret, and how I felt like I was used by my doctors," she said thoughtfully. It made her realize, "If they're shutting me up just for talking about my experience, they're very well doing the same to other people in that situation."

It's hard to speak up, Chloe admitted. "There's the social pressure of all that, and then just the shame of admitting this life-changing decision you made was wrong, and painstakingly attempting to go back after all the physical and identity-related changes."

I told her I thought she was very brave for trying to talk to her doctors about it.

"Thank you," she said simply. "It's just not something I can stay silent about."[20]

CHAPTER 8

He

Ritchie

"I want to tell everyone what they took from us, what irreversible really means, and what that reality looks like for us," shared Ritchie Herron, a biological man who lived as a woman for a decade:

> No one told me any of what I'm going to tell you now. . . .
>
> I have no sensation in my crotch region at all. You could stab me with a knife and I wouldn't know.
>
> The entire area is numb, like it's shell shocked and unable to comprehend what happened, even 4 years on. . . .
>
> No one told me that the base area of your penis is left, it can't be removed—meaning you're left with a literal stump inside that twitches.
>
> When you take Testosterone and your libido returns, you wake up with morning wood, without the tree.
>
> I wish this was a joke. . . .

And thats something that will never come back and one of the reason why i got surgery.

My sex drive died about 6 months on HRT and at the time I was glad to be rid of it, but now 10 years later, Im realising what im missing out on and what I won't get back. . . .

Because even if i had a sex drive, my neo vagina is so narrow and small, i wouldn't even be able to have sex if i wanted too.

And when I do use a small dilator, I have random pockets of sensation that only seem to pick up pain, rather than pleasure. . . .

Any pleasure I do get comes from the Prostate that was moved forward and wrapped in glands from the penis, meaning anal sex isnt possible and can risk further damage. . . .

Then theres the dreams. I dream often, that I have both sets of genitals, in the dream I'm distressed I have both, why both I think? I tell myself to wake up because I know its just a dream.

And I awaken into a living nightmare. . . .

In those moments of amnesia as I would wake, I would reach down to my crotch area expecting something that was there for 3 decades, and it's not.

My heart skips a beat, every single damn time. . . .

Then theres the act of going to the toilet. It takes me about 10 minutes to empty my bladder, it's extremely slow, painful and because it dribbles no matter how much i relax, it will then just go all over that entire area, leaving me soaken. . . .

So after cleaning myself up, I will find moments later that my underwear is wet—no matter how much I wiped, it slowly drips out for the best part of an hour.

I never knew at 35 I ran the risk like smelling like piss everywhere I went. . . .

Now i get to the point where im detransitioned and the realisation that this is permanent is catching up with me.

During transition, I was obsessive and deeply unwell, I cannot believe they were allowed to do this to me, even after all the red flags. . . .

I wasn't even asked if I wanted to freeze sperm or want kids. In my obsessive, deeply unwell state they just nodded along and didnt tell me the realities, what life would be like. . . .

And finally, theres dilation, which is like some sort of demonic ceremony where you impale yourself for 20 agonising minutes to remind you of your own stupidity. . . .

This isn't even the half of it. And this isn't regret either, this is grief and anger.

Fuck everyone who let this happen.[1]

It's hard to overstate the anguish expressed in that harrowing story, which went viral on Twitter when Ritchie posted it in June 2022.

Since then, he has repeatedly spoken out against the dangers of quick affirmations. Unlike the other detransitioners in this book, Ritchie lives in the United Kingdom, and his surgery was performed through the UK's National Health Service (which he plans to sue).

Since he has shared his mental and physical anguish so publicly, Ritche must endure the rage of activists and peers who believe he has betrayed them by speaking to conservative outlets—largely the only media interested in telling the stories of detransitioners.

"I'm tired," he wrote in an April 2023 Twitter thread, reflecting on the "purity testing, the purposeful misrepresentation" that he has been subjected to. "Few actually give a shit about the human factor," he wrote. "Most only care if their 'side' is right, even though there are no sides, just dozens of factions. I belong to none of them."

Ritchie said he still hates his body. In fact, he hates it more than he did before surgery: "I don't want to be a balding hairy eunuch with breasts," he reflected, "it's quite a devastating thought.... I'm stuck as I am, and going back isn't really possible. People still see me as trans, and frankly I don't think I care anymore."

Ritchie just wanted to be helped with his severe mental health issues. But here he is today, still intensely struggling. He calls himself a "pariah of pariahs," or "at best...a token disaster to fawn over...."

"[I don't know] what my future holds, it doesn't really matter at this point, what's done is done," Ritchie says. "All I know is we deserve justice for what happened to us, and I'm doing everything I can to make that a reality."[2]

This book has thus far focused on the stories of young women who tried to transition to become boys or men. But I would be remiss if I did not also share the stories of some biological men who, like Ritchie, also tried to cross this divide.

Walt

Walt Heyer, author of *Trans Life Survivors*, is one of the most prominent detransitioners. Walt's book is a sobering look at some of the emails he has received from the "hundreds" of people who have written to him about "the biggest mistake" of their lives. But his story is a little different from the others we have examined, since his transition attempt took place decades ago—meaning that it was devoid of the social media influence so central to the other stories.

April 2023 marked forty years since Walt's therapist told him that a "sex change" was the only solution to his mental distress.

"Unfortunately, I followed his advice, obtained cross-sex hormones, and underwent surgery," Walt wrote in a March 2023 piece. "As I learned through my painful experience, 'gender-affirming treatment' (GAT), also known as 'gender-affirming care,' is medical fraud and malpractice."[3]

Walt shared with me that his grandmother dressed him as a girl in a purple dress when he was between the ages of four and six. Though Walt initially enjoyed the extra attention he received from his grandmother, he said her actions later caused him to experience severe gender dysphoria.

"Affirmation of cross gender/sex identities is child abuse," he told me, "and I have been dealing with the consequences in my life for 75 years."

Walt, who had been diagnosed with gender dysphoria, told me that he underwent cross-gender hormone therapy and obtained a surgical gender change in 1983 at age forty-two. He shared that though he lived as a woman for eight years, he still experienced gender dysphoria during that time and eventually became suicidal.

Walt ultimately detransitioned in 1999 and underwent psychotherapy to "resolve having been sexually abused and cross dressed and affirmed by my grandmother."[4]

"Through hard work and effective psychological counseling, I resolved the wounds of the past and my desire to be a woman dissipated," he wrote in a January 2020 piece for The Federalist. "I re-identified as Walt Heyer legally and socially, removed the breast implants, and with the support of an amazing group of friends, built my life anew, this time on psychological wholeness."

Walt went on to get married to a woman and has now been happily married for over twenty-five years. But the suffering he experienced throughout his attempted transition process haunted him, spurring him to find ways to support others who were going through what he had.[5]

In addition to his writings on transgender issues, Walt runs the website Sex Change Regret. That site is dedicated to raising awareness about people who regret their transitions, and to helping other detransitioners understand that they are not alone.[6]

Not only does he regret his own gender transition—he is strongly opposed to encouraging children who might want to transition and calls such affirmation "child abuse." "The idea [that] you can change your gender/sex is a folly," he said in our 2020 interview. "It destroyed my body, caused my divorce and ended my career, all for nothing, a total waste of my life during the 8 years as 'Laura.'

"It is categorically impossible for anyone to change their innate chemistry," Heyer insisted to me. "Telling them they can is emotional, psychological and even social child abuse over the long term. Thousands are de-transitioning because they were affirmed in an identity that was not who they are. It will continue to be a disaster for many years to come."[7]

Walt has watched the transgender movement progress over the past few decades. He was once told that detransitioning is rare—but his Sex Change Regret website has proven to him that this is not the case.

"The same thing is happening to people today, except at younger ages," he writes. "I know. I get their emails.

"In the decades following my surgery, instead of the 'gender' industry dying out, it has run rampant—devaluing, dehumanizing, and destroying thousands of lives," Walt said. "When I fell for the scam, the patients were exclusively adult men. Today, the industry targets vulnerable adolescents of both sexes influenced by the emotional and physical throes of puberty, who can't be expected to grasp the long-term consequences, such as infertility, bone density loss, and heart problems."[8]

"Abel"

"Abel Garcia" is another young man whose life was drastically changed in this way.[9]

"Abel" grew up in California. He shared with me that his parents came to the United States illegally when his mother was pregnant with him. He largely keeps the rest of his family life private (such as whether he has siblings), but he did say that his parents were Catholic, as were his grandparents. "My parents were religious, but not as religious as my grandparents," he said. "And I was the least religious."

Abel went to public school, but his family moved a ton within Central and Southern California while he was growing up, so he found it a little difficult to make friends. He does not describe himself as being super interested in either typically male or typically female activities as a kid—he played soccer in kindergarten and elementary school, but he largely liked to be alone and played video games when he was able.

He never really had a social media presence, Abel said, and if he spent time on the internet, it was on YouTube or Facebook. But around elementary school, he began wondering whether he was actually a guy. His grandfather, father, and cousins were pretty masculine, and coming from a "very masculine, very machismo" Mexican culture, Abel felt that he was coming up short. "For some reason, I assumed that if I can't be the *most* masculine person, I must have been born a woman," he said.

It was this "most" that stuck out to me and that Abel emphasized repeatedly as he discussed his childhood. "I wish I had known that I don't have to be the most masculine boy or man and that it's okay to be not the most masculine," Abel told me at the end of our conversation. "I wish I would have known that."

He describes himself as very empathetic and a bit more emotional than most boys his age, and these aspects of his personality confused him. "I was also very shy, very quiet, timid," Abel added. "Not your typical boy. And I was very observant and deep into my thoughts. I guess the best way I can explain is, I was very aware of myself, hyper-aware of myself and the people around me."

Abel says he was raised by his grandparents for the first few years of his life, since his parents were usually busy working in the Central California fields. Eventually his father got a better-paying job and was able to support the family, so Abel's mother became his primary caregiver.

Abel didn't tell anyone that he wondered if he was really a woman until after he had graduated high school. As he explained to me, he spent about a decade holding that inside. And unlike all the female detransitioners I have spoken with, Abel says he didn't talk to anyone on the internet about his musings (he also didn't really have access to the internet until late middle school because of his family's financial situation).

Abel doesn't know why he was so influenced internally when others were influenced externally, but he did bring up that many detransitioners have been discussing the correlation between gender dysphoria and autism. "I know one thing with a lot of the other detransitioners is [that] a lot of them say they are autistic," he said. "I've never been tested myself, personally. But that seems to be a correlation." Maybe, Abel speculated, he was on the spectrum himself, and that had something to do with his hyper-self-awareness at a young age. But he doesn't know.

Abel continued to think about all this as he went through high school. When he had graduated high school and was in his first semester of college, deciding what to do with the rest of his life, he thought to himself, *It's now or never. I can go see medical professionals, see what is going on.* He wanted to find out what his thoughts meant. *Can I get help?* he wondered.

Eventually Abel was directed towards his local LGBT center. "And that's how, I guess, my story begins," he reflected.

He spoke to someone at the center and told them that he felt like he might have been born in the wrong body, and that he wanted to talk to someone and see what would happen. They gave him an appointment, set him up with a therapist, he told me. And during his very first appointment with the therapist, she affirmed to him that he was transgender, Abel said.

"She just affirmed you, straight up?" I asked.

"Yep," he replied.

"How did you feel?" I asked.

"I was shocked, honestly," he said. "But then again, because it was a therapist, I was raised to always trust medical professionals because again, they are medical professionals and I had no reason to doubt them, especially since I don't have the same background."

The therapist also told Abel that she would get him the letter needed to begin his transition that same day if he wanted it, promising him that she "didn't want to gatekeep" him (that's a phrase I encounter often on transgender websites and in "gender-affirming care" contexts). But when he said he needed more time to think about it, she didn't push him to do anything further—"for that day at least," he said.

"I took her word…but part of me, in the back of my head, was skeptical," Abel said. "I told her I didn't want to accept the letter right away. I wanted to take a bit more time to process everything, to make sure everything was accurate and there were no mistakes."

He continued seeing the therapist for a few months. A few months earlier, Abel had told his mother that he believed he was transgender and that he was going to see a therapist to try to transition. He had also asked her not to tell his father, he told me. "She cried," he said. "Asked, what if I'm wrong? There's a possibility of being wrong. I told her, no I'm not wrong. I was one of those kids, no, I know everything."

He didn't want his dad to know because he knew his father wouldn't take it well. "And I was right," Abel said. "My mother eventually told him," he added. "And unfortunately my dad did the worst idea he could ever think of."

Abel's father couldn't believe his ears when his wife told him that his son wanted to transition to become a girl. He wanted to cure his son of such thoughts. Around May 2016, when Abel was nineteen years old, his father told him that he needed to go to Mexico for a dentist appointment that involved anesthesia, and he needed Abel to come with him to drive him back. So Abel got in the car and drove across the border with his father. "I believed him because I had no reason to doubt my father," he said.

They went to the dentist, and then his father suggested they go get some food. "He eventually gets directions for a location, and on our way there, that's when I started to get some red flags," Abel said. "But I did not care, because I was an angsty teenager." Eventually they parked, and his father walked away from the car saying he would be right back—he just needed to check out the restaurant. Abel waited in the car until his father came back, and then they went into the building together. The building was completely black—you couldn't see anything from the outside to the inside, Abel told me. And once they were inside, he realized that it wasn't a restaurant. They were not going to lunch.

"He took me to a brothel," Abel said.

Abel's father told him to pick one of the women. The boy was shocked and caught incredibly off guard. "I was a shy kid," he said. "I was very quiet, very reserved, very awkward, and nervous near women."

Abel didn't know what to do. So he asked his father, "Which one do you recommend?" Then Abel randomly picked one of the women. "I don't remember which one," he said. "And I don't remember how many there were."

Abel and the prostitute began to walk away together, but as they turned the corner, his father asked for the prostitute to hold back a moment.

Abel was told to go into a specific room, but he said all his "red flags were going off" and he didn't trust anything in the moment. So he hid around the corner and overheard his father tell the prostitute in Spanish, "Take good care of him. It's his first time."

Abel says the situation was traumatizing. He doesn't really remember what happened next. It was his first time to have sex; he was in a Mexican brothel with a strange woman, a prostitute; and his father was waiting outside to see how it was going to go.

"She tells me to undress, and because I am ashamed of my body at the time, I am questioning myself, and I was also a little fat, so I didn't want that to be seen. Eventually I undress," he told me. "I don't remember much, but I know that she was doing her job. And I don't recall much, but let's just say, nothing happened. We did it, but nothing really happened," he explained.

"Eventually we got a loud bang on the door, which I guess meant we were out of time or we were running out of time. Either way, it doesn't really matter because I could not perform. Honestly," he asked, "who's going to perform in that situation when it's forced upon you by your own father?"

Abel felt that his father would be ashamed of his son for failing in this way with the prostitute. So he asked her to lie for him. "I asked her, 'Tell my father it went well, it was the best thing you ever had. Blah blah blah.' She does cover for me, lied to my father, straight to his face."

His father paid the prostitute $100, Abel said.

On the way home, Abel's father kept bringing up the brothel and the prostitute, trying to talk to him about it. Furious, overwhelmed, and upset, Abel desperately didn't want to talk about it, but he also didn't want his father to know that he had hated his first sexual encounter. So he lied again, saying that he enjoyed it, that they should go back, and that they should bring one of his uncles.

"What are you thinking at this point?" I asked him. "As you are in the car on your way home?"

"I was thinking, I hate my father," Abel responded. "How dare he do that? You as a father should be protecting your children, not harming your children. I don't care whether you assume that I'm gay, or that my mother told you that I was going to transition. Why would you assume that's the best course of action? . . .

"I lost respect for my father at that moment," he said. "There's no way any child would forgive their parents right there, right then, if they did that."

But Abel's father believed him when he said that he had enjoyed the brothel experience and wanted to go back for round two. "He was happy," Abel said.

He guesses that his father eventually told his mother, "I took Abel to sleep with a prostitute, and he's cured now." But he isn't sure. He hasn't asked, and he doesn't really want to. "That incident was the straw that broke the camel's back," he said. "It made me jump off the deep end."

He hadn't been 100 percent on board to transition, but after the brothel incident, he decided that transitioning was the best route to "get away from the trauma."

So Abel got a prescription for hormones. And a few months later, he got the hormones themselves. He said he had health insurance, but it wasn't accepted because his hormones weren't considered medically necessary. So he had to pay out of pocket. He doesn't remember exactly how much the hormones cost, but he believes it was less than $100 since he had a $100 bill that day.

Abel's doctor did a scan of his hand to check "my bone age just to make sure I was good," Abel said. He doesn't remember the full conversation with the doctors about the hormones. But the weirdest part of the experience came next, according to Abel.

"My doctor had told me there was a transgender woman, male to female, who worked within the clinic as their transgender member to help new transgender patients," he said, noting that the doctors asked if he wanted to speak to this trans-identifying person about the potential side effects of the hormones. "So I said sure, that's fine."

This trans-identifying person, a biologically male individual who identified as a transgender woman, came out and talked to Abel. A few seconds into the conversation, the clinic worker asked Abel to "stand up and do a little twirl" for him. Abel felt awkward, but he got up and did a little twirl as he was asked. The trans-identifying clinic worker then said that yes, by looking at Abel's body structure, he could tell that Abel "should have been born a woman."

Abel found the experience incredibly odd. Now he views it as almost a "grooming" move. "This was the first time I had ever been groomed, I guess," he explained.

He took his prescription to a local pharmacy, he told me, where he paid out of pocket and obtained the pills—estradiol. Initially he took one milligram of estradiol. Later on, it went up to four milligrams of estradiol, and after four milligrams, he switched to injectables.

"I was told it was healthier for my liver to do injectables," he said, "since obviously pills go through the liver and eventually take a toll on it. And the injections, I would get a better result of estrogen into my system since it was more direct."

Not long after he started taking estradiol, Abel noticed that his skin was much softer. He wasn't breaking out in acne as much as he used to. The fat on his body began to redistribute, and he began developing a more breast-like chest. And though he didn't have much facial hair, even that drastically slowed down.

"I was very happy. I was very proud of what I was doing at the time," he explained. "I was being affirmed by everyone, and so I was assuming that I was doing the right thing."

Before he began seeing a therapist, Abel had experienced doubts about whether he was ready for surgeries. "I don't know if it was my conscience, if I was going insane, a voice in my head... religious people are saying it was the voice of God," he said thoughtfully. "But I told myself I wanted to wait five years before I got breast implants, and [I wanted to wait] ten years before I got that bottom surgery (penile inversion, loss of my genitals to create a wound, whatever you want to call it)."

Abel met with a doctor and told him that he was ready for breast implants. He eventually wanted to get facial and bottom surgery, he told the doctor, but not for ten years.

A few weeks afterwards, Abel said, he received not one but two letters in the mail congratulating him on being approved for both top and bottom surgery. "I think I got like one or two more letters in the mail from my insurance saying, 'Hey, don't forget you have this appointment. Don't forget to make this appointment for bottom surgery!'"

I asked Abel if he thinks his insurance company was purposefully pushing him towards these surgeries.

"Oh, definitely," he said.

The day of his surgery, the day that he went in to get breast implants, Abel said he was a little scared. But he thought this was what he wanted.

He doesn't remember much about the surgery. And he says his friend drove him home.

At first Abel's recovery went pretty smoothly. Then he began to notice issues. "My right chest, or right nipple, or whatever you want to call it, I noticed it went numb...I don't think I even brought it up. Because I thought that it was going to come back to sensation. But it never did, and it never came back.

"It really doesn't help either way now, because they had to cut so much off so both my nipples are numb.... Honestly if you wanted to stab me in the chest, if I wasn't looking I probably wouldn't know until I looked down."

Abel hadn't even known that this was a possibility. No one had told him, he said. "Because it is this ideology, I would assume it's best for them not to say anything just in the small possibility the person they talk to is very offended, which unfortunately is 99 percent of their clients," he told me, when I asked why no one had explained these possible side effects to him. "Everyone gets easily offended."

As an example of doctors acting on ideology, Abel told me a story about a young lady he knew who wanted to become a man. She was very overweight, Abel said, and her surgeon said he would not perform a double mastectomy on her unless she lost some weight. Outraged, the girl found another surgeon. And the surgery predictably did not go well. Something went wrong during her surgery, and during recovery her scars began gushing blood or some kind of liquid. "She had so many issues," Abel told me.

Overall, from September 2020 to March of 2022, Abel said he spent a total of $7,105.42, including on doctor visits and two surgeries after he decided to detransition—one to remove the implants and one to reconstruct his chest. That included a $2,535 fee to save his nipples. During the breast implant surgery, the doctors had to remove his nipples at one point. The surgeon saved them and put them back on "where they needed to go," Abel said.

Abel also shared that he had been trying to become a cop, but he failed the police academy. So he started working for the chief of police as a volunteer. And, wanting to build a better relationship between the transgender community in the area and the police, he went to talk to a nonprofit transgender group about how that group could collaborate with the police.

"They didn't like my questioning," he said. "They accused me of acting like a cisgender woman. And here's the most shocking part," Abel added, "the person that I spoke to was the person who had me do a twirl in front of [him] a few years prior....

"I thought they were just having a bad day," he said of the people at the transgender clinic. "So I came back the next day, and same situation. And I didn't realize then, but they called the chief of police and filed a complaint against me, that I was harassing them."

This took place about two months before Abel got his surgery.

After the surgery, he was only happy with what he had done for about three months. "Life happened. One day I wake up and I realize, 'What the hell am I doing to myself?'"

Abel had grown out his hair all the way down his back. At this point, he was "passing" as a woman. "If you want to take a religious point of view, God speaking to me, or my own conscience or my own voice...it all had built up from right before I went to therapy, and it just came crashing in all at once," Abel said.

"I woke up, went to the bathroom and looked at myself, realizing I was just destroying my body. No matter what I would have done, if

I would have continued getting my face done, my genitals removed, even if the world recognized me as a woman, and I was able to present well enough that I was able to lie to the world, that deep down inside of me, I was always going to be a man.

"At best, I would have been a caricature of what I believed a woman was, because no matter what, in the end, I would never know what it is to be a woman. I would only have an idea what it is just from my own stereotypical idea of a woman, my own caricatures, the idea of a woman. Even if I was able to replicate a decent amount of it in the end, being a woman is more than what the caricature of my mind had."

Abel went to talk to his doctor. His doctor told him to talk to his therapist, Abel says, and his therapist suggested he was not having doubts about being transgender but was just experiencing childhood traumas coming back up.

"I don't have childhood trauma, not that I'm aware of," Abel exclaimed to me. "I think that's when I had just realized this was all just insanity," he said. "So I just told her, 'You know what, I forgot to mention, I have a new job. Unfortunately, the hours are much different, so I won't be able to come back as often.' That was my excuse to never see her again," he said.

"I need a new therapist," Abel said he told his doctor. "My last one is crazy."

To Abel's chagrin, he found that his insurance would cover his transgender surgeries—but not his detransition. At this point he was working with a male therapist, who cautioned Abel not to be too cavalier with his detransition. You don't know the potential side effects of what could happen to your body, Abel said the therapist told him.

"You probably already noticed the drastic difference of wanting to transition and wanting to detransition," Abel added. "When I wanted to transition, everything's already set in stone for me. From the moment I start to one Sunday with surgeries and past that. But for me to detransition, there's roadblocks every half centimeter so I would not be able to get any proper help."

Abel began to drink heavily. In fact, he became an alcoholic. He had lost hope.

It wasn't until a 2018 incident at a party where he "royally fucked up" that Abel realized he needed to get it together. Abel didn't share exactly what happened at the party, but he said that it shook him enough to make him realize that he needed to change things.

In December 2020 he decided to surgically detransition—to get his breast implants removed.

"How have you been doing since then?" I asked him.

"My emotions ebb and flow, up and down, however you want to say it," he shared. "And now, due to my past history of alcoholism and just because of how everything has gone, I try not to think about my decisions, what's happened to me, because I know my mind can go into deep places, deep, dark places, and I'd rather not go there. I try to keep myself busy by overworking myself to death, figuratively speaking, and sleeping as long as I can, and helping others."

I asked Abel how he thinks his new transition will affect his life going forward. He isn't totally sure—there are many physical side effects that he is trying to understand.

"The left half of my body has tremors," he said. "Unfortunately, I don't know when they will happen. They come every so often. My genitals have atrophied (which means they've shrunk) so it's really hard to use a restroom. And unfortunately, when I do have to relieve myself, even if I relieve myself completely, there's still enough urine left that I urinate over myself. I don't know if I can have kids due to the atrophy of my genitals and the time that I was on hormones."

Abel also said he has astigmatism in his left eye, which is making him almost blind in that eye, "or at least the eyesight has degraded drastically in a short amount of time." He has had doctors check on it, and the eye doctor told him that they've seen stuff like this, but they can't confirm or deny that it is due to the hormones. "I would assume that it is, because I want to say it is, but who knows," he said.

Abel has begun speaking out against gender ideology. He's friends with Chloe, and with Prisha, allied in their mutual agreement to fight back against this movement that harmed them so grievously.

Abel believes he has two possible routes going forward.

"Scenario one," he said thoughtfully. "Working with Chloe, working with other detransitioners, in the end we win against this insanity, I am able to live a comfortable life through the compensation of the medical system who chose to harm me and others. And I can live somewhat peacefully that way.

"Or option two," he added. "We all lose, because it is a system we are fighting in. Who knows from there? It can go very dark, I would assume."

That second alternative is scary. But Abel seemed optimistic. "We are picking up momentum," he said. "I would say that people are starting to wake up to how insane this is. And out of everyone right now, the most public individual is Chloe, and she's able to move everyone's hearts, which is a good thing."

His advice for young people and parents?

"Don't do what my father did," he quickly advised. Then: "Support your child, but don't support them regarding any form of transition, since that will play into their mindset. Monitor who they are hanging out with, both physically in real life and on social media and on the internet."

Abel reflects that his attempt to transition happened very quickly. But nowadays, he emphasized, it is worse. "Everything's set in stone," he said. "From the moment you see a medical professional."[10]

Thankfully, Abel didn't get the bottom surgeries that had been pushed on him.[11] Some of these surgeries, according to UVA (University of Virginia) Health, include penile skin inversion vaginoplasty "with or without scrotal skin grafting," revision vaginoplasty "using small bowel or the rectosigmoid colon," and "secondary genital reconstruction."[12]

A vaginoplasty surgery will typically take between seven and ten hours, according to Johns Hopkins Medicine, which describes the procedure thus: "Vaginoplasty involves rearranging tissue in the genital area to create a vaginal canal (or opening) and vulva (external genitalia), including the labia. To create the vaginal canal, the surgeon uses a combination of the skin surrounding the existing penis along with the scrotal skin. Depending on how much skin is available in the genital area, the surgeon may need to use a skin graft from the abdomen or thigh to construct a full vaginal canal."[13]

After the procedure, FOLX warns, you will have to care for your newly instated tissue to make sure it will survive: "All types of vaginoplasty where a canal is made require dilation."

What is dilation? Essentially, it's the "lifelong commitment" to stick different-sized dilator-type tools into your faux vagina to make sure that it doesn't close up. "Dilation prevents the vaginal walls of the canal from sticking to each other and prevents stenosis, or the canal from becoming too narrow and tight for penetration," FOLX explains. "If not dilated, the buildup of discharge and graft tissue that doesn't survive can lead to an infection. Dilation also helps stretch the pelvic muscles around the canal to maintain width/girth and minimize pain with penetration."[14]

For biological men who have undergone this surgery, going to the bathroom is a whole new ball game, Johns Hopkins Medicine acknowledges. Their website emphasizes to patients that "for the rest of your life," you will have to "wipe front to back" when "wiping with toilet paper or washing the genital area.... You may notice some spraying when you urinate," Johns Hopkins Medicine notes. "This is common and can be addressed with physical therapy to help strengthen the pelvic floor. A physical therapist can help you with exercises, which may help improve urination over time."[15]

Johns Hopkins Medicine claims that this surgically constructed vagina is sexually functional, though patients must wait twelve weeks after surgery to engage in sexual activity and "sensation is not guaranteed."

The average depth of a surgically constructed vagina depends on patient preference and anatomy: "On average, the constructed vaginal canal is between 4 and 6 inches deep. Vaginal depth is dependent on the amount of skin available in the genital area before your vaginoplasty. This varies among individuals, and some patients may need skin grafts. Some patients may request a no-depth or minimal-depth vaginal canal, which is also possible."

In a stomach-churning story for the Christian Post in April 2023, my friend Brandon Showalter reported on the death of an eighteen-year-old boy who had undergone a vaginoplasty.

"In 2016, this boy participated in a 'linchpin' Dutch study, and prior to going under the knife, doctors had arrested his natural puberty with hormone-blocking agents," Brandon explains. "Due to this intervention, his secondary sex characteristics did not develop normally." The boy's genitals had not matured, so there wasn't any usable tissue for surgeons to "fashion a simulacrum of a vagina during the penile inversion surgery," Brandon explained.

"When this is the case, surgeons routinely use a swatch of bowel tissue, which smells of excrement given the presence of fecal bacteria. The Dutch medical report explains that problems arose within 24 hours of the surgery, a laparoscopic intestinal vaginoplasty, and the boy developed lethal necrotizing fasciitis, a condition where flesh-eating germs spread throughout his body causing sepsis and, ultimately, his death," Brandon wrote. "An investigation into the boy's death revealed that the strain of E. Coli that made his organs fail was from his own intestine."[16]

Activist Chris Elston, who advocates for the protection of children and young people from gender ideology, compiled a Twitter thread that included gruesome photos of the boy's infection, Brandon noted. The boy's "maimed private anatomy was seen by millions of users and has been retweeted tens of thousands of times."

We've already discussed how some detransitioners feel about these tragic images going viral on social media, and about descriptions using this kind of language. But there is no denying the emotional response that these images provoke, the action, legislation, and protesting they provoke, or the influential eyeballs they arrest.

One conservative commentator viewed the images with horror, calling them "Frankenstein level stuff."

"I agree," billionaire Elon Musk replied. "This is super messed up."[17]

CHAPTER 9

The Aftermath: Dealing with Betrayal

Helena

Helena was absolutely terrified to tell her parents what she had realized. But as she gradually recognized that her experience was a "phenomenon," rather than a singular personal failing of her own, she began to feel strengthened.

And when they invited her to come visit them back in their hometown in spring of 2018, she decided she would tell them. "I felt myself growing more and more nervous as the day of my flight approached, and on that day, I was a wreck," Helena wrote. "The airport in my hometown has a long hallway that requires maybe ten minutes to traverse from the terminal to baggage claim."

She adds, "I distinctly remember my walk down this corridor and seeing my parents as two little dots at the very end. The dots grew and their image came into focus, and with every step I felt more afraid, my heart pounding in my chest, stomach churning, and a dizziness overcoming my body. At about 50 meters away, my vision blacked out for a few seconds! That's how terrified I was to admit to my parents what I had realized!"

At dinner that night, they asked her, "What's new?"

So she told them.

"It was an awkward conversation, but at least they didn't say 'I told you so,'" she reflects. "They didn't say much; maybe they didn't know what to say. They did say they were glad to hear it though and that they thought detransitioning was the right decision. My brother was fairly silent throughout, and later that night I heard him say to his gaming friends on Discord, 'Sooo, my sister isn't trans anymore.'"

Helena is thankful that she has not dealt with permanent damage to her body, as many other young detransitioners must live with.

The hardest part, she says, "has been coming to terms with the bad decisions I made that made my emotional struggles much more painful, my ability to socially adjust and have healthy relationships much more difficult, and generally took my life in an unexpected direction that has been *very* hard to climb out of.

"In many ways I am still climbing out of it," she shares. "The years following my initial decision to detransition have been fraught with challenges that…have required me to mature beyond my age. I am very thankful for that, and am growing to truly enjoy and respect myself, but it has also made finding my place in the world difficult."

She's still dealing with many of the original problems that led her to identify as trans in the first place, Helena says. Things like "social weaknesses, anxieties about not fitting in, poor body image, unresolved childhood grief, shame, and conflicts in my family."

And she believes that even if testosterone hadn't taken such a damaging toll on her mind, the act of identifying as transgender and attempting transition was "an act of immense self-harm. Emotions are a way for the unconscious, all sensing body to communicate to the part of us that experiences conscious thought information about how our environment and the people around us affect us," she wrote. "In order to move through and overcome painful emotions, we must first acknowledge the core emotion that is occurring and have compassion towards ourselves for feeling the emotion in the context within which it is occur[r]ing. Trans identity took me far away from this into blaming and punishing my body for the emotions I was feeling," Helena explains. "It resulted in an even wider disconnect from understanding the conditions that led me to feel such sadness, fear, and grief. Transitioning made my mental health much, much worse. Not better. It was a 'fuck you' to the hurting child inside of me. It was telling her that she didn't matter. It was telling her that I hated her and wanted to annihilate her. It was an act of war against myself."

And that war comes at a cost, Helena says. "In the aftermath, there are fires to put out, ashes and debris to clean up, towns to rebuild and ground to fertilize so that life may exist once again. Having just been at war, these necessities of the aftermath feel insurmountable; the body and mind [are] too exhausted."

In one of Helena's most heartbreaking reflections, she describes feeling like she had "just woken up from a five-year spell and was suffering amnesia," and was transported back into the consciousness of her fifteen-year-old self—"like all the years of being trans were not really me, and the real me [lay] dormant under it all, finally able to come forward once the false persona disintegrated. Being the 'real me' again, years out from detransitioning at this point, I still can't fully wrap my head around having been consumed by that false persona. It doesn't really feel like that was me. And it makes me sad that I did feel the need to reject myself to such a degree as to completely dissociate from who I was, because I quite like myself now, actually. I recognize that many of my qualities that have made certain aspects of life more difficult also make me unique in a very powerful way."

Helena wants others to know that her story is no fluke. She is not, as she wrote, "uniquely troubled or irresponsible."

"What I am though, is fortunate, because there are others for whom the harm has been exponentially worse."[1]

Helena has become one of the most articulate voices on this issue, engaging in public speaking appearances, writing, doing interviews with reporters, and more. Her Substack offers a variety of insights into the topic, though she has stepped back a bit after experiencing burnout from the high demand for her insights.

"The trans movement is a very dark topic, and I take it very personally," she wrote in July 2022, explaining why she was taking a step back. "I feel it deeply every time I read or hear the story of someone who has been or is being seriously hurt by gender ideology, especially when that comes from friends or people I have come to care for from a distance. I feel a sense of duty and obligation to fully witness the suffering of people who have been seriously hurt in a way that I never was but came very close to being. It's kind of like survivor's guilt."[2]

I asked Helena what role she plans to play in the gender discourse going forward, and what her vision of "the good life" looks like.

"I don't have any plans for the future in regards to this as of right now," she told me. "I don't know if or when that will change. My vision for a good life is to focus on healing from the things that made me vulnerable to this and other hurtful experiences in the first place."

Asked what she would tell her young teenaged self, Helena was honest: She doubts she would have listened to any advice, even from someone like herself, when she was beginning her transition. "I was thinking out of pure emotion and lack of development, which is why I advocate for institutions to put safeguards that would protect children, teenagers, and vulnerable young adults from harm," she said. "But it would be nice to have a way to communicate to my younger self that the source of my pain isn't me, it's experiences that I wasn't able to fully process or understand at the time that I was blaming on myself and my body," Helena reflected. "But again, a teenager wouldn't listen to that."[3]

Chloe

As "Abel" pointed out, Chloe has become one of the highest-profile advocates for young people who, like herself, went through a transition at a young age. She speaks at conferences, rallies, on television, and to reporters for stories. Chloe is also a "patient advocate" for the medical group Do No Harm, a group of physicians, healthcare professionals, medical students, patients, and policymakers pushing to protect health care from ideology.[4]

"It's quite the change," she told me, as we discussed her relatively new role. "Especially because I was a super shy kid in school, for the most part." But she feels like it has been healthy for her to open up, both emotionally and socially.

"Just practicing my socialization, it's helping develop a lot of skills. And it's just been a nice experience, meeting all these wonderful people, and other people who have been through what I have, and getting to bond over that. All these parents and politicians, all these amazing people...despite all our differences, we're all fighting on this one front," she said. "It's not something I had ever really seen before. It fills me with a lot of hope."

Chloe answers questions thoughtfully, taking her time before she speaks. The result is that everything she says comes out slowly and deliberately. She is a powerful speaker.[5]

When I worked with her to share her story in a Daily Signal video, we asked her to do a "straight to cam" interview. We wanted her to look straight into the camera and make eye contact with the viewer, so that every single person who watched would see her resolute face and hear her grave young voice explain exactly what this ideology had done to her. I asked her what message she might have for other people who are in the same boat as she was, particularly when she was deciding whether or not to go through with her surgery.

"I think the best thing to do is to wait," she said simply.

"If I were to go back in time and speak to my twelve-year-old self?" she pondered. "Well, the first thing I would tell her is to get off her butt, get off social media, and get into a sport or a school club, so she isn't thinking so much about these kinds of things. I would let her know that she's worth so much more than her body, and the way that she presents herself, and the way that she thinks other people perceive her," Chloe continued. "And that it's infinitely more important that she spends time with her family and her friends and getting involved in her community."

She reflected that for young people, it can be very difficult to understand one's feelings, to "introspect well enough to be able to tell where these feelings might really be coming from.

"A belief that a lot of people hold around gender dysphoria is that it's innate and that it makes you the opposite sex, and that gender identity is an innate thing," she said. "But a lot of the time there are comorbidities, there are things that facilitate the development of gender dysphoria." Young people who want to transition might have issues that they don't even know about—just like she did. And, Chloe believes, most children will naturally desist over time and find that they become more comfortable with their biological sex as they mature.

Chloe also reflected on her acquaintances in the transgender community. "I find that a lot of the other transgender people that I was friends with, especially the ones who were around my age, they weren't very close to their families," Chloe said. "They had some sort of family trauma, or they had been abused or assaulted at a young age. And they were often fearful of the world.

"They were very pessimistic about a lot of things," she added. "They were afraid to go out into the world, even to go out to school and get involved. But really, once you get past that fear and you really become involved with your community and the people around you, it only gets so much better from there."

Chloe's story is troubling and sad, but her conversational demeanor is cheerful, borderline spunky. As we chatted, I pointed this discrepancy out to her and asked her what keeps her so cheerful and brave.

"I've gone through a lot of hardships, and I don't think anything else in my life has affected me nearly as much as transitioning and stopping transitioning has," she told me. "But I've managed to keep my head up. I would attribute that mostly to having people around me who I know really support me and care about me," Chloe added. "That's often hard to come by, and I think I'm pretty lucky in that regard, but it's really important for people to find that community."[6]

Prisha

Many of those who once felt themselves to be the transgender darlings of the medical establishment are now finding that they cannot get any medical professionals to help them deal with the fallout of their transition—at all.

"I was under the impression that my doctors, who were transitioning me, loved me. They said they didn't want me to die, they were saving my life, they were worried about me, and they wanted me to be healthy and happy," Prisha said, as Kelsey Bolar reported in a heartbreaking February 2023 piece for The Federalist. "Clearly, they don't love me. As soon as it's not profitable, they don't want to help."

Most of Prisha's medical complications are tied to her endocrine system, which makes hormones and releases them into the blood, regulating almost every process in the body, including metabolism, growth, development, emotions, mood, sexual drive, sleep, and more.

"I was hoping that if I could get my endocrine system working, I could be on less psychiatric medicine because low testosterone and estrogen will cause depression and anxiety, both of which I'm medicated for and don't really like being medicated for," Prisha told Bolar. She was hoping that estrogen supplements might help redistribute muscle and fat, and thereby help solve the pain she's been experiencing for the past few years. And she had been hopeful it would help with her hair loss, body hair growth, sore throat, inability to sing, and problems with her reproductive system—which has gotten so bad that she can't even use tampons anymore. "I used to be able to, and now I can't," she told Bolar. "And that sucks. There's pain, there's irregular periods, and atrophy."

But all the medical professionals she calls turn her away. "I could call and be rejected every single day," she said.[7]

Prisha has shared her heartbreaking journey on social media. There have been many days when I opened Twitter to see Prisha posting about being rejected by yet another medical provider.

"I have my appointment with Plume tomorrow," she tweeted hopefully on January 29, 2023. "Hope it goes well! I'm really used to being rejected by doctors by now.... I'm going to be honest with them and see if they help detransitioners because no doctor I can find in person will help me."[8]

The very next day she tweeted: "Plume ghosted me. I'll upload a video soon. I'm losing it."[9]

She's not alone.

"When I detransitioned I realized how 'good' trans people have it," wrote social media user Susana, whose username is @detransfemcel.

"There are so many spaces for trans people, and everyone accepted it when I told them I was trans. I transitioned after a year of 'therapy' which trans people call gatekeeping but when I detransitioned, the real gatekeeping started.

"I had no ovaries and my endocrinologist didn't want to help me," she said. "I couldn't legally change my name back. There are no support groups. So where is the transphobic society? Why am I not accepted as my birth sex if everyone hates trans people so much?"[10]

Chloe also described this experience to me. As she tries to deal with the physical effects of her transition, she's struggling to find any doctors who can help her figure out what is going on. And since Kaiser is both her healthcare provider and her insurance provider, if she goes outside of them, she told me, she's not going to be covered. So things will be expensive.

I expressed to her my surprise that legitimate, life-affirming doctors hadn't approached her, at least privately, to offer her their expertise, particularly considering how high-profile Chloe has become in recent months. She seemed unsurprised. "There's a lot of pressure from the industry as a whole," she said. "You could get your license or your job taken away just for not affirming a patient."

Some of that pressure comes from groups like the Human Rights Campaign (HRC) and its Healthcare Equality Index, which sways the practices of hospitals and healthcare facilities across the United States by scoring them on whether they are adopting ideological pro-LGBTQ+ policies.[11] "Over time and due to a decade of advancement in LGBTQ+ inclusion in daily life, healthcare facilities have worked harder than ever to increase their work to provide equitable care for the LGBTQ+ community," the HRC boasts, "and now the [Healthcare Equality Index] survey reflects and promotes these efforts through its scoring criteria."[12]

The Healthcare Equality Index objectives make it clear that to be scored well, healthcare institutions must prove they are inclusive of

LGBTQ patients, cultivate inclusive workplaces by promoting LGBTQ policies and benefits, and engage publicly with the LGBTQ community.

Inclusivity may mean allowing patients or employees to use the restroom that aligns with their gender identity, rather than biological sex, or providing access to "gender-affirming care."

The index also punishes hospitals that allow "discriminatory treatment that is in conflict with their non-discrimination policy" and requires hospitals to offer the same treatments to treat gender dysphoria as the hospital offers to treat other medical conditions. That means, as the Washington Free Beacon noted, that if a hospital uses puberty blockers to treat early puberty, it also must allow their use for children who "identify" as transgender.

If you're familiar with the HRC and its work, you'll notice the Healthcare Equality Index's similarities to the Corporate Equality Index,[13] another Human Rights Campaign initiative, which is thought to be behind Bud Light's financially disastrous decision to use a biological male who "identifies" as a transgender woman, Dylan Mulvaney, as its public face.[14]

Bud Light's parent company, Anheuser-Busch, was formerly honored with HRC's "Best Place to Work for LGBTQ+ Equality" title.[15] But HRC removed Anheuser-Busch from the list and suspended the company's Corporate Equality Index score over Bud Light's response to public outrage over its promotion of Mulvaney, a biological man, as a woman.[16]

The Corporate Equality Index has even infected the likes of Fox News: I reported in May of 2023 that for the past several years, Fox has received a perfect score on the Corporate Equality Index.[17] A former Fox News employee told me that the company frequently mentions its perfect score in employee training materials. And according to Fox's company handbook policies on gender transition,

Fox News employees are allowed to use restrooms that align with their gender identity, permitted to dress in alignment with their preferred gender, and must also be addressed by their preferred name and pronouns in the workplace.[18]

"All these people that believe in [gender] ideology should be concerned that there's a huge monopoly," Chloe insisted, "not only on the studies and the so-called science around this, but all the corporations are on this. A lot of these people are the same people who are anti-corporation, pseudo-socialists, and yet when a big corporation sells pride stuff, it's a good thing?

"They don't really believe in [gender] ideology," she hypothesized. "I don't think anybody can truly believe that you can actually be the opposite sex. That's something that's so deeply ingrained in us, in our psychology and physiology. And every part of us...our bodies are centered around our sex. And they can make up as many terms as they like...assigned female at birth, assigned male at birth.... I think it shows that biology, in a way, it triumphs over all."[19]

Luka

Shortly after she stopped taking testosterone, Luka went to see a doctor at her university gender clinic about getting some blood work done. She wanted to see how the doctor could help her.

When I asked whether the doctor was open to hearing about her struggles, Luka said that the doctor was kind and nice to her, and that she did try to help her. "But she was also like...'I have no idea what to do with you. There is absolutely no protocol for this.'"

The doctor isn't wrong—there really isn't any known protocol for detransitioning.

As Luka put it, "There's barely medical protocol for transitioning, let alone when people go back. And a big reason for that is a lot of people who detransition kind of just disappear from the clinic and never come back.... I really think that doctors prefer it if we just stop coming in and disappear when we do transition, because then they don't have to face the reality that it's happening," Luka said. "It's easy to say it never happens when you don't have to face what you've done to a person."

She also thinks that the doctors' pride is involved. "It must be a lot to feel like you are helping people, and then realize that you might have been harming them."

I pressed her on this, asking if she thinks that the doctors really do think they are helping people.

"The vast majority of them definitely think that they're doing the right thing," she said. "But there are a few that are more activists than doctors. I don't even know if they see patients anymore.... Even then, I don't think they are evil. I just think they're maybe misguided and their refusal to listen to the people who have gone out the other side of this medical industry and have regretted it will probably come back to haunt them."

She also speculated about why detransitioners just kind of disappear from gender clinics and don't come back, suggesting that most detransitioners have a deep-rooted fear that "the people who did this to us will not help us if we detransition." For some, Luka said, this fear is grounded in experience. They go back to their gender clinics and find that doctors are more willing to call them crazy for *wanting to detransition* than these doctors were when they wanted to transition in the first place.

I asked her if this distrust is prompted by doctors who are pushing transitioning on children.

She emphatically said yes: "It's just a fear that someone so willing to go along with activist talking points on [something like] children transitioning won't help us when we come out and say we've regretted it. There's a lot of distrust among the [detransitioner] community for doctors who would [transition children], even more to the ones who say things like *Children know who they are and we need to believe them*," she said. "That kind of talking point, in my opinion, is extremely dangerous."

When I asked her why she thought it was dangerous, Luka exclaimed, "Kids believe a lot of things about themselves that just blatantly aren't true. They're still growing and developing in their identity. And it's also unreasonable to ask a thirteen-year-old who you're about to put on puberty blockers, 'Have you thought about having children?' because they can't make that decision!" Children can't fully comprehend and consent to the long-term effects of some of these procedures, Luka insisted. "I couldn't understand what the long-term impacts of testosterone would be at sixteen. That's why I felt like it hit me like a bus when I turned twenty."[20]

Luka also thinks that there is a cognitive dissonance problem with some of these doctors performing such surgeries and procedures, particularly on children. She did a TV interview a while back where she was on a panel with a few doctors. One of the doctors on the panel was in favor of "slowing everything down," Luka said. But a more radical doctor on the panel was pushing "believe children when they tell you about this stuff" talking points, Luka said.

According to Luka, that doctor was Meredithe McNamara, who is an assistant professor of pediatrics at the Yale School of Medicine and formerly worked as a pediatrician at the University of Chicago. She did not respond to my requests for comment.[21]

"She would not even look me in the eyes, let alone acknowledge my presence," Luka said. "It was obvious enough to the point where I noticed it. And when I tried to say hi or make eye contact with her, she would not meet my eyes."

"Why?" I asked.

"I honestly don't know," Luka said slowly. "If you have to look someone in the eyes who's been through this and has been harmed by it, and you do these practices, it's going to make you think about things that maybe you don't want to think about.

"Because it's really easy to just parrot the same talking points over and over again when you don't have to look into the eyes and interact with someone who was harmed by it.

"And I think that's the thing with some of these doctors, if they've only seen detransitioners through social media, it's very easy to just use a mute button and not have to deal with these thoughts and continue believing that you're the hero doctor saving children from committing suicide if they didn't transition."

Luka reflected that for many really little children, if they are struggling with their gender, the "vast majority of them will grow out of it as they go through puberty." But what she really doesn't understand is the narrative: *If you do not let your child transition, they will kill themselves.*

"Do we not have any way of protecting young people if they're suicidal?" she asked. "Because I've had friends who are suicidal and they seem to have like protections in place that don't involve cosmetic surgery. Clearly we have protocols for that that [don't] involve affirming whatever that person who is struggling with this says.…

"One thing I've always thought about was, I dealt with really bad depression. And no one affirmed my depression. No one was like, 'Oh, you want to stay in bed all day because your brain is telling you to stay in bed all day.' No one did that.

"But they were like, 'Oh, your brain is having issues with your gender. Cool, we are going to listen to you on that one.' Every other mental health struggle I dealt with, it was not affirmed. But for some reason this one was, and that one led down a direct path to surgery and hormones."

Luka emphasized that she was never suicidal even when she was really depressed. But the talking point was still used to push her transition on her parents. And, in light of all her mental health struggles, she understands why her parents fell for it.

Luka's message to young people or children who are considering transition: Wait. "Use your teenage years to really connect with your body, and learn that yeah, you are uncomfortable, but this is you," she recommends. "Learn to love that. Dress how you want, that doesn't mean you need to change your name, and stuff like that. Find hobbies that make you happy."

Another point she thinks young people considering transitioning should think about: attempted gender transitions consume your childhood and your teenage years. You'll spend a ton of time at the doctor. "I feel like what a lot of people don't realize is, my teenage years kind of got ruined with a lot of medical appointments and constant doctor visits," Luka emphasized. She urges young people to focus on getting through high school and into college (if that is their goal), exercising, eating well—"all that good, wholesome stuff that doesn't involve turning to a predatory medical industry.

"Thinking about your gender constantly and thinking about how others refer to you, that isn't healthy," Luka insists. "Constantly being on alert for the right name and pronouns and making sure no one uses the wrong words to refer to you, that takes up such a large portion of your brain.

"It could be filled with so much better things."

Luka also urges parents to build more trust with their children. "Try and stay close to them, even when they're teenagers."

She believes that part of the reason that it was so easy for her to get sucked in online, and ultimately preyed upon, was the fact that her parents were going through a divorce. The emotional distance between herself and her parents allowed her to get caught up in things she should never have been exposed to, especially at such a young age. "It was a messy one and I didn't feel like I could trust them," she said of her parents' divorce. "At the time, at least just be aware of what [your children are] doing online. Be close to them. Do family activities."

Interestingly, Luka repeatedly brought up how parents should respond to their children wanting to dress as another gender. She urges parents to not push back too hard against their children dressing rather gender neutral: "Let them know that they can dress gender-nonconforming, but that doesn't mean they need to change gender now."[22]

I also asked these detransitioners about their thoughts on the phrase "gender-affirming care" used by media and activists to describe, and encompass, and mask transgender sex-change procedures and hormones.

Luka thinks it is a phrase that is "paraded out" so that people don't have to "face the reality of what it actually means." To Luka, gender-affirming care is "a feel-good term to use so you do not have to face the reality that a sixteen-year-old is getting their breasts cut off." She joked, "It sounds positive! It sounds nice. It's a nice thing for media outlets to report on as a way of [saying], 'Why would you take this away from children?' And cause a little panic about it like that.

"I don't think it's accurate," Luka said. "I think it's one of those terms that can be easily bent to mean whatever you want in the scope of 'gender-affirming care.' Because I've seen a lot of things called 'gender-affirming care,' it's one of those ever-shifting definitions that doesn't seem to really be helpful to anyone on any side of this debate."

Luka isn't a fan of using phrases that contain words like "mutilation"—cautioning that the way some media describe detransitioners paints them as broken human beings. "That's also not helpful language," she said. "Going around calling the detransitioners mutilated and destroyed and ruined. That's not helpful either. And it makes a lot of us not want to go back on social media and talk about things."

She has heard the phrase "sex-denying care" thrown around. We both laughed at that, since it is a little tongue in cheek, and very obviously takes one side of the issue. "It's funny and kind of accurate," she said.

Pretty much every detransitioner mentioned in this book suggested to me that using the phrase "gender-affirming care" is an attempt at manipulation—to control the rhetoric on the issue.

Luka criticized the "media circus" that has resulted from legislation seeking to ban puberty blockers and hormones for children: the media cries foul, accusing lawmakers of wanting to ban "gender-affirming care" for children when the legislation merely makes children wait for puberty blockers and hormones until eighteen years of age.

Luka has seen advocates sling around the word "conversion therapy" unfairly too, she said. The suggestion that someone should go to therapy to figure out whether their gender dysphoria is coming from other issues seems pretty practical, but Luka has noticed that activists have begun claiming that this is a form of conversion therapy.

"It is the only standard of care I've seen where self-diagnosis is not only valid but encouraged," she said.[23]

Prisha wants young people to know that puberty is not a disease.

"Being a mentally ill teenage girl is the hardest thing I've ever done," she reflects. But she emphasizes that there is not a "cure" for puberty. For mental illness, Prisha pushes young people to see a therapist, but a real therapist, not a "gender-affirming" therapist.

"Going through puberty, you are going to hate your body, and that doesn't mean anything is wrong," she says. "You don't have to change it. It's awkward, it's difficult. It really is. That's valid. And I see you. But there's not a cure. You don't medicalize yourself because you're experiencing that."

To parents, she has a very similar message: to empathize with how huge this experience feels for young people without affirming their misconceptions. What your child is experiencing might seem crazy (and it shouldn't be affirmed), but it is also the biggest and "worst thing they've ever experienced," she says.

"They're going through something big, and it doesn't have to be labeled as trans," she says. "Just tell them that the sickness or the issue is actually just being normal and going through puberty because it's hard."[24]

CHAPTER 10

The Future

S o what comes next for these men and women? It depends. Some of them, like Ritchie, are still suffering intensely as they attempt to discern what their future will look like. Others are determined to hold the institutions and individuals who tore their lives apart to account through speaking out publicly, or lawsuits, or both. Some simply want to live peacefully, to resume normalcy, and to grow old with another person who cherishes them for who they truly are.

The detransitioners whose stories are detailed in this book are very brave individuals. Those who have shared their stories publicly have experienced horrifying amounts of hate and venom for just disclosing the facts of their lived experiences. If they go so far as to take a stand against gender ideology, the vitriol becomes much worse.

"Shut the fuck up TERF." That's a typical message that Watson, another outspoken detransitioner, says she has received in response to frequent Twitter posts about detransitioning.

"Fucking idiot."

"Suck me."[1]

The hate takes its toll. Many detransitioners who post on social media are quick to emphasize that though they oppose gender ideology, they are not "TERFs," an acronym that stands for "trans exclusionary radical feminists" and that was often utilized in the frenzied backlash over J. K. Rowling's defense of biological sex.

You can be accused of being a "TERF" for pretty much any remark that critiques gender ideology, but the phrase suggests that the gender-critical person is a feminist who is "transphobic," or hates transgender people. Pro-trans activists are quick to sling the insult around on social media, to the point where those on the receiving end have begun to just shrug it off, or even to embrace the label.

"Every time the media reports on sex offenders with the words 'her penis' a new terf is born," Helena joked in a February 2022 tweet.[2]

"Trans people have to accuse me of being paid off and puppeteered by Big Terf because they can't mentally handle someone who was one of them for 5 years authentically changing their mind and being so effective at breaking the spell for countless normal people," she added in May 2022. "Sorry transgender bros, if you have to resort to delusional conspiracy theories, it's over," she tweeted. "It'll be easier if you admit it now and denounce your cult and the transing of kids before the entire society realizes what's going on and turns against you."[3]

But despite the attacks, the mere presence of detransitioners on social media has been massively impactful.

On "DeTrans Awareness Day" in March of 2022, detransitioners flooded Twitter with their stories. Their testimonies came amid national controversy over Republican Texas governor Greg Abbott's claim that transgender surgeries and hormones for children are dangerous and amount to "child abuse."

- "I started taking testosterone at 18 because i was tired of not fitting in with other girls so thought i'd make a better man instead," tweeted Allie. "An autism diagnosis later and it all makes sense now."

- "I was vulnerable, desperate, and young," shared Michelle. "On top of that, I had people online telling me 'if you think you're trans, you are' and 'cis people don't think about gender this much.' I heard the 'only 1% regret it' statistic, and I thought I'd be fine. That could never be me. What reasons did I have to not trust them?" she asked. "Why would so many people tell me things that weren't true? Why would my doctors go along with it if I weren't really a man? Why would therapists risk my mental health if they weren't sure whether I would benefit from transition?"

- "Why are we doing this? Why are we talking about detransition," asked Watson. "Because it is important. Because it is *happening.* The stories will not be easy to accept—medical scandals never are. But that doesn't mean they should be ignored. Quite the contrary, actually."[4]

The amount of clamor that detransitioners created that day was hard to ignore. They did it again in 2023. And throughout 2022 and 2023, Chloe and other detransitioners participated in multiple rallies that drew national attention, including the Rally to End Child Mutilation with The Daily Wire in Nashville[5] and the Detransition Awareness Day rally in Sacramento, California.[6]

"I was met with hatred by the same people who encouraged and celebrated every milestone in my transition," Chloe said, speaking passionately to the crowd in Nashville. "I was told that I was a nuisance at best, and a harmful force to other, real transgender people at worst, just for admitting my mistake. They said to me that I was only a spoiled brat, who manipulated and hurt my parents and family. They said that I didn't deserve to go on testosterone or undergo mastectomy.

"Now, that part is true," she told the crowd. "Because I deserved so much better."[7]

Prisha has devoted much of her time lately to testifying before state lawmakers about the dangers of transition for young people. In April 2023, for example, both she and Chloe testified in Ohio on HB68, the Enact Ohio Saving Adolescents from Experimentation Act. State lawmakers had invited her to speak, she wrote in a Substack story detailing her experience. Prisha's story includes selfies of Prisha and Chloe beaming into the camera with another detransitioner named Xandra.

Prisha describes how the Democratic Ohio state lawmakers tried to portray her testimony as irrelevant, since she was not from Ohio: "Representatives asked me where I received my care and if it was in Ohio. I told them that if they waited until a detransitioner came from their [states], that means someone is hurt and the state has failed. I also mentioned the lack of medical care and insurance coverage for detransitioners."[8]

Chloe was the first detransitioner to file a U.S. lawsuit against the medical providers who permanently altered her life. Represented by attorneys with the Center for American Liberty, in addition to Dhillon Law Group and LiMandri & Jonna LLP, Chloe is suing Kaiser Foundation Hospitals, the Permanente Medical Group, Lisa Kristine Taylor, M.D., Hop Nguyen Le, M.D., and Susanne E. Watson, Ph.D., for medical negligence.[9]

The complaint, filed in the Superior Court of California, County of San Joaquin, on February 22, 2023, sums her story up succinctly:

> This case is about a team of doctors…who decided to perform a mutilating, mimicry sex change experiment on Chloe, then a thirteen-year-old vulnerable girl struggling with complex mental health co-morbidities, who needed love, care, attention, and regular weekly psychotherapy, not cross-sex hormones and mutilating surgery….
>
> Under Defendants' "care," between ages 13–17 years, Chloe underwent harmful transgender transition, specifically, off-label puberty blockers and cross-sex hormone "treatment," and a radical double mastectomy of her healthy breasts….
>
> Defendants blindly ramrodded Chloe through this transition "treatment," ignoring her extensive co-morbidities, her declining mental health condition, and the failure of her social and academic functionality to improve after each predetermined sequence of social, hormonal and surgical "gender affirmation treatment." Put another way, Chloe was not responding to treatment and Defendants ignored this fact.[10]

The lawsuit tears into the doctors and medical providers, accusing them of failing to provide Chloe and her parents with proper informed consent processes, such as regular therapy sessions and assessment of Chloe's mental health conditions. And the suit claims that the hospitals, doctors, and therapists "obscured and concealed" vital information on transgender surgeries and hormones for young people like Chloe.

What kind of vital information? According to Chloe's legal complaint, that information includes the significant health risks for biological women taking high dosages of testosterone and puberty blockers and the conflicting or lack of studies in this area, evidence showing that these treatments have "poor mental health outcomes," the significant likelihood that Chloe wouldn't get the outcome she desired, the possibility that she would regret her choices and want to desist and detransition, and "the lack of accurate models for predicting desistence and detransition."

Chloe's lawyer hammered home that the doctors, medical providers, and hospitals that Chloe worked with "falsely represented" that her gender dysphoria would not resolve unless she chemically and surgically transitioned—and that she represented a high risk of suicide unless she transitioned.

"These were materially false representations," the lawsuit states, specifically pointing to the infamous phrase: "Would you rather have a dead daughter, or a live son?"

"This unethical form of coercion reflects a lack of understanding of suicide risk, or a deliberate decision to misrepresent suicide risk," the complaint says. "Defendants' coercion, concealment, misrepresentations, and manipulation are appalling and represent an egregious breach of the standard of care. This misconduct also constitutes fraud, malice, and oppression."[11]

Chloe's lawyers argue that patients like Chloe represent a significant "monetary benefit" to those in the transgender transitioning industry. "Chloe underwent tens of thousands of dollars of so-called medical treatment," they point out. And if she had continued down this path, the lawsuit emphasizes, she "would have represented a monetary benefit to the Defendants of tens of thousands of additional dollars in terms of follow-up lifelong treatment and in terms of further risky surgeries to construct fake genitalia."

These doctors had a large monetary incentive to get patients to transition as soon as possible, the lawyers argue: "Patients like Chloe, who would have naturally desisted from their gender dysphoria by adulthood, represent a significant lost monetary potential if they are not medically treated when symptoms first present. It is well known that the vast majority of patients who start transition through puberty blockers go on to further transition through life altering cross-sex hormones and surgery.

"It appears that the lucrative nature of transition treatment, rather than sound medical evidence and Chloe's wellbeing, represented a substantial factor motivating Defendants' ill-formed advice to start Chloe on the transition path."[12]

Chloe continues to speak out on the topic, even in the face of harsh criticism. The *New York Times* took a stab at her reputation, headlining its May 2023 hit piece "How a Few Stories of Regret Fuel the Push to Restrict Gender Transition Care." In that piece, Maggie Astor wrote, "As Republican-controlled state legislatures have passed over a dozen bills banning transition care for minors this year and have moved to restrict care for adults, Ms. Cole and fewer than 10 activists like her—people who transitioned and then changed course— have become the faces of the cause, according to a *New York Times* review of news coverage and legislative testimony.

"These activists are fixtures at legislative hearings and rallies," Astor continued. "Their experiences have been splashed across conservative media as cautionary tales. In Wyoming, a lawmaker named his bill to ban transition care for minors 'Chloe's Law.'"

And then Astor added, "Most people who transition do not change course. And yet, the influence of these activists has been striking."

Astor suggested that lawmakers are using such stories to weaponize parental fears and target transgender youth. "Their stories of regret and irreversible physical transformation have tapped into strong emotions about rapidly shifting gender norms—from hardened prejudice to parental worry," the *New York Times* writer warned. "Lawmakers have used these accounts to override objections from all major medical associations, which oppose bans on transition care, as well as testimony from the far larger number of transgender people who say transitioning improved their mental health."

Chloe wisely did not return the *Times*' requests for comment. Neither did Prisha, who is also named in the story. But the story in and of itself was an acknowledgment: Detransitioners cannot be ignored anymore. They, and their stories, are influential.[13]

And they are charging the battlegrounds that gender ideologues thought they had so securely captured.

The Lawsuits

Given the venomous hate and pushback that detransitioners receive, it should surprise no one that there are not that many detransitioner lawsuits out there yet.

There is Chloe's lawsuit, of course. Chloe's lawyers work for the Center for American Liberty, which is headed by Harmeet K. Dhillon, the head of Dhillon Law Group. Dhillon is also representing "Kayla Lovdahl" in a suit filed in June of 2023 against the Permanente Medical Group, Kaiser Foundation Hospitals, Dr. Lisa Kristine Taylor, Dr. Winnie Mao Yiu Tong, Susanne Watson, Ph.D., and Dr. Mirna Escalante.[14] Kayla Lovdahl is her current legal name, by which she is identified in her lawsuit, but she now goes by Layla Jane.

Layla Jane is now nineteen years old, but she attempted to transition to become a man when she was between twelve and seventeen years of age.

In their lawsuit, filed June 14, 2023, Layla Jane's attorneys explained what her former providers had done to this twelve-year-old girl:

> This case is about a team of doctors (i.e. the Defendants) who decided to perform a damaging, imitation sex change experiment on Kayla, then a twelve-year-old vulnerable girl struggling with complex mental health co-morbidities, who needed care, attention, and psychotherapy, not cross-sex hormones and mutilating surgery.
>
> . . . critical facts establish that Defendants should not have recommended or performed transition "treatment" on Kayla and that Defendants thereby breached the standard of care in this regard.
>
> . . . Defendants falsely and authoritatively represented . . . that she represented a high-risk of suicide unless she transitioned. These were material, false representations. Defendants coercion, concealment, misrepresentations, and manipulation . . . represent an egregious breach of the standard of care. This misconduct also constitutes fraud, malice, and oppression.[15]

Like many of the other young people mentioned in this book, Layla had a history of mental health issues as a child. Layla's issues included anxiety, depression, gender dysphoria, appetite changes, trouble with bullying, anger, confusion about puberty, cutting, nausea, irritability, mood swings, and suicidal ideation, according to the complaint in her case.

She "came out" as transgender at eleven years old and expressed the desire to transition to the opposite sex. Even though at least one of her initial providers said that she couldn't start hormones until age sixteen or undergo surgery until age eighteen (per Kaiser's official policies), Dr. Watson, Dr. Taylor, and Dr. Tong allegedly approved her for both cross-sex hormones and a double mastectomy at ages twelve to thirteen, according to the legal complaint. This was done "without adequate psychological evaluation," Layla's lawyers allege.[16]

Like so many others, Layla's parents were also presented with the infamous false dilemma: "it is better to have a live son than a dead daughter."[17]

And so Layla began puberty blockers and testosterone at age twelve and had both her breasts removed through a double mastectomy at age thirteen, according to her lawyers.[18]

Her mental health comorbidities naturally did not resolve with these steps. According to her complaint, she "continued to have the following symptoms: hyperventilation, nausea, nightmares, anger outbursts in which Kayla would punch holes in the wall, suicidal ideation, appetite swings, energy swings, excessive anxiety or worry, excessive fear of social situations, repeated nightmares, and explosive temper outbursts."[19]

She's at increased risk of infertility. And she'll never be able to breastfeed a baby.[20]

I've reached out to all the doctors and hospitals that are specifically mentioned in these two suits. None of them responded to my requests for comment (which is not unusual when dealing with lawsuits).

Investigations Begin

The legal filings come as pediatric gender clinics across the country are facing increased scrutiny for their practices.

Missouri attorney general Andrew Bailey's office launched an investigation into the Washington University Transgender Center at St. Louis Children's Hospital.

News of his investigation came after a whistleblower (Jamie Reed, a self-described "queer" leftist woman) came forward saying that the center is using experimental drugs on children, giving out puberty blockers and cross-sex hormones without individualized assessment, and even giving these drugs to children without their parents' consent.[21]

Her allegations were first made public through a story in The Free Press,[22] a relatively new website published by journalist Bari Weiss. Weiss, who is by no means a traditional conservative, resigned from the *New York Times* in July 2020 over the publication's ideological fixation on a "predetermined narrative." As she wrote at the time, "Showing up for work as a centrist at an American newspaper should not require bravery."[23] The publication of Reed's whistleblower allegations in The Free Press seems wise: activists and lawmakers who are quick to pigeonhole or ignore revelations published in obviously conservative outlets had to pay attention.

Reed, who is married to a biological man who identifies as a transgender woman, detailed her allegations in a twenty-three-page affidavit submitted to the attorney general.

She had been working for Washington University for seven years and had taken a job in "the Center" (the Washington University Pediatric Transgender Center) because she supports "trans rights and firmly believed [she] would be able to provide good care for children at the Center who are appropriate candidates to be receiving medical transition. Instead," she wrote, "I witnessed the Center cause permanent harm to many of the patients."[24]

As Reed explains in her sworn affidavit, "During my time at the Center, I personally witnessed Center healthcare providers lie to the public and to parents of patients about the treatment, or lack of treatment, and the effects of treatment provided to children at the Center. I witnessed staff at the Center provide puberty blockers and cross-sex hormones to children without complete informed parental consent and without an appropriate or accurate assessment of the needs of the child. I witnessed children experience shocking injuries from the medication the Center prescribed. And I saw the Center make no attempt or effort to track adverse outcomes of patients after they left the Center."

Reed says she raised concerns for years, but the center's doctors told her to stop. And in the fall of 2022 both the center and the university administration told her to "get with the program or get out." She explains, "Because the Center was unwilling to make any changes in response to my concerns, I left the Center in November 2022 and accepted employment elsewhere within Washington University."[25]

Reed's allegations are horrifying. But those familiar with the stories of detransitioners will not find them wholly surprising. She claims that from 2020 to 2022, the center began medical transitions for over six hundred children—and about 74 percent of those were young girls.

Their procedures were largely paid for by private insurance, Reed said, but she believes that the center also billed state and federal publicly funded insurance programs (and she allegedly witnessed staff discomfort about sending bills to publicly funded insurance programs dismissed).[26]

"Children come into the clinic using pronouns of inanimate objects like 'mushroom,' 'rock,' or 'helicopter,'" she explained. "Children come into the clinic saying they want hormones because they do not want to be gay. Children come in changing their identities on a day-to-day basis. Children come in under clear pressure by a parent to identify in a way inconsistent with the child's actual identity." And in all these cases, Reed said, the doctors at the center put the kids on puberty blockers or cross-sex hormones.

"In one case where a girl was placed on cross-sex hormones, I found out later that the girl desired cross-sex hormones only because she wanted to avoid becoming pregnant," Reed said. "There was no need for this girl to be prescribed cross-sex hormones," the whistle-blower said. "What she needed was basic sex education and maybe contraception. An adequate assessment before prescribing hormones would have revealed this fact. But because the doctors automatically prescribe cross-sex hormones or puberty blockers for children meeting the bare minimum criteria, this girl was unnecessarily placed on drugs that cause irreversible change to the body."

In another example that Reed provided, a patient underwent a double mastectomy at St. Louis Children's Hospital. Only three months later, the female patient reached out to the surgeon and asked for her breasts to be "put back on," Reed said. She had clearly not understood that getting her breasts removed was actually a "forever" move—she could never undo it. "Had a requisite and adequate assessment been performed before the procedure, the doctors could have prevented this patient from undergoing irreversible surgical change," Reed said.[27]

She added, "It is my belief that the Center does not track these outcomes because they do not want to have to report them to new patients and because they do not want to discontinue cross-sex hormone prescriptions. The Center never discontinues cross-sex hormones, no matter the outcome."[28] Reed said that on several occasions, doctors at the center continued prescribing hormones and puberty blockers "even when a parent stated that they were revoking consent."[29]

"The Center does not require children to continue with mental health care after they prescribe cross-sex hormones or puberty blockers and even continues those medications when the patients directly report worsening mental health after initiating those medications," she told the Missouri attorney general.[30] She also said that she has personally seen puberty blockers worsen children's mental health, writing, "Children who have not contemplated suicide before being put on puberty blockers have attempted suicide after."[31]

Reed also claimed that she saw center providers lie to both parents and the public about the treatments for children and their effects on children, specifically related to surgeries: "Doctors at the Center also have publicly claimed that they do not do any gender transition surgeries on minors.... This was a lie. The Center regularly refers minors for gender transition surgery. The Center routinely gives out the names and contact information of surgeons to those under the age of 18. At least one gender transition surgery was performed by Dr. Alison Snyder-Warwick at St. Louis Children's Hospital in the last few years."[32]

I reached out to Dr. Snyder-Warwick and St. Louis Children's Hospital on this point. They did not respond to my requests for comment.

The center also lies about puberty blockers, Reed said. "The Center tells the public and parents of patients that the point of puberty blockers is to give children time to figure out their gender identity," Reed told the attorney general. "But the Center does not use puberty blockers for this purpose. Instead, the Center uses puberty blockers just until children are old enough to be put on cross-sex hormones. Doctors at the Center *always* prescribe cross-sex hormones for children who have been taking puberty blockers."[33]

Reed slammed the center for telling parents and the public that it makes individualized decisions based on each person's needs. The center's doctors "always" push puberty blockers and hormones on children meeting their criteria, she said. "Doctors at the Center believe that every child who meets four basic criteria—age or puberty stage, therapist letter, parental consent, and a one-hour visit with a doctor—is a good candidate for irreversible medical intervention," she said. "When a child meets these four simple criteria, the doctors always decide to move forward with puberty blockers or cross-sex hormones. There were no objective medical tests or criteria or individualized assessments."[34]

Reed alleges that Dr. Chris Lewis, a doctor at the center, gives patients a drug called Bicalutamide. According to Reed, the drug "has a legitimate use for treating pancreatic cancer, but it has a side effect of causing breasts to grow, and it can poison the liver." According to Reed, "There are no clinical studies for using this drug for gender transitions, and there are no established standards of care for using this drug."[35] In addition, she said, "I know of at least one patient at the Center who was advised by the renal department to stop taking Bicalutamide because the child was experiencing liver damage. The child's parent reported this to the Center through the patient's online self-reporting medical chart (MyChart). The parent said they were not the type to sue, but 'this could be a huge PR problem for you.'"[36]

Dr. Chris Lewis did not respond to my requests for comment.

Attorney General Bailey's office, which is being assisted by the Missouri Department of Social Services and Division of Professional Registration, began an investigation into the allegations about two weeks before they went public, as Bailey's office said in a press release in February. "As Attorney General, I want Missouri to be the safest state in the nation for children," he said at the time. "We have received disturbing allegations that individuals at the Transgender Center at St. Louis Children's Hospital have been harming hundreds of children each year, including by using experimental drugs on them. We take this evidence seriously and are thoroughly investigating to make sure children are not harmed by individuals who may be more concerned with a radical social agenda than the health of children."[37]

And following his announcement of the investigation, Attorney General Bailey launched an online tip line where "those who have experienced harm from gender transition interventions or witnessed troubling practices at transition clinics in Missouri can submit their concerns," encouraging victims or their parents to reach out to the attorney general's office if they "believe that they or someone they know have been subject to illegal or abusive behavior surrounding gender transition intervention procedures."[38]

Senator Josh Hawley of Missouri, a Republican, also launched an investigation into potential malpractice regarding children at the Washington University Transgender Center in a February 9 letter to the university: "Starting immediately, your institutions must take steps to preserve all records, written and electronic, regarding gender-related treatments performed on minors since the opening of the Center. Additional oversight inquiries and outreach will follow."[39]

Hawley's letter also noted that the hospital had advised a school district to avoid requiring parental notification about children participating in chest-binding (according to emails obtained by the group Parents Defending Education [PDE] through a public records request).[40]

The senator said in a social media post that same day that the chancellor of Washington University in St. Louis "was appalled by these reports of child sterilization & mistreatment" and had promised to fully cooperate with investigations.[41]

It is hard to overstate what a big deal this all is, coming after years of gaslighting and scoffing from leftist lawmakers and activists on the topic.

Many commentators had weighed in on the matter with pivotal and ball-moving observations. But a whistleblower from within? This was groundbreaking.

The Missouri attorney general calling children pushed into these life-changing procedures "victims": groundbreaking. The nation, corporate media, and the medical establishment being forced to grapple with the allegations and with the possibility that the public's eyes are being opened to the cultish aspects of gender ideology: groundbreaking.

As part of his investigation, Attorney General Bailey's office demanded records from Planned Parenthood of the St. Louis Region and Southwest Missouri on its "gender-affirming care" program: "TRANSforming Community, TRANSforming Care."[42] The records request, according to the *Kansas City Star*, asked for information and documents on Planned Parenthood's hormone and puberty blocker policies as well as for the youngest age of those who have been receiving these treatments through Planned Parenthood.

Planned Parenthood accused the attorney general of acting from political motivations and asking for things outside the scope of his power and asserted that its program in question "is designed by and for the trans and non-binary community and extends gender-affirming care to all Planned Parenthood locations in the St. Louis area, Springfield and Joplin."[43]

In a May 2023 phone interview, Bailey told me that "Planned Parenthood and others have fought us to keep concealed any safeguards they might have in place to protect patients and protect children. So we're in court fighting them out over that," he said. "And in response, we've promulgated an emergency rule to provide some baseline of protection and to shine the light of truth on the fact that there are zero FDA approvals or clinical trials showing the safety or effectiveness of cross-sex hormones and puberty blockers to treat gender dysphoria."

To his knowledge, he had not heard whether Planned Parenthood clinics were involved in the surgical side of gender transitions. But he noted that after his office promulgated the emergency rule, Planned Parenthood started advertising pop-up clinics, encouraging people to come seek gender treatments.

"This is a left-wing, woke ideology masquerading as medicine," he said. "The mainstream media wants to convince you that it's somehow normal and proper and prudent and ignores the fact that European countries have curtailed these procedures because they understand that they're experimental and that the long-term negative implications outweigh that short-term benefit."[44]

The previous fall, in September 2022, The Daily Wire's Matt Walsh had exposed videos and archived webpages from Vanderbilt University Medical Center (VUMC) describing one doctor's promotion of "big money maker" trans surgeries and hormone treatments, as well as "apparent threats against medical professionals who dare object for religious reasons" (as Daily Wire reporter Amanda Prestigiacomo reported at the time).

One of these videos shows VUMC Clinic for Transgender Health's Dr. Shayne Sebold Taylor saying in a lecture: "It's a lot of money. These surgeries make a lot of money," before explaining that a chest reconstruction surgery can garner $40,000 per patient. A person merely on routine hormone treatment, whom Taylor might see only a few times a year, "can bring in several thousand dollars," she added, "and actually makes money for the hospital."

Taylor goes on to cite the Philadelphia Center for Transgender Surgery to describe how vaginoplasty surgeries (in which doctors attempt to create a vagina on a biologically male patient after removing the penis, testicles, and scrotum)[45] can rake in $20,000 for a medical establishment—a figure Taylor guesses is an "underesti-mate.... And the female-to-male bottom surgeries, these are huge money makers," she adds, before saying that such surgeries could bring in "up to $100,000" for VUMC and noting that some clinics are entirely supported by such surgeries. "These surgeries are labor intensive, there are a lot of follow-ups, they require a lot of our time, and they make money," she added, according to the video. "They make money for the hospital."[46]

Taylor hasn't responded to my requests for comment.

Walsh also exposed a video of Vanderbilt health law expert Ellen Wright Clayton delivering a lecture to staffers in which she warns that any "conscientious objection" to transgender surgeries or procedures will be met with "consequences." If staff don't want to participate in the surgeries? Maybe they shouldn't be working for Vanderbilt, Clayton suggests. "If you are going to assert conscientious objection, you have to realize that that is problematic," Clayton said, according to the video. "You are doing something to another person, and you are not paying the cost for your belief. I think that is a … real issue.… I just want you to take home that saying that you're not going to do something because of your conscientious—because of your religious beliefs, is not without consequences, and should not be without consequences," she adds, according to the videos. "And I just want to put that out there.… If you don't want to do this kind of work, don't work at Vanderbilt."[47]

When I covered this story in the fall of 2022, I reached out to Clayton about her remarks. "No," she responded, when asked to comment on the videos. She hasn't responded to my more recent inquiries.

Further, VUMC has a program called "Trans Buddy," which matches patients with "trained peer advocates"[48]—or, as Walsh described them, "trans activists from the community who attend appointments with trans patients, monitoring the doctors to guard against 'unsafe' behavior such as misgendering."[49]

The Daily Wire host also flagged videos from the university medical centers discussing hormone treatments for children as young as thirteen and double mastectomies for adolescent girls.

Walsh's exposé, done through a viral Twitter thread and backed up by Daily Wire reporting, ignited a firestorm on social media. "Vanderbilt got into the gender transition game admittedly in large part because it is very financially profitable," Walsh warned. "They then threatened any staff members who objected, and enlisted a gang of trans activists to act as surveillance in order to force compliance. They now castrate, sterilize, and mutilate minors as well as adults, while apparently taking steps to hide this activity from the public view," he added. "This is what 'health care' has become in modern America."[50]

VUMC responded with a statement claiming they were victims of posts misrepresenting the facts, emphasizing that VUMC requires parental consent to treat minor patients and insisting that they never refuse parental involvement in transgender procedures for minors. Referring to the video of Clayton, the statement continued: "Our policies allow employees to decline to participate in care they find morally objectionable, and do not permit discrimination against employees who choose to do so. This includes employees whose personal or religious beliefs do not support gender-affirming care for transgender persons." VUMC added, "We have been and will continue to be committed to providing family-centered care to all adolescents in compliance with state law and in line with professional practice standards and guidance established by medical specialty societies."

And Vanderbilt University distanced itself from the controversy. University spokesman John O'Brien told me that VUMC—Vanderbilt University Medical Center—has been a separate legal entity from Vanderbilt since 2016. "As such, Vanderbilt University has no role in medical decisions and patient care."[51]

Walsh's exposé prompted multiple lawmakers, including two prominent Tennessee Republicans, Senator Marsha Blackburn and Governor Bill Lee, to call for investigations into the matter.[52] The VUMC Pediatric Transgender Clinic took down its website page following backlash over Walsh's findings.[53]

"The 'pediatric transgender clinic' at Vanderbilt University Medical Center raises serious moral, ethical, and legal concerns," Lee said at the time. "We should not allow permanent, life-altering deci-sions that hurt children or policies that suppress religious liberties, all for the purpose of financial gain. We have to protect Tennessee chil-dren, and this warrants a thorough investigation."[54]

In response to demands from lawmakers, Vanderbilt's Pediatric Transgender Clinic agreed to pause all gender transition surgeries on minors, pending a review.[55] C. Wright Pinson, the deputy CEO and chief health system officer at Vanderbilt University Medical Center, also revealed that the clinic had performed about five "gender-affirming surgical procedures per year" since it opened in 2018, all with parental consent, according to The Daily Wire.[56]

Christina Buttons, reporting for The Daily Wire, spoke with a source who suggested this was not true, claiming to "have first-hand knowledge that at least 10 minors have received double-mastectomies this year—double what VUMC says is their average."[57] But neither Christina nor I was able to confirm this claim.

Pinson also emphasized that the clinic was relying on the guidance of "leading medical specialty societies" such as the World Professional Association of Transgender Health (WPATH) and the Endocrine Society.

In June 2023, Vanderbilt University Medical Center turned over medical records for trans-identifying patients to the Tennessee attorney general's office. Those records were related to the state's investigation into "billing for transgender care services provided to individuals enrolled in State-sponsored insurance plans," VUMC said in a notice to its patients.[58] It appears that VUMC wanted word to get out about the attorney general's request—in a press release, Attorney General Jonathan Skrmetti's office empha-sized that its investigation is focused not on the patients, but on VUMC and on certain providers. "VUMC started producing medical records more than six months ago," Skrmetti's office said.

"This Office has kept the investigation confidential for almost a year and was surprised by VUMC's decision to notify patients. The Attorney General has no desire to turn a run-of-the-mill fraud investigation into a media circus."[59]

CHAPTER 11

The Alternative

There is so much to be learned from the stories of people like Luka, Prisha, Chloe, Helena, and "Abel." And I'm incredibly grateful to them for being so vulnerable about such a traumatic and emotional part of their lives.

Though their paths ahead may be difficult, these individuals are thankful that they escaped the gender ideology cult.

Not everyone made it.

The story I'm about to share is that of Yaeli Mozzelle Galdamez, a young girl who identified as a boy named "Andrew," or "Andy."

California school authorities affirmed Yaeli's claim that she was a transgender boy. They called her Andrew as she asked and referred to her using male pronouns.[1] When her mother discovered this and pushed back, the Los Angeles County Department of Children and Family Services (DCFS) removed her from her mother's care.

Yaeli ultimately knelt in front of a train, raised her arms above her head, and watched as the train hurtled towards her. She was nineteen years old.

Authorities had to pick up pieces of the young girl's body from all over and around the tracks. When her grieving mother asked to see her daughter, she was told that no part of the girl would be recognizable.[2]

I spoke with Yaeli's mother, Abby Martinez. She has repeatedly shared Yaeli's story in the hope that others may learn from it. Almost every time she speaks about her daughter, she is visibly shattered by her grief. It is hard to speak with her, or listen to her, without sharing her emotion.

Abby tells me that she is the oldest daughter in a family of nine children, born and raised in El Salvador. She came to the United States around age eighteen to live with her cousin, where she met Rigo Galdamez, Yaeli's father. He was a little older than she was, Abby told me, and a paralegal in a law firm. They married in 1991, according to a September 15, 2016, Los Angeles County Department of Children and Family Services (DCFS) Jurisdiction/Disposition Report.

Her husband was very jealous, Abby told DCFS—describing him as emotionally and verbally abusive—calling her names, isolating her from her female friends, accusing her of seeing other men, and, ultimately, physically hurting her. "It got too ugly," she said. "I didn't want that life. It wasn't good for me or [the children]."[3]

Abby finally took the children back to El Salvador when Yaeli was six, as she told my colleague Virginia Allen in a March 2022 interview.[4] They lived in El Salvador for five years, visited California in the summer, and finally moved back in 2011, settling down in Arcadia, where Abby worked as a nanny and for her church. (She told DCFS that the family attended weekly.)[5]

Abby says she never reconciled with her husband. She told DCFS in 2016 that he was "currently homeless and very ill" due to a blood infection and had lost his job in 2010.

Rigo still made appearances in the family's life, however—Abby told me that he would occasionally show up at the door wanting to spend time with the family. Abby did not leave him unmonitored with the children, but told DCFS that he "acts like a good guy in front of the kids."

Yaeli reportedly adored her father. Her mother said she was "the closest child to her father," and her sister described her to DCFS as "Daddy's little girl."[6]

Yaeli Becomes Andrew

As a young girl, Yaeli used to dress up as a princess, her mother tearfully shared in her Daily Signal interview. "She loved to dance, sing, and she was very artistic."

But when Yaeli entered her teens, she began to use social media more and more. Her mother watched this with anxiety, noticing how depressed her daughter was becoming. And then she started noticing that Yaeli was cutting herself.[7]

Struggling with depression in her early teen years, Yaeli made friends with a biologically female high school student who would later identify as a boy and go by the name Caden, according to the 2016 Department of Children and Family Services Jurisdiction/Disposition Report. That friend, formerly named Arianna, was a student a few years ahead of Yaeli. Arianna suggested to her that she might be depressed because she was transgender.

"Caden's mother, Mercedes, is known to be very supportive of this process in both Caden, and presumably Andrew," the report says. "Caden has a good friend Nate, who is also supportive of this process for Andrew."[8]

Yaeli began attending an LGBTQ club at her high school, according to her mother, who says that the club affirmed to her what she had been questioning: she was a boy.

Her school counselor also affirmed this, Abby said, and Yaeli began "socially transitioning."

Abby had no idea. But she knew that her daughter was struggling dramatically both mentally and academically.

According to the Jurisdiction/Disposition Report, Yaeli began cutting herself on the arms with a "razor or something sharp, like a paper clip," around age thirteen. In eighth grade, she attempted to take her own life by overdosing on allergy medicine, the report says. This was her first suicide attempt, and it resulted in her being sent to "a mental hospital for one week."

"It was all right," Yaeli said, according to the report. "It made me realize I was not the only one to go through this." After this, Arcadia High School provided Yaeli with a therapist, the report says.

The paperwork also notes that Abby was concerned that "Yaeli was not sleeping, using the iPad constantly, was tired during the day and not focusing on schoolwork, in addition to being very moody" and was "wearing black clothing, experimenting with 'emo' styles."

At age fifteen, Yaeli again tried to take her life, by overdosing on "31 pills—Advil and something else."

"I didn't get sick," Yaeli is quoted saying in the report. "I wrote suicide notes and my mom called the police and an ambulance came." Yaeli was again hospitalized.

And in October 2015, after an argument with her mom, Yaeli was found by police on the 210 Freeway overpass. The police prevented her from jumping, according to DCFS, and Yaeli was hospitalized for one week for the third time.[9]

Abby said she finally asked Arcadia High School for help because Yaeli's grades had become so bad. She also wanted to inform them about Yaeli's mental health struggles and suicide attempts, and to ask school officials to keep an eye on anything concerning.

So you can imagine her shock when she discovered that the school was well aware that her daughter identified as transgender. As Abby told me: "I never [would have] imagined that what they were doing is trying to make her believe that once she goes through the [gender] transition that life was going to be different."

Yaeli was fifteen at this point, a freshman in high school. Up until this point, her mother had had no idea that she was identifying as transgender—one of Abby's other daughters had told her that Yaeli "thinks she likes girls," but Abby just thought Yaeli was going through typical teenage *Who am I?* identity struggles.

So Abby took Yaeli out to eat and pressed her to share what was going on.

Yaeli finally admitted, "I don't want to talk about it because you guys are not going to be supportive," her mother said.

"Well, we don't know," Abby says she told her daughter. "So, if you tell us what's going on I'll be more than happy to help you. I'd do anything to help you, Yaeli. The only thing that I need, and I wanted it for you, is to see the happy girl that used to be before."

"I'm not a girl," Yaeli finally told her. "I'm a boy."[10]

California Gets Involved

Things became worse as Yaeli's family grappled with this startling news. They didn't know what to do.

In the 2016 Department of Children and Family Services Jurisdiction/Disposition Report, Yaeli's sister Katherine (who was twenty-four at the time) stated that her mother was trying to make Yaeli as "comfortable as possible" and that Abby had taken Yaeli shopping for boys' clothes. She also said that Abby had been "trying very hard ever since this started" and was currently going to therapy with Yaeli.[11]

The family wasn't following Yaeli's wishes and calling her "Andy," according to Yaeli's sister Raziel, who was seventeen at the time. But they all wanted her to be happy. Several of Yaeli's siblings say in the DCFS report that Yaeli had hurt their mother physically and that she had a pattern of lying to get what she wanted.[12]

On July 27, 2016, Yaeli's therapist "Jackie" came to the house to walk and talk with her (as was their custom, Abby said). Yaeli asked her mother if she could bring her iPad with her on the walk with the therapist, saying that she wanted to take some photos.[13]

The entire family was concerned about Yaeli's iPad usage. Their testimony describes her staying "up all night" on the internet, "not sleeping much at night." Abby told her oldest daughter Katherine that she had seen Yaeli sexting people, and her brother Benjamin described his older sister as "addicted" to the device, according to the DCFS Jurisdiction/Disposition Report.[14]

Abby allowed her to take the iPad on the condition that she would give it back when she got home, and Yaeli agreed.

But when she got home from her walk, Yaeli told her mother that her therapist had a different opinion: "Jackie said I bought the iPad with my own money so I can keep it."

"We made an agreement, so please give me the iPad," Abby said, according to her testimony in the DCFS Jurisdiction/Disposition Report.

Then Yaeli lost it and began hurling insults at her mother. "You're not my mother. You're nothing to me. You're not my mother, so why should I give it to you?"

Abby says that she tried to reason with her daughter, and that Razi backed her up. Yaeli fled to her room, stuffed the iPad in her pants, and curled up into a ball in a fetal position first on her bed, then on the floor. Abby tried to take the iPad away from her, and Yaeli bit her mother's finger (Razi backs that claim up in the report). As

Abby pulled her hand away, she said she accidentally swiped it against Yaeli's face.

DCFS and Yaeli would say that Abby had slapped Yaeli on the mouth, and that Abby had previously slapped her daughter on several other occasions. "Such physical abuse was excessive and caused the child unreasonable pain and suffering," the DCFS report says. "The child does not want to return to the mother's home and care, due to the physical abuse of the child by the mother. Such physical abuse of the child by the mother endangers the child's physical health, safety and well-being, creates a detrimental home environment and places the child Yaeli, at risk of serious physical harm, damage, danger and physical abuse."[15]

Yaeli's seventeen-year-old sister Razi told DCFS that the allegation was false. "The only one who was getting hurt was my mom."

Abby believes that Yaeli's "older, trans-identifying friend" was coaching Yaeli on what extreme things she should say so that DCFS would remove her from her home.

Benjamin, fourteen at the time, described his sister as emotionally volatile, saying she had thrown things at him and had hurt him, Razi, and his dog in past fights: "She thinks she's always right. She can't be wrong.... Yaeli took a screwdriver and stabbed my mom's door.... She has no respect for my mom."[16]

The testimony in the DCFS Jurisdiction/Disposition Report further states that after Abby took the iPad from Yaeli, Yaeli continued demanding the iPad, but when her mother ignored her requests, she finally left and went on her computer.

The next day was a Thursday, according to the DCFS report. Yaeli was in a good mood and attended a church youth group. On Friday, she went shopping with her mother and siblings, and Abby bought Yaeli three shirts that she wanted.

On Saturday, Abby and Yaeli went to their local farmer's market. Yaeli spent some time on the computer and then suggested to her mother that they watch TV together. Abby, according to the report, said she had to finish cleaning a room and would meet Yaeli on the sofa.

But then Yaeli disappeared. Abby looked all over the house and outside, calling for her daughter without response. Eventually, panicked and crying after three hours of searching, around 2:00 p.m. she called the police.

"She later saw her neighbor's security camera footage which showed that Yaeli went out the front door and ran into a familiar car…which quickly drove off," the Jurisdiction/Disposition Report states. Benjamin told DCFS the car belonged to Arianna (who went by Caden) and Arianna's mother.[17]

Abby would learn that Arianna and her mother had taken Yaeli to the police station—she arrived at Arcadia police station "as a runaway" at 10:00 pm on Sunday, July 31, 2016, where she "stated she did not want to return to her mother's care," the report says.[18]

Yaeli told police that being in her verbally abusive mother's home made her suicidal, the report said, and that she identified as a male and called herself "Andy."

After this, DCFS would contact Abby. Yaeli was placed in a group home. "I'm better here" at the Junior Blind group home, the sixteen-year-old Yaeli stated to DCFS. "I get to be myself, and it's more comfortable for me. I will be Andrew, a male. I'd rather be happy rather than miserable for them," she continued, apparently referring to her family. "I never felt comfortable in my body. I tried to be girly, but that didn't make me comfortable."

She did not want to go back home, she said, and the only people she wanted to see were Caden and Nate—the two friends who had encouraged her transition.[19]

The contributions to the Department of Children and Family Services Jurisdiction/Disposition Report by Ione Mieure, Yaeli's school psychologist, are revealing. Mieure stated that she met with Yaeli (whom she calls Andy) every week for two years and was aware that Yaeli was depressed. She also said that Yaeli told her that she had "always identified as a boy. He was very sure of who he was," Mieure said of Yaeli, using male pronouns. "When DCFS got involved and [therapist] Jackie was involved his grade[s] really improved."

Mieure shared that she had become "very concerned" about Yaeli's mental health and safety in relation to her family. "His mother is highly religious," Mieure warned. "Andy had no freedom and [Abby] wouldn't allow him to have independence. It was very stifling. He was feeling very desperate…. Andy wants nothing more than to be truly accepted by his mother."

Mieure advocated for Yaeli to be taken from her family: "I believe Andy needs to live in an environment where he's accepted for being transgender," she told DCFS. "His emotional well-being and safety is inextricably tied to being accepted."[20]

Mieure is still employed by Arcadia School District, I confirmed in April 2023. She did not respond to multiple requests for comment.

Abby's children tried to advocate on behalf of the family in statements to DCFS.

"My mom's a good mom and she tries her best," Raziel said.

"We're trying to get by, and work on it," Katherine said in her statement. "You don't want to make decisions that you regret." Katherine also pointed out that Yaeli had many unresolved issues with her father, emphasizing that she used to be "Daddy's little girl."

"Yaeli used to be a very bad liar, but I think she is practicing," her little brother said of her. "She exaggerates and makes things up. She wants everything her way, she'd betray our trust…. My mom is really nice and pushes her to do better, and for us to do our best. She's there when we need her, and she makes time for us."[21]

Yaeli had long suffered from mental health struggles. The DCFS Jurisdiction/Disposition Report notes that her grades in school suffered dramatically on account of her depression (documented as recently as March 2016) and that she had been prescribed Seroquel and Prozac over the past few years (though at the moment of the report Yaeli said she didn't need psychotropic medication).

But that same DCFS report describes Yaeli as "healthy, with no medical problems" and looking forward to "taking male hormones and eventually getting surgeries to become a male."[22]

"Evidently, the accusations had the desired effect," *National Review*'s Madeleine Kearns wrote in a *Spectator World* piece on Yaeli and Abby. "In 2016, the DCFS declared the allegations of emotional abuse against Abigail 'substantiated' and placed Yaeli in a group home. (Curiously, Abigail—whom the judge deemed a threat to Yaeli—was permitted to retain custody of her other minor children and to continue working as a nanny.)"[23]

For two weeks after she was placed in the group home, Yaeli refused to have visits with her family, the DCFS Jurisdiction/Disposition Report says. When she finally agreed to a three-hour visit with her mother, the young girl left the room after ten minutes, saying it was "too intense." A second visit was arranged, and this time Abby brought Yaeli's dog. Yaeli allegedly told DCFS that she felt more comfortable that time since there was "at least one staff member monitoring the visit."[24]

Yaeli was sixteen years old at the time. In her Daily Signal interview, Abby alleged that the social worker involved in Abby's visits with Yaeli told Abby that she couldn't talk about God—or she wouldn't be allowed to see her daughter.

Abby tearfully reflected on the logic she said was behind the state's decision to take her child from her: *"If we keep [Yaeli] out of your home, she [will] have more chance to survive. She's not going to try to commit suicide."*[25]

"The scenario is complicated enough, considering that Andrew's mother was raised a Christian in a church that did not accept LGBT values," the DCFS assessment reads. "It is clear that at this time Yaeli/ Andrew is content to be out of the family home."

Abby pleaded for her child, drawing on her maternal instincts and intimate knowledge of her daughter. "Yaeli just wants freedom," she told DCFS. "She doesn't want me to say this isn't good for you, it's the wrong path. I could say yes to everything you want, but that's not being a good parent. I'm here to protect and feed you, take you to school, tell you what's right and wrong...."

"The therapist told me to let her go, but she wasn't mature enough to choose the right people," Abby insisted, referring to a therapist named in the DCFS Jurisdiction/Disposition Report as Jackie. "I let her go but when I did she always did something she's not supposed to do.... I didn't have a good feeling about these people [Caden, Nate, Mercedes] and Yaeli acted suspiciously [with them]. I talked to her about the dangers of drugs, sex.

"Yaeli is one of a kind who wants to be free and she's very smart," she continued. "I love Yaeli to death, but she was going in the wrong direction. Yaeli is trying to find her identity.... Yaeli was going online to sex and pornography sites. She should not put that in her brain at this age.... I told Yaeli she needed to talk to God. 'Nothing is making you happy, so ask God.'" And finally: "She doesn't want to be with us even though she knows we love her."

As of September 2016, Yaeli's group home had already made her an appointment with the Children's Hospital transgender program and scheduled a meeting with the nonprofit RISE program. "Fortunately, child Andrew will receive a lot of education and support on transgender issues," the DCFS report states.

That report, signed by social workers Jill Kaufman and Norma Dison and submitted to DCFS director Philip Browning, recommends that the court declare Yaeli a dependent of the court and suitably place her.[26]

So Yaeli lived away from her family for almost three years. DCFS helped her get started taking cross-sex hormones, testosterone, to begin her medical transition. She legally changed her name to Andrew. But she was still deeply depressed.

"She was taking the [cross-sex] hormones; she was not happy. She changed her name, [but] was not happy," Abby said. "She adopted a dog because that was going to make her happy. None of it, everything that they've done, didn't work."[27]

Abby couldn't find a good attorney to represent her at the time, "To at least be there and talk to the judge, and say, you know, we need a psych evaluation. You want to help her? Give her some medical treatment. Mental health. The issue," Abby added, pointing to her brain, "is here."

"I wish the system, instead of spending millions of dollars on these kids, having them in foster care, [would] support us as a parent and gave us the tools that we need. I just didn't want to lose my daughter."[28]

Kearns reported in her piece for *Spectator World* that DCFS director Philip Browning was confident that Yaeli would be happier if she underwent a gender transition.[29] (Browning, who retired from LA DCFS in 2016 and went to work for consulting firm Capstone Solutions, tells me he has no memory of the case. See my interview with him, below.)

According to a July 2017 DCFS Status Review Report, Yaeli had requested that she be placed in a foster home, but no home was available. Yaeli was going to therapy at the Center for Transyouth Health Development at the Children's Hospital of Los Angeles with medical therapist Jamie Julian, LCSW, the report says.

"Ms. Julian states that during the time she has worked with Andrew, he has never wavered on wanting to do hormone treatment/therapy," according to the report. "Ms. Julian states that she works with Andrew on all the feelings and the distress that might be caused by the transition process."[30]

As one might imagine, Abby was struggling with the loss of her child, firmly convinced that taking male hormones would not be helpful to her daughter. And things only got worse. On January 17, 2017, Abby was ordered by the court to complete conjoint counseling and family counseling, as well as to attend a transgender support group for parents at Children's Hospital Los Angeles. She was referred to three LGBT support groups: Transforming Family, Gay and Lesbian Support Groups for Christians, and Pasadena Pride Center. Each of these groups supports transitions. Abby ultimately didn't go.[31]

The court authorized Yaeli to begin testosterone treatment on June 2, 2017—"the medical authorization was signed," the DCFS medical evaluation says.[32]

Abby recalled with anger and frustration the moment that the paperwork for Yaeli to begin hormone treatment was signed in front of her, describing how one of the California DCFS workers smiled and said that Abby could no longer hold up Yaeli's transition.

"She signed that just right there in front of me," Abby told me tearfully. "Oh gosh, I was crying. I knew that was not what my daughter needs."

"I cried," she said, her voice shaking. "I felt like they tied my hands. I couldn't do anything to defend my own child.... They feel like it's not your child."[33]

On June 20, 2017, a clinical social worker completed a reunification assessment for Abby and Yaeli, according to the report. That assessment found that there was a "low" risk level of any future abuse, and its resulting recommendation was that Yaeli return home to her family.

And yet this didn't happen. The unnamed clinical social worker or social workers used "discretionary override to change the recommendation to continue services in order to allow for more time for Andrew and mother to make amends and continue on the path of progress that they were previously on," the Status Review Report states.[34]

A judge overruled Abby's objections and O.K.'d Yaeli to begin testosterone treatment, Kearns reported. Yaeli's older sister Katherine shared with Kearns that the state paid for half of Yaeli's treatment until the young girl turned eighteen. After that, she had to pay her own way. "They left her halfway," her sister said.

And the testosterone caused Yaeli significant pain. "These hormones cause changes in your body," Katherine told Kearns. "Her joints, her muscles, she had asked my mum for CBD oils to help relax because she would just be in so much pain."

Abby would frequently reach out to her daughter, bringing her food or reminding her that she loved her. She wouldn't call her daughter Andrew, but as a compromise, she stored her daughter's contact in her phone as "God Perfect Plan."

In one heartbreaking text exchange posted by the *Daily Mail*, apparently in reference to Abby bringing her daughter food, Abby texted Yaeli, "You know that you are not [alone] and I'm always there for you."

"You don't know how much this means to me mama," Yaeli texted back. "Like I literally have tears in my eyes."

In another exchange, she tells her mother: "Thank you so so much mama. You don't know how much this means to me like I'm really crying right now [out of] happiness. This really means a lot to me. I know I'm not perfect either and I can be difficult sometimes but I do really love you mama."

"I [love] you too mi amor," her mother replied, with heart and praying hand emojis. "And I just want the best for you."

In another set of text messages, from January 28, 2019, Yaeli lovingly texted her mother a lengthy message about how thankful she was for her.

"I love you and I'm proud of everything you've done," she said. "I haven't told you this often but I'm really happy to have you as my mom. You mean the world to me."[35]

"This Pain Never Goes Away"

DCFS had taken Yaeli away from Abby based on allegations of emotional abuse, Kearns reported. But in August 2019, DCFS told Abby that it had changed the status of those allegations from "substantiated" to "inconclusive." Why? DCFS wouldn't tell me (or Kearns).

"The gesture was too little, too late," Kearns wrote. "Yaeli's mental health was deteriorating."

"In a sane world, skepticism of transgender ideology would not automatically forfeit constitutionally protected parental rights," Kearns noted, describing multiple lawsuits around the country that deal with schools circumventing parents in pushing gender ideology on children. "Neither a school nor the state is entitled to drive a wedge between a child in distress and their family, simply because that family disagrees with current LGBT doctrine. Yet that is exactly what's happening across the country."[36]

Abby told our Daily Signal team that on September 4, 2019, she felt uneasy—"weird."

"I felt like I have a pain in my chest," she said. "I didn't know why. I was sad, but super sad, like something was taken away from me."

So she called Yaeli. No response. Then she texted her. Thankfully, Yaeli replied.

"I was like, 'Oh my God, she's O.K.,'" Abby said, one hand on her heart.

"I'm so glad you replied, how are you doing?" she asked her daughter.

"Oh I'm good, Mama," Yaeli replied. Abby said her daughter told her a little bit about her day and about work and then stopped replying. Abby hoped that Yaeli was in the shower or had just gotten caught up in something else.

"That was the last text that I received from her."

The next morning around 8:15, as she drove home from dropping her son off at school, Abby received a phone call. "Are you Yaeli Galdamez's mom, a.k.a. Andrew?" she was asked. Then she was told: "I need you to park the car."

"My heart went like crazy," she said. "I got off at the first exit. I parked my car."

"Tell me, where is my daughter, I want to go see her," she begged the person on the phone, who was calling from the coroner's office.

Abby was sobbing at this point as she shared her story on camera with The Daily Signal team.

"I'm so sorry, but you're not going to be able to see her," the person responded.

"Why?" begged Abby. "What hospital is she in, I just want to see her."

And then she was told that her daughter had taken her own life. Yaeli had thrown herself in front of a train.

"I got out of the car, I was screaming like crazy," the distraught mother said, tears streaming down her face. "I was screaming, I said, 'No, I want my daughter!'"

But Yaeli was gone.[37]

Madeleine shared with me the coroner's report detailing Yaeli's death.

The details made me sick. According to officers on the scene, a freight train was traveling westbound at approximately thirty-eight miles per hour on the morning of Wednesday, September 4, 2019, when the engineer saw Yaeli "lay down on the north set of tracks."

Yaeli was first seen sitting on her knees, then lying down onto her back, with her head facing south and her legs out in front of her.

The engineer sounded the horn and set the emergency brakes. But it was too late.

The train ran over Yaeli.

"The freight train was located resting on the north set of railroad tracks," one officer stated in the coroner's report. "The 1st engine was facing west and I was unable to see the rear of the train. There was blood and brain matter on the engine on the gas tank of the 1st engine."

There was blood smear and some brain matter on the north side of the crossing, just south of the north tracks. Located feet west along the north set of tracks and just south of the north set of tracks were multiple pieces of brain matter, human debris, pieces of skull, pieces of ribs, and blood splatter. Amongst the debris, was the decedent's right hand and part of her right arm, which was located just south of the north set of tracks. Her forearm was located inside a sweatshirt and there was a black beanie with the sweatshirt. Located just south of her forearm was a piece of a fractured rib. Located a few feet northwest of her right arm, was the decedent's left arm, torso, and legs. Located just east of her torso was a kidney, and located a few feet southwest of her torso, just south of the north set of train tracks were multiple pieces of brain matter, an unknown piece of one of her organs, a piece of skull, and other human debris. Located feet west of the decedent's torso was her other kidney. There were multiple pieces of brain matter extending feet west just south of the north set of train tracks. Located feet south of the north set of train tracks was a large piece of skull. Located a few feet north-west of that large piece of skull, in the middle of the north set of train tracks was part of the decedent's rib cage, her right shoulder, and part of her right arm. Located a few feet west of her rib cage, was the decedent's left sneaker and part of a fractured rib. Located southwest of that piece of fractured rib, south of the north set of train tracks, were multiple blood marks leading up to the decedent's head. The decedent's right sneaker was located on the north set of train tracks, feet west of the 57 Freeway.

Her head was "traumatically amputated at the neck." Her right arm was "traumatically amputated just below the elbow," and found lying just south of the tracks. Her left arm was "almost traumatically amputated, and was attached to the torso by a piece of skin."

The coroner's report goes on and on, describing injuries so extensive that authorities concluded that Yaeli could not be positively identified visually.

"The decedent is probably Yaeli Mozelle Galdamez and Andrew Elijah Martinez both with a DOB of 04/23/2000," the report concludes.

Following standard practice, the coroner's office called Abby and informed her that her nineteen-year-old daughter had taken her own life: "On Thursday, 09/05/2019 at 0815 hours, I tentatively notified Silvia Martinez, the decedent's mother, of her daughter's death via telephone."

Abby would ultimately obtain a physical copy of this gruesome and graphic coroner's report detailing the gory last moments of her daughter's short life, illustrations of how Yaeli's body would have been impacted by the train, and bluntly graphic descriptions of her scattered remains.[38]

She was told not to see the body because there wasn't much left of her daughter to see.

She still has the report, and shared photographs of it with Madeleine, who in turn shared them with me —"live" photos that allow for a flash of a moment to see through the eyes of a bereaved mother looking down on the heartbreakingly blunt, brutishly plain explanations of her daughter's demise.

"They are monsters," she told me, when we discussed the adults in Yaeli's life who guided her down this path. "None of the stuff that they allowed her to do worked. At the end, they took my child."

There was a resolute glint to her eyes, though she continually wiped away her tears, when she addressed what she wants others to learn from her story as she spoke with our Daily Signal team.

"I want everyone to know that the system is taking our children away," she said. "They are not helping them. My daughter was a number. It's all political. It's in their agenda. LGBTQ used her to collect money from wealthy people, just to tell the story, that her mom didn't support her and that's why she ended up in a group home, because she was transgender and I never accepted that. And that was a lie."[39]

The Department of Children and Family Services didn't back down after Yaeli's death. They issued a statement calling her "Andrew M." and expressing condolences not only to Yaeli's family and her friends but "as well as to the LGBTQIA community which advocates relentlessly to protect its youngest and most vulnerable members from such tragedies."[40]

And shortly after Yaeli's death, the Los Angeles County Board of Supervisors approved a motion, authored by Supervisors Hilda Solis and Sheila Kuehl, to further strengthen a "system of support" and "ensure the success of every foster youth who identifies as LGBTQ+."[41]

What does that entail? DCFS told me, in an April 2023 email response to my inquiry about how they were implementing "gender-affirming care" for foster children, that it has "aggressively pursued the implementation of inclusive, gender-affirming laws, policies and supportive services for LGBTQ+ youth."

This includes formalized contracts between DCFS and the Los Angeles LGBT Center, Penny Lane Centers, The Help Group, and the Long Beach LGBTQ Center.

"Affirming services are intended to uplift a youth's sexual orientation and gender identity," the DCFS email said.

"Therapy, leadership and mentorship programs, crisis intervention services, support groups, training and education also will be provided to youth, their families and caretakers through these organizations."

DCFS is "fiercely committed" to this work, they assured me.[42]

Ryan Foran, spokesman for the Arcadia School District (the district in which Yaeli's school was), denied to The Daily Wire that Yaeli's school had encouraged her to medically transition. Foran claimed that such a suggestion was "categorically false."

Foran, who ultimately did not respond to my requests for comment, also denied to The Daily Wire that the school had failed to appropriately treat Yaeli's mental health issues. "Furthermore, a claim suggesting our school or a staff member did not properly treat a student's severe depression is both completely inaccurate and troubling as our schools and staff would not be authorized or medically qualified to treat clinical depression," he added.

"However, our staff works tirelessly to provide and suggest resources, when appropriate, to help connect students and families with licensed mental health professionals to treat conditions such as clinical depression. We have a very caring staff that is dedicated to providing a safe, nondiscriminatory school environment for all students. We also continually provide resources to promote the healthy mental, emotional, and social well-being of all students."[43]

In early April 2023 I spoke with former DCFS director Philip Browning, who submitted the September 2016 Jurisdiction/Disposition Report on Yaeli's progress transitioning away from her family.[44] We spoke for about twenty minutes. I asked him about Yaeli, and about her mother's allegations.

Throughout the course of our phone call, Browning repeatedly claimed he could not recall anything about Yaeli's story or death, saying that he had dealt with many similar cases. He suggested that DCFS would never recommend a child for medical transition without proper parental involvement.

"I don't know about this case at all," he said at the beginning, "I don't recall that case," later on, and "I can't speak to that situation."

"I think we are both cognizant that this was an upsetting case," I said, noting that I had the DCFS report in front of me with his name on it. "I'm a little surprised that you don't remember it."

"Well it's been a number of years," he responded. "We had thousands of cases."

"Do you mind if I text you the news story and see if you remember?" I asked.

When he responded in the affirmative, I texted him a link to the *Daily Mail*'s coverage of Yaeli's death while we were still on the phone. "It won't open," he said.

I told him I had another one, and sent him The Daily Signal's story. "Won't open either," he said. "Maybe if I put that into a desktop, maybe that would work."

I expressed willingness to wait while he checked the links on his desktop, but he responded, "I'm not able to do that at this minute."

"Why not?" I asked.

"I've got some other things that I'm working on, frankly," he said, stuttering slightly, before starting to question me about The Daily Signal.

"Wait," I said. "You're willing to talk to me about The Daily Signal but you're not willing to Google the actual story right now?"

"Yeah, I uh, have some other things that I have to do," he said. "Mary Margaret, I did call you back…if I didn't want to talk about it, I would have hung up when you mentioned [her] name. I think I've been very clear."

"It sounds like you are afraid to talk about what I actually want to know," I told him.

We went back and forth a few more times. Then we got off the phone.

It is worth noting that, though he said he could not remember the specific case, Browning repeatedly told me that he is certain others would have been involved in giving Yaeli the O.K. to transition. He specifically noted that DCFS's psychiatrist on staff—"one of the only child psychiatrists that worked for a child welfare program in America"—would absolutely have been involved.

"I feel sure that if any discussion or review were to occur about a situation like that, the psychiatrist would certainly have been involved," he said.[45]

Abby wants the system to change. She truly wants to help children to navigate puberty and sexuality in this turbulent age, to provide them with the mental health resources that they need.

"I know that I'm not the first one," she said in spring 2022. "Maybe there [are] many parents, moms that are struggling with this with the school system, with DCFS, and we can't do anything with them. It's like they tied our hands to do something with our children. They take it away like they belong to them.

"I don't want any parent to go through this," she said. "This pain never goes away."[46]

AFTERWORD

Since I began writing *Detrans*, around Christmastime of 2022, Chloe, Prisha, and Luka have all filed their own lawsuits suing the medical professionals who transitioned them.

These lawsuits name numerous therapists, doctors, and institutions that were involved in these tragedies. It cannot be emphasized enough how momentous these suits are—they are huge, huge steps forward in holding the medical establishment accountable, and I strongly commend the lawyers who brought them about, particularly Harmeet Dhillon and the attorneys at the Center for American Liberty and Campbell Miller Payne.

Chloe, Prisha, Luka, Helena, "Abel," Ritchie, Walt, and many other detransitioners continue to publicly share their lived experiences in the best ways they know, in social media posts, livestreams, Substacks, public testimony before lawmakers, videos, speeches at rallies, and more.

I believe the tide is turning, if it has not already turned, on this issue. How can it be possible to hear these stories without, at the very,

very least, advocating for caution? How is it possible to hear of detransitioners' sufferings without wishing that someone, anyone, had stood up for them as they floundered down this path?

Is it possible to think of these people, so young, lost, afraid, so heavily burdened, without longing to dry their tears and tell them that they need not maim themselves in order to live happy and fulfilled lives?

I truly believe that reading and understanding these real, lived stories of detransitioners makes it impossible to advocate for such destructive practices, particularly for children.

And that is why I wrote this book.

ACKNOWLEDGMENTS

I am grateful to The Daily Wire for permission to reprint portions of my reporting originally published by them, including "Catholic Chicago Hospital Chose Ideology over Biology in Treating Biological Girl Who Believed She Was Male"; similarly grateful to The Daily Signal for permission to reprint portions of my reporting originally published by them, including "He Went Undercover to Expose 'Rubber-Stamping' of Trans Surgeries"; and grateful to the Daily Caller News Foundation for permission to reprint portions of my reporting originally published by them, including "'It Destroyed My Body': Here's Why This Former Trans Woman Regrets His Gender Transition."

I would like to extend a very heartfelt thanks to Jay Richards, Katrina Trinko, Rob Bluey, and The Heritage Foundation for their abundant support of this project. Their encouragement and backing allowed me to devote the time and resources to this book that it deserved.

Many thanks to the others who provided advice, guidance, and support throughout this project, including Abigail Shrier, Mary Rice Hasson, Terry Schilling, Brandon Showalter, and my colleagues Samantha Aescheris and Virginia Allen. Of course, none of these individuals bears responsibility for the content of this book, which is solely mine.

I'm also incredibly grateful to Tom Spence, Regnery, Tony Lyons, and Skyhorse Publishing for bringing my book into reality, and to Elizabeth Kantor for her gracious and thorough editing.

And, of course, many thanks to my family and close friends for their patience, support, and prayers.

Notes

Introduction

1. Lindsey Tanner, "How Common Is Transgender Treatment Regret, Detransitioning?," Associated Press, March 5, 2023, https://apnews.com/article /transgender-treatment-regret-detransition-371e927ec6e7a24cd9c77b5371c6ba2b.
2. "GLAAD Media Reference Guide 11th Edition," GLAAD, https://glaad.org /reference; "Glossary of Terms," Human Rights Campaign, updated May 31, 2023, https://www.hrc.org/resources/glossary-of-terms.
3. Angela Dallara, "Fact Sheet: Reporter Guide to Covering Transgender People, Topics, and Legislation," GLAAD, March 23, 2023, https://glaad.org/fact-sheet -evidence-based-healthcare-transgender-people-and-youth.
4. "GLAAD Media Reference Guide."
5. Jen Christensen, "Gender-Affirming Care, a 'Crucial' Process for Thousands of Young People in America," CNN, updated April 25, 2023, https://www.cnn .com/2022/04/21/health/gender-affirming-care/index.html.
6. Anne Branigin, "An Idaho Bill Would Criminalize Medical Treatments for Trans Youths. It Echoes Abortion Bans," *Washington Post*, March 11, 2022, https: //www.washingtonpost.com/lifestyle/2022/03/11/idaho-transgender-medical -treatment-bill.
7. Andrew Demillo, "Sanders Signs Arkansas Trans Care Malpractice Bill into Law," Associated Press, March 14, 2023, https://apnews.com/article/huckabee-sanders -transgender-malpractice-lgbtq-arkansas-41b7cd39b167b3bf2f3796d8be37ecf6.
8. Ibid.
9. Lisa Littman, "Individuals Treated for Gender Dysphoria with Medical and/or Surgical Transition Who Subsequently Detransitioned: A Survey of 100 Detransitioners," *Archives of Sexual Behavior* 50 (2021): 3353–69, https://doi .org/10.1007/s10508-021-02163-w.
10. ADM Rachel Levine (@HHS_ASH), "Gender-affirming care is medical care…," Twitter, August 19, 2022, 11:35 a.m., https://twitter.com/HHS_ASH/status /1560651684694589440?s=20.
11. "Gender-Affirming Care and Young People," U.S. Department of Health and Human Services, Office of Population Affairs, March 2022, https://opa.hhs.gov /sites/default/files/2022-03/gender-affirming-care-young-people-march-2022.pdf.
12. "Discrimination on the Basis of Sex," U.S. Department of Health and Human Services, Office of Civil Rights, January 20, 2023, https://www.hhs.gov/civil-rights /for-individuals/sex-discrimination/index.html.

13. "Lesbian, Gay, Bisexual, and Transgender Health: Health Services," Centers for Disease Control and Prevention, July 18, 2023, https://www.cdc.gov/lgbthealth/health-services.htm.

14. "National Survey on LGBTQ Youth Mental Health 2021," The Trevor Project, https://www.thetrevorproject.org/survey-2021.

15. "Glossary of Terms."

16. M. Clarke et al., "Gender-Affirming Care Is Trauma-Informed Care," The National Child Traumatic Stress Unit, 2022, https://www.nctsn.org/sites/default/files/resources/fact-sheet/gender-affirming-care-is-trauma-informed-care.pdf.

17. Kareen Matouk and Melina Wald, "Gender-Affirming Care Saves Lives," Columbia University Department of Psychiatry, March 30, 2022, https://www.columbiapsychiatry.org/news/gender-affirming-care-saves-lives.

18. Leor Sapir, "'Trust the Experts' Is Not Enough: U.S. Medical Groups Get the Science Wrong on Pediatric 'Gender Affirming' Care," Manhattan Institute, October 17, 2022, https://manhattan.institute/article/trust-the-experts-is-not-enough.

19. Leor Sapir, "Finland Takes Another Look at Youth Gender Medicine," Tablet, February 21, 2023, https://www.tabletmag.com/sections/science/articles/finland-youth-gender-medicine.

20. Mary Margaret Olohan, "UK's National Health Service Finds Most Youths 'Identifying' as Trans Are Going through 'Transient Phase,'" The Daily Signal, October 24, 2022, https://www.dailysignal.com/2022/10/24/uks-national-health-service-finds-most-youths-identifying-trans-are-going-transient-phase-biden-pushes-trans-surgeries-kids.

21. "About the Review," The Cass Review, https://cass.independent-review.uk/about-the-review.

22. Eleanor Hayward, "Tavistock Gender Clinic 'to Be Sued by 1,000 Families,'" *The Times*, August 11, 2022, https://www.thetimes.co.uk/article/tavistock-gender-clinic-to-be-sued-by-1-000-families-lbsw6k8zd.

23. Robin Respaut and Chad Terhune, "Putting Numbers on the Rise in Children Seeking Gender Care," Reuters, October 6, 2022, https://www.reuters.com/investigates/special-report/usa-transyouth-data.

24. David Gortler, telephone interview by the author, May 22, 2023.

25. "Risk of Pseudotumor Cerebri Added to Labeling for Gonadotropin-Releasing Hormone Agonists," Food and Drug Administration, July 1, 2022, https://www.fda.gov/media/159663/download.

26. Mary Harrington, "Boston Children's Hospital's Transgender Insanity Reveals How Unhinged Elites Make Money off Our Kids," *New York Post*, August 24, 2022, https://nypost.com/2022/08/24/boston-childrens-hospitals-transgender-insanity-elites-profit-from-kids.

27. "Service Update," Planned Parenthood of Great Northwest, Hawai'i, Alaska, Indiana, Kentucky," 2023, https://www.plannedparenthood.org/planned-parenthood-great-northwest-hawaii-alaska-indiana-kentuck/patients/health-care-services/hrt-hormone-therapy-for-trans-and-non-binary-patients; see also "A

Guide to Hormone Therapy for Trans People," NHS, 2007, 10, https://www
.scottishtrans.org/wp-content/uploads/2013/06/NHS-A-Guide-to-Hormone
-Therapy-for-Trans-People.pdf.

28. Julia Johnson, "Blackburn Seeks Action after Doctor Touts Profits of Transgender
Surgeries on Video," *Washington Examiner*, September 22, 2022, https://www
.washingtonexaminer.com/restoring-america/community-family/blackburn-doctor
-profits-transgender-surgeries-video.

29. "JK Rowling Dismisses Backlash over Trans Comments: 'I Don't Care about My
Legacy,'" BBC News, February 22, 2023, https://www.bbc.com/news
/entertainment-arts-64729304.

30. See, for example, Prisha (@detransaqua), "It's almost his constant bullying…,"
Twitter, September 5, 2023, 5:33 a.m., https://twitter.com/detransaqua/status
/1698992676085858689?s=20; Chloe Cole (@ChoooCole), "Getting a lot more
hate recently…," Twitter, August 17, 2022, 4:24 p.m., https://x.com/ChoooCole
/status/1559999676966793221?s=20.

31. Mary Margaret Olohan, "White House: 'Early' Trans Surgeries, Hormones Are
'Crucial' for Kids, Teens Who Identify as Trans," The Daily Wire, March 31, 2022,
https://www.dailywire.com/news/white-house-early-trans-surgeries-hormones-are
-crucial-for-kids-teens-who-identify-as-trans.

32. Littman, "Individuals Treated for Gender Dysphoria," 3364.

Chapter 1: The Slippery Slope

1. Prisha Mosley, telephone interview by the author, December 22, 2022.

2. Kelsey Bolar, "Mentally Ill Teen Betrayed by Health Professionals Who
Recommended Testosterone and 'Top Surgery,'" Independent Women's Forum,
https://www.iwf.org/identity-crisis-stories/prisha-mosley.

3. Prisha (@detransaqua), "I'm ready to share this…," Twitter, April 22, 2023, 3:26
p.m., https://twitter.com/detransaqua/status/1649857304500801536.

4. Prisha Mosley, telephone interview by the author.

5. Bolar, "Mentally Ill Teen Betrayed."

6. Complaint and Jury Demand, *Charlie Mosley, a.k.a. Prisha Mosley, a.k.a. Abigail
Mosley, Plaintiff, v. Eric T. Emerson, MD; Piedmont Plastic Surgery and
Dermatology, P.A.; Brie Klein-Fowler; Family Solutions, PLLC; Shana Gordon;
Tree of Life Counseling PLLC; Martha Fairbanks Perry, MD; and Moses Cone
Medical Services, Inc., Defendants*, General Court of Justice, Superior Court
Division, State of North Carolina, County of Gaston, filed July 17, 2023, available
at https://www.documentcloud.org/documents/23882834-prisha-mosley
-complaint.

7. Prisha Mosley, telephone interview by the author.

8. Abigail Shrier, *Irreversible Damage: The Transgender Craze Seducing Our
Daughters* (Washington, D.C.: Regnery Publishing, 2020), 25–49, 135–42, 206–8,
212–20, citing L. Littman, "Parent Reports of Adolescents and Young Adults

Perceived to Show Signs of a Rapid Onset of Gender Dysphoria," *PLOS ONE* 14, no. 3 (August 16, 2018), https://doi.org/10.1371/journal.pone.0202330.

9. Abigail Shrier, "When Your Daughter Defies Biology," *Wall Street Journal*, January 6, 2019, https://www.wsj.com/articles/when-your-daughter-defies-biology-11546804848.

10. Lori Lamothe, "What Is Kik and Why Is It a 'Predator's Paradise'?," Medium, August 1, 2022, https://medium.com/politically-speaking/what-is-kik-and-why-is-it-a-predators-paradise-e6a00469d58d.

11. Luka Hein, telephone interview by the author, December 27, 2022.

12. Complaint for Medical Malpractice, Waiver of Panel Review, and Demand for Jury Trial, *Luka Hein, Plaintiff, v. UNMC Physicians, the Nebraska Medical Center, Nahia J. Amoura, M.D., Perry Johnson, M.D., Stephan Barrientos, M.D., and Megan Smith-Sallans, Defendants,* District Court of Douglas County, Nebraska, filed September 13, 2023, available at https://libertycenter.org/wp-content/uploads/2023/09/Luka-Hein-District-Court-Complaint-9-13-23-filed.pdf.

13. Chloe Cole, telephone interview by the author, January 13, 2023.

14. See Complaint for Medical Negligence and Jury Trial Demand, *Chloe E. Brockman a/k/a Chloe Cole v. Kaiser Foundation Hospitals, Inc., a California Corporation, the Permanente Medical Group, Inc., a California Corporation, Lisa Kristine Taylor, M.D., an Individual, Hop Nguyen Le, M.D., an Individual, Susanne E. Watson, Ph.D., an Individual, and Does 1 through 50, Inlcusive, Defendants,* Superior Court of California, filed February 22, 2023, 2, available at https://libertycenter.org/wp-content/uploads/2023/02/Complaint1.pdf.

15. Chloe Cole, telephone interview by the author.

16. "What Is Autism Spectrum Disorder?," Centers for Disease Control and Prevention, https://www.cdc.gov/ncbddd/autism/facts.html.

17. Christina Buttons, "How Autistic Traits Can Be Mistaken for Gender Dysphoria," buttonslives (Substack), March 24, 2023, https://buttonslives.substack.com/p/how-autistic-traits-can-be-mistaken.

18. Sharon Kirkey, "Are Autistic Children More Likely to Believe They're Transgender? Controversial Toronto Expert Backs Link," *National Post*, January 12, 2017, https://nationalpost.com/health/are-autistic-children-more-likely-to-believe-theyre-transgender-controversial-toronto-expert-backs-link.

19. Jimmy Nsubuga, "Transgender Children Could Actually Be Autistic, Suggests Psychologist," *Metro*, January 12, 2017, https://metro.co.uk/2017/01/12/transgender-children-could-actually-be-autistic-suggests-psychologist-6376900.

20. Kenneth Zucker, telephone interview by the author, April 2023.

21. *Transgender Kids: Who Knows Best?*, BBC Two Films, January 12, 2017, https://www.dailymotion.com/video/x58s24i.

22. Chloe Cole, telephone interview by the author.

23. Chloe Cole, "DETRANSITIONER Chloe Cole speaks at The End Child Mutilation Rally in NASHVILLE," YouTube, October 21, 2022, https://www.youtube.com/watch?v=ARP_XmPRhzc.

24. Chloe Cole, telephone interview by the author.

25. Complaint, *Chloe E. Brockman v. Kaiser Foundation Hospitals*, 8.

26. Chloe Cole, telephone interview with the author.

27. Helena Kerschner, telephone interview by the author, April 2023; Helena Kerschner, email interview by the author, April 10, 2023.

28. Helena Kerschner, "Escape from Womanhood," The Scroll (Substack), February 22, 2022, https://thedailyscroll.substack.com/p/escape-from-womanhood.

29. Prisha Mosley, telephone interview by the author.

30. Niki Fritz, Vinny Malic, Bryant Paul, and Yanyan Zhou, "A Descriptive Analysis of the Types, Targets, and Relative Frequency of Aggression in Mainstream Pornography," *Archives of Sexual Behavior* 49, no. 8 (November 2020): 3041–53, https://pubmed.ncbi.nlm.nih.gov/32661813.

31. Ana J. Bridges et al., "Aggression and Sexual Behavior in Best-Selling Pornography Videos: A Content Analysis Update," *Violence against Women* 16, no. 10 (October 2010): 1065–85, https://pubmed.ncbi.nlm.nih.gov/20980228.

32. Mary Margaret Olohan, "Pornography and Sex Trafficking Are 'Completely Interwoven,' Activists Warn," The Daily Caller, February 9, 2020, https://dailycaller.com/2020/02/09/pornography-sex-trafficking-relationship.

33. *The Public Health Harms of Pornography* (Washington, D.C.: National Center on Sexual Exploitation, 2018), 4, https://endsexualexploitation.org/wp-content/uploads/2021/04/NCOSE_SymposiumBriefingBooklet_1-28-2.pdf.

34. Ibid., 12–15.

35. Prisha Mosley, telephone interview by the author.

36. Kerschner, "Escape from Womanhood."

37. Prisha Mosley, telephone interview by the author.

38. Chloe Cole, telephone interview by the author.

39. Helena Kerschner, telephone and email interviews by the author.

Chapter 2: Encouragement

1. "2. What Do Gender Dysphoria and Transgender Mean?," The Heritage Foundation, May 18, 2020, https://www.heritage.org/gender-identity/2-what-do-gender-dysphoria-and-transgender-mean.

2. Ryan Anderson, *When Harry Became Sally: Responding to the Transgender Moment* (New York: Encounter, 2018), 95.

3. "What Is Gender Dysphoria?," American Psychiatric Association, August 2022, https://www.psychiatry.org/patients-families/gender-dysphoria/what-is-gender-dysphoria.

4. Prisha Mosley, telephone interview by the author, June 28, 2023.

5. Independent Women's Forum (@IWF), "Prisha Mosley testified before the South Carolina Senate…," Twitter, March 24, 2023, 2:55 p.m., https://twitter.com/IWF/status/1639340072020344857?s=20.

6. "Prisha Mosley's Testimony to South Carolina Senate," Person & Identity, March 24, 2023, https://personandidentity.com/prisha-mosleys-testimony-to-south-carolina-senate.

7. Kelsey Bolar, "Mentally Ill Teen Betrayed by Health Professionals Who Recommended Testosterone and 'Top Surgery,'" Independent Women's Forum, https://www.iwf.org/identity-crisis-stories/prisha-mosley.

8. Prisha Mosley, telephone interview by the author, June 28, 2023.

9. Helena Kerschner, telephone interview by the author, February 9, 2022.

10. Helena, "By Any Other Name: The Story of My Transition and Detransition," prude posting (Substack), February 19, 2022, https://lacroicsz.substack.com/p/by-any-other-name.

11. Helena, "Tumblr: A Call-Out Post," 4th Wave Now (Tumblr), March 20, 2019, https://4thwavenow.com/2019/03/20/tumblr-a-call-out-post/.

12. Helena, "By Any Other Name."

13. Chloe Cole, "DETRANSITIONER Chloe Cole Speaks at the End Child Mutilation Rally in NASHVILLE," YouTube, October 21, 2022, https://www.youtube.com/watch?v=ARP_XmPRhzc.

14. Georgia Wells, Jeff Horwitz, and Deepa Seetharaman, "Facebook Knows Instagram Is Toxic for Teen Girls, Company Documents Show," *Wall Street Journal*, September 14, 2021, https://www.wsj.com/articles/facebook-knows-instagram-is-toxic-for-teen-girls-company-documents-show-11631620739.

15. Jeff Horwitz and Katherine Blunt, "Instagram Connects Vast Pedophile Network," *Wall Street Journal*, June 7, 2023, https://www.wsj.com/articles/instagram-vast-pedophile-network-4ab7189.

16. "How Instagram's Algorithm Connects and Promotes Pedophile Network" *Tech News Briefing* (*Wall Street Journal* podcast), June 8, 2023, https://www.wsj.com/podcasts/tech-news-briefing/how-instagrams-algorithm-connects-and-promotes-pedophile-network/a683c0b4-2e6f-4661-9973-10bd455db895.

17. See Complaint for Medical Negligence and Jury Trial Demand, *Chloe E. Brockman a/k/a Chloe Cole, an Individual, Plaintiff, v. Kaiser Foundation Hospitals, Inc., a California Corporation, the Permanente Medical Group, Inc., a California Corporation, Lisa Kristine Taylor, M.D., an Individual, Hop Nguyen Le, M.D., an Individual, Susanne E. Watson, Ph.D., an Individual, and Does 1 through 50, Inclusive, Defendants*, Superior Court of the State of California, filed February 22, 2023, 8–9, available at https://libertycenter.org/wp-content/uploads/2023/02/Complaint1.pdf. Chloe discussed these events with me as well. Chloe Cole, telephone interview by the author, June 2023.

18. Chloe Cole, telephone interview by the author.

19. Complaint, *Chloe E. Brockman v. Kaiser Foundation Hospitals*, 9.

20. Virginia Allen, "Social Media Gave Me the Idea 'I Could Be a Boy.' Chloe Cole's Journey into and out of Transgenderism.," The Daily Signal, January 11, 2023, https://www.dailysignal.com/2023/01/11/social-media-gave-me-idea-i-could-be-boy-chloe-coles-journey-transgenderism.

21. Ann P. Haas, Philip L. Rodgers, and Jody L. Herman, *Suicide Attempts among Transgender and Gender Non-Conforming Adults, Findings of the National Transgender Discrimination Survey* (Los Angeles: The Williams Institute, January 2014), 2, https://studylib.net/doc/13499004/suicide-attempts-among-transgender -and-gender-non-conform.

22. Laurel Duggan, "'Emotional Blackmail': Transgender Suicide Stats Are 'Exaggerated' and Can Increase Suicide Risk, Psychiatrists Say," The Daily Caller, December 20, 2022, https://dailycaller.com/2022/12/20/transgender-suicide-rate -psychiatrists.

23. Alison Clayton, "Gender-Affirming Treatment of Gender Dysphoria in Youth: A Perfect Storm Environment for the Placebo Effect—the Implications for Research and Clinical Practice," *Archives of Sexual Behavior* 52, no. 2 (November 14, 2022): 483–94, https://link.springer.com/article/10.1007/s10508-022-02472-8#ref-CR15.

24. Luka Hein, telephone interview by the author, December 27, 2022. See also Complaint for Medical Malpractice, Waiver of Panel Review, and Demand for Jury Trial, *Luka Hein, Plaintiff, v. UNMC Physicians, the Nebraska Medical Center, Nahia J. Amoura, M.D., Perry Johnson, M.D., Stephan Barrientos, M.D., and Megan Smith-Sallans, Defendants*, District Court of Douglas County, Nebraska, filed September 13, 2023, available at https://libertycenter.org/wp -content/uploads/2023/09/Luka-Hein-District-Court-Complaint-9-13-23-filed .pdf.

25. Prisha Mosley, telephone interview by the author, December 22, 2022.

26. Bolar, "Mentally Ill Teen Betrayed."

27. "Transgender 'Health' Doctors Prescribe Puberty Blockers to Minors as Young as Eight Years Old and Irreversible 'Cross-Gender Hormones' to Minors as Young as 14 Years Old," Project Veritas, April 19, 2023, https://www.projectveritas.com /news/wpath-connected-transgender-health-doctors-prescribe-puberty-blockers -to.

28. Prisha Mosley, telephone interview by the author, December 22, 2022.

29. "About Us: Meet Our Team: We Exist for You," Tree of Life Counseling (Greensboro, North Carolina), https://tlc-counseling.com/tree-of-life-greensboro -nc-jacksonville-nc/home-2/about-us.

30. "USA Gender Therapists," FTM Help Desk (Tumblr), https://f-2m-help.tumblr .com/therapy2.

31. Complaint and Jury Demand, *Charlie Mosley, a.k.a. Prisha Mosley, a.k.a. Abigail Mosley, Plaintiff, v. Eric T. Emerson, MD; Piedmont Plastic Surgery and Dermatology, P.A.; Brie Klein-Fowler; Family Solutions, PLLC; Shana Gordon; Tree of Life Counseling PLLC; Martha Fairbanks Perry, MD; and Moses Cone Medical Services, Inc., Defendants*, General Court of Justice, Superior Court Division, State of North Carolina, County of Gaston, 39, https://www .documentcloud.org/documents/23882834-prisha-mosley-complaint.

32. Ibid., 14.

33. "Transgender 'Health' Doctors Prescribe Puberty Blockers to Minors."
34. Ibid.
35. Helena, "By Any Other Name."
36. Ibid.
37. Helena Kerschner, telephone interview by the author.
38. Helena, "By Any Other Name."
39. Complaint, *Chloe E. Brockman v. Kaiser Foundation Hospitals*, 10.
40. "How To Bind Your Chest: Tips, Tricks, and Safety While Binding," FOLX Health, April 15, 2022, https://www.folxhealth.com/library/how-to-bind-your -chest-tips-tricks-and-safety-while-binding.
41. "About Us," McLean Clinic, https://www.topsurgery.ca/about.
42. "Health Consequences of Chest Binding," McLean Clinic, https://www.topsurgery .ca/blog/health-consequences-chest-binding.
43. Ibid.; "How to Bind Your Chest."
44. Complaint, *Chloe E. Brockman v. Kaiser Foundation Hospitals*, 10.

Chapter 3: Getting the Hormones

1. Jill A. Crank, "Informed Consent Model for Gender Affirming Hormone Therapy," Johns Hopkins Medicine, March 16, 2021, https://affirm.blogs .hopkinsmedicine.org/2021/03/16/informed-consent-model-for-gender-affirming -hormone-therapy.
2. Helena, "By Any Other Name: The Story of My Transition and Detransition," prude posting (Substack), February 19, 2022, https://lacroicsz.substack.com/p/by -any-other-name.
3. Florence Ashley, "Gatekeeping Hormone Replacement Therapy for Transgender Patients Is Dehumanising," *Journal of Medical Ethics* 45, no. 7 (July 2019): 480–83, https://pubmed.ncbi.nlm.nih.gov/30988174.
4. Mary Margaret Olohan, "Catholic Chicago Hospital Chose Ideology Over Biology in Treating Biological Girl Who Believed She Was Male, De-Transitioner Says," The Daily Wire, https://www.dailywire.com/news/catholic-chicago-hospital-chose -ideology-over-biology-in-treating-biological-girl-who-believed-she-was-male-de -transitioner-says.
5. Helena, "By Any Other Name."
6. Olohan, "Catholic Chicago Hospital Chose Ideology."
7. Julie Rovner, "Planned Parenthood: A Thorn in Abortion Foes' Sides," NPR, April 13, 2011, https://www.npr.org/2011/04/13/135354952/planned-parenthood -makes-abortion-foes-see-red.
8. Samantha Allen, "The Attack on Planned Parenthood Hurts Transgender People, Too," The Daily Beast, January 10, 2017, https://www.thedailybeast.com/the -attack-on-planned-parenthood-hurts-transgender-people-too.
9. "Gender Affirming Care," Planned Parenthood, https://www.plannedparenthood .org/get-care/our-services/gender-affirming-care.

10. "Gender Affirming Hormone Therapy," Planned Parenthood of Illinois, Services & Patient Resources, https://www.plannedparenthood.org/planned-parenthood -illinois/patient-resources/gender-affirming-hormone-therapy.

11. "Gender Affirming Care Services Patient Guide," Planned Parenthood Mar Monte, December 8, 2020, https://www.plannedparenthood.org/uploads/filer_public/7e /fa/7efac779-c916-4b58-b6c6-909962d348be/20201208_v01_gender_affirming _care_services.pdf.

12. Juliana Kim, "How Gender-Affirming Care May Be Impacted When Clinics That Offer Abortions Close," NPR, August 14, 2022, https://www.npr.org/2022/08 /14/1115875421/gender-affirming-care-abortion-clinics.

13. Archived link: "Gender Affirming Hormone Care," Planned Parenthood of Central and Western New York, November 19, 2018, Internet Archive Wayback Machine, https://web.archive.org/web/20181119223028/https://www.plannedparenthood .org/planned-parenthood-central-western-new-york/patient-resources/our-services /gender-affirming-hormone-care.

14. Melanie Israel, "Planned Parenthood Is Providing Fewer Breast Screenings, Wellness Exams, and More Abortions, Transgender Services," The Heritage Foundation, February 26, 2021, https://www.heritage.org/life/commentary /planned-parenthood-providing-fewer-breast-screenings-wellness-exams-and-more.

15. Allen, "The Attack on Planned Parenthood."

16. *Relentless. 2021–2022 Annual Report*, Planned Parenthood, 10, 29, https://cdn .plannedparenthood.org/uploads/filer_public/25/ed/25ed2675-fbbc-453b-8b35 -f8ddaa025b57/281222-ppfa-annualreport-c3-digital.pdf.

17. Allen, "The Attack on Planned Parenthood."

18. Olohan, "Catholic Chicago Hospital Chose Ideology."

19. Helena, "By Any Other Name."

20. Olohan, "Catholic Chicago Hospital Chose Ideology."

21. "Aetna Expands Gender-Affirming Surgery Coverage for Transgender Women," CVS Health, January 26, 2021, https://www.cvshealth.com/news/health-insurance /aetna-expands-gender-affirming-surgery-coverage-for-transgender-.html.

22. Landon Mion, "CVS 'Gender Transition' Guide Says Employees Must Use Preferred Pronouns, Can Use Bathroom Reflecting Identity," Fox Business, April 15, 2023, https://www.foxbusiness.com/economy/cvs-gender-transition-guide -employees-preferred-pronouns-bathroom-reflecting-identity.

23. Julia Jacobs, "Transgender Woman Says CVS Pharmacist Refused to Fill Hormone Prescription," *New York Times*, July 20, 2018, https://www.nytimes .com/2018/07/20/us/cvs-pharmacy-transgender-woman-nyt.html.

24. Alex Boyer, "New Dallas Clinic Partners with Walgreens to Offer Free Services for LGBTQ+ Community," Fox 4 News, July 6, 2022, https://www.fox4news. com/news/new-dallas-clinic-partners-with-walgreens-to-offer-free-services-for -lgbtq-community.

25. Jan S. Redfern and Michael W. Jann, "The Evolving Role of Pharmacists in Transgender Health Care," *Transgender Health* 4, no. 1 (April 11, 2019): 118–30, https://doi.org/10.1089/trgh.2018.0038.

26. "Life-Changing Healthcare for the Gender-Diverse Community," Plume, https://getplume.co/about-plume.

27. "Transmasculine: Masculinizing Resources," FOLX Health, https://www.folxhealth.com/gender-affirming-care/transmasculine; "Ensuring Access," FOLX Health, https://www.folxhealth.com/price-list.

28. "Transfeminine: Feminizing Resources," FOLX Health, https://www.folxhealth.com/gender-affirming-care/transfeminine; "Ensuring Access," FOLX Health, https://www.folxhealth.com/price-list.

29. "Informed Consent Considerations for Estrogen HRT," FOLX Health, March 2, 2021, https://www.folxhealth.com/library/informed-consent-considerations-for-estrogen-hrt: "To keep the non-permanent changes to your body, you will need to take your hormones for life"; "Informed Consent Considerations for Testosterone HRT," FOLX Health, March 2, 2021, https://www.folxhealth.com/library/informed-consent-testosterone-hrt: "To keep the non-permanent changes to your body, you will need testosterone for life."

30. Mary Margaret Olohan, "He Went Undercover to Expose 'Rubber-Stamping' of Trans Surgeries," The Daily Signal, June 7, 2023, https://www.dailysignal.com/2023/06/07/he-went-undercover-expose-rubber-stamping-trans-surgeries.

31. Ibid.

32. "Gender-Affirming Surgery Letters 101," FOLX Health, November 1, 2022, https://www.folxhealth.com/library/gender-affirming-surgery-letters-101.

33. Olohan, "He Went Undercover."

34. Olohan, "Catholic Chicago Hospital Chose Ideology."

35. "Trans Health Services," Chicago Women's Health Center, https://www.chicagowomenshealthcenter.org/trans-health; "Gender Development Program," Lurie Children's Hospital of Chicago, https://www.luriechildrens.org/en/specialties-conditions/gender-development-program.

36. Complaint for Medical Negligence and Jury Trial Demand, *Chloe E. Brockman a/k/a Chloe Cole v. Kaiser Foundation Hospitals, Inc., a California Corporation, the Permanente Medical Group, Inc., a California Corporation, Lisa Kristine Taylor, M.D., an Individual, Hop Nguyen Le, M.D., an Individual, Susanne E. Watson, Ph.D., an Individual, and Does 1 through 50, Inclusive, Defendants,* Superior Court of California, filed February 22, 2023, 10, available at https://libertycenter.org/wp-content/uploads/2023/02/Complaint1.pdf.

37. "Hypogonadotropic Hypogonadism," Penn Medicine, https://www.pennmedicine.org/for-patients-and-visitors/patient-information/conditions-treated-a-to-z/hypogonadotropic-hypogonadism.

38. "Freedom of Information Act Request: Off-Label Puberty Blockers," America First Legal, September 29, 2022, https://aflegal.org/wp-content/uploads/2023/02/09.29.2022-FOIA-Request.pdf.

39. "America First Legal Sues Biden's FDA for Illegally Hiding Records Regarding the Off-Label Use of Puberty Blockers and Cross-Sex Hormones on Children," America First Legal, February 28, 2023, https://aflegal.org/america-first-legal-sues

-bidens-fda-for-illegally-hiding-records-regarding-the-off-label-use-of-puberty
-blockers-and-cross-sex-hormones-on-children.

40. "Risk of Pseudotumor Cerebri Added to Labeling for Gonadotropin-Releasing Hormone Agonists," Food and Drug Administration, July 1, 2022, https://www.fda.gov/media/159663/download.
41. Complaint, *Chloe E. Brockman v. Kaiser Foundation Hospitals*, 16.
42. Kelsey Bolar, "Mentally Ill Teen Betrayed by Health Professionals Who Recommended Testosterone and 'Top Surgery,'" Independent Women's Forum, https://www.iwf.org/identity-crisis-stories/prisha-mosley.
43. Ibid.
44. Marc Siegel, Georeen Tanner, and Perry Chiaramonte, "Detransitioning Becomes Growing Choice among Young People after Gender-Affirming Surgery," Fox News, December 19, 2022, https://www.foxnews.com/health/detransitioning-becomes-growing-choice-young-people-gender-affirming-surgery.
45. Bolar, "Mentally Ill Teen Betrayed."
46. Prisha Mosley, telephone interview by the author, December 2022.

Chapter 4: The Hormones Set In

1. "Testosterone Therapy for Gender Affirmation," UCLA Health, https://www.uclahealth.org/sites/default/files/documents/26/testosterone-info-english.pdf?f=58f86701.
2. Prisha Mosley, telephone interview by the author, December 22, 2022.
3. "Testosterone HRT & Bottom Growth," FOLX Health, February 17, 2021, https://www.folxhealth.com/library/testosterone-bottom-growth.
4. "Bottom Growth and Genital Changes on Testosterone," Plume, September 9, 2022, https://getplume.co/blog/bottom-growth-and-genital-changes-on-testosterone.
5. "9 Myths You Might Have Believed about Testosterone HRT," FOLX Health, May 10, 2022, https://www.folxhealth.com/library/9-myths-you-might-have-believed-about-testosterone-hrt.
6. Prisha Mosley, telephone interview by the author, December 22, 2022.
7. "Testosterone HRT & Bottom Growth."
8. "Testosterone Therapy for Gender Affirmation."
9. Prisha Mosley, telephone interview by the author.
10. "Testosterone Therapy for Gender Affirmation."
11. "9 Myths You Might Have Believed."
12. Prisha Mosley, telephone interview by the author.
13. Helena, "By Any Other Name: The Story of My Transition and Detransition," prude posting (Substack), February 19, 2022, https://lacroicsz.substack.com/p/by-any-other-name.
14. Helena Kerschner, telephone interview by the author, February 9, 2022.
15. Helena, "By Any Other Name."

16. "9 Myths You Might Have Believed."

17. Helena, "By Any Other Name."

18. *Ethical and Religious Directives for Catholic Health Care Services*, 6th edition (Washington, D.C.: United States Conference of Catholic Bishops, June 2018), https://www.usccb.org/about/doctrine/ethical-and-religious-directives/upload/ethical-religious-directives-catholic-health-service-sixth-edition-2016-06.pdf.

19. Lauretta Brown, "U.S. Bishops Approve Plan for Guidance to Health Care Institutions on Transgender Issues," Catholic News Agency, June 16, 2023, https://www.catholicnewsagency.com/news/254597/us-bishops-approve-plan-for-guidance-to-catholic-healthcare-institutions-on-transgender-issues.

20. Michael Hichborn, *CommonSpirit Health and the Sex-Change Industry* (Partlow, Virginia: Lepanto Institute, 2023), https://www.lepantoin.org/wp/wp-content/uploads/2023/06/CommonSpirit-Report-6.9.2023-FINAL.pdf.

21. Brown, "U.S. Bishops Approve Plan."

22. Mary Margaret Olohan, "Catholic Chicago Hospital Chose Ideology Over Biology in Treating Biological Girl Who Believed She Was Male, De-Transitioner Says," The Daily Wire, https://www.dailywire.com/news/catholic-chicago-hospital-chose-ideology-over-biology-in-treating-biological-girl-who-believed-she-was-male-de-transitioner-says.

23. Ibid.

24. Mary Margaret Olohan, "PhRMA, Pfizer Funded LGBT Index Scoring Hospitals for Promoting Gender Ideology," The Daily Signal, May 24, 2023, https://www.dailysignal.com/2023/05/24/phrma-pfizer-funded-lgbt-index-scoring-hospitals-promoting-gender-ideology.

25. Ibid.

26. Helena, "By Any Other Name."

27. Luka Hein, telephone interview by the author, December 27, 2022. See also Complaint for Medical Malpractice, Waiver of Panel Review, and Demand for Jury Trial, *Luka Hein, Plaintiff, v. UNMC Physicians, the Nebraska Medical Center, Nahia J. Amoura, M.D., Perry Johnson, M.D., Stephan Barrientos, M.D., and Megan Smith-Sallans, Defendants*, District Court of Douglas County, Nebraska, filed September 13, 2023, available at https://libertycenter.org/wp-content/uploads/2023/09/Luka-Hein-District-Court-Complaint-9-13-23-filed.pdf.

28. Christine Rousselle, "Health Alert for Women: Early Use of Birth Control Pills Linked to Higher Rates of Depression, Study Finds," Fox News, June 13, 2023, https://www.foxnews.com/lifestyle/health-alert-women-early-use-birth-control-pills-linked-higher-rate-depression-study.

29. Emily Stearn, "Warning over New Gen Z TikTok Trend Urging Women to Quit the Pill Because It 'Makes You Ugly, Fat and Depressed'—so What's the Truth about the Claims?," *Daily Mail*, April 26, 2023, https://www.dailymail.co.uk

/health/article-12015015/Warning-new-TikTok-trend-urging-women-quit-Pill
-makes-ugly-fat.html.

30. Intentionlifestyle (Jeanna), "Attraction on the Pill: If You Went through This You're
    Not Alone," TikTok, April 22, 2023, https://www.tiktok.com/@intentionlifestyle
    /video/7224965609858010411.

31. V. Michelle Russell, James McNulty, Levi Baker, and Andrea Meltzer, "The
    Association between Discontinuing Hormonal Contraceptives and Wives' Marital
    Satisfaction Depends on Husbands' Facial Attractiveness," *Proceedings of the
    National Academy of Sciences of the United States of America* 111, no. 48
    (November 17, 2014): 17081–86, https://doi.org/10.1073/pnas.1414784111.

32. Pam Belluck, "F.D.A. Advisers Say Benefits of over-the-Counter Birth Control Pill
    Outweigh Risks," *New York Times*, May 10, 2023, https://www.nytimes.com
    /2023/05/10/health/fda-otc-birth-control-pill.html.

33. See Complaint for Medical Negligence and Jury Trial Demand, *Chloe E. Brockman
    a/k/a Chloe Cole, an Individual, Plaintiff, v. Kaiser Foundation Hospitals, Inc.,
    a California Corporation, the Permanente Medical Group, Inc., a California
    Corporation, Lisa Kristine Taylor, M.D., an Individual, Hop Nguyen Le, M.D.,
    an Individual, Susanne E. Watson, Ph.D., an Individual, and Does 1 through 50,
    Inclusive, Defendants*, Superior Court of the State of California, filed February
    22, 2023, 16, available at https://libertycenter.org/wp-content/uploads/2023/02
    /Complaint1.pdf.

34. Chloe Cole, interview by the author, Washington, D.C., January 9, 2023.

35. Complaint, *Chloe E. Brockman v. Kaiser Foundation Hospitals*, 22–23.

36. Chloe Cole, interview by the author.

37. Complaint, *Chloe E. Brockman v. Kaiser Foundation Hospitals*, 16.

38. Chloe Cole, interview by the author.

39. Complaint, *Chloe E. Brockman v. Kaiser Foundation Hospitals*, 17.

40. Virginia Allen, "Social Media Gave Me the Idea 'I Could Be a Boy.' Chloe Cole's
    Journey into and out of Transgenderism," The Daily Signal, January 11, 2023,
    https://www.dailysignal.com/2023/01/11/social-media-gave-me-idea-i-could-be
    -boy-chloe-coles-journey-transgenderism.

41. Chloe Cole, "DETRANSITIONER Chloe Cole Speaks at The End Child
    Mutilation Rally in NASHVILLE," YouTube, October 21, 2022, https://www
    .youtube.com/watch?v=ARP_XmPRhzc.

42. Complaint, *Chloe E. Brockman v. Kaiser Foundation Hospitals*, 21.

Chapter 5: Surgery

1. Luka Hein, telephone interview by the author, December 27, 2022. See also
   Complaint for Medical Malpractice, Waiver of Panel Review, and Demand for
   Jury Trial, *Luka Hein, Plaintiff, v. UNMC Physicians, the Nebraska Medical*

Center, Nahia J. Amoura, M.D., Perry Johnson, M.D., Stephan Barrientos, M.D., and Megan Smith-Sallans, Defendants, District Court of Douglas County, Nebraska, filed September 13, 2023, available at https://libertycenter.org/wp-content/uploads/2023/09/Luka-Hein-District-Court-Complaint-9-13-23-filed.pdf.

2. Brooke Vuong et al., "Outpatient Mastectomy: Factors Influencing Patient Selection and Predictors of Return to Care," *Journal of the American College of Surgeons* 232, no. 1 (January 2021): 35–44, https://doi.org/10.1016/j.jamcollsurg.2020.09.015.

3. Luka Hein, telephone interview by the author. See also Complaint for Medical Malpractice, Waiver of Panel Review, and Demand for Jury Trial, *Luka Hein v. UNMC Physicians*.

4. Azeen Ghorayshi, "More Trans Teens Are Choosing 'Top Surgery,'" *New York Times*, June 21, 2023, https://www.nytimes.com/2022/09/26/health/top-surgery-transgender-teenagers.html.

5. James Reinl, "EXCLUSIVE: Miami Sex-Change Surgeon Who Dubs Herself 'Dr Teetus Deletus' Is Reported to Consumer Watchdog for 'Deceptively' Luring 'Vulnerable' Teens into Transgender Operations with Gimmicky TikTok Video Blitz," *Daily Mail*, October 13, 2022, https://www.dailymail.co.uk/news/article-11303919/Florida-sex-change-surgeon-dubs-Dr-Teetus-Deletus-REPORTED-consumer-watchdog.html.

6. Sidhbh Gallagher (drsidhbhgallagher), "This is Masculoplasty plus -a technique we developed -where we combine a reverse tummy tuck at the same time as top surgery to smooth out the upper belly…," Instagram, May 16, 2023, https://www.instagram.com/p/CsTq_WtrkcH/?hl=en.

7. Sidhbh Gallagher (drsidhbhgallagher), "Intestinal vaginoplasty is often considered a backup option for patients who have lost a previously created vagina…," Instagram, May 16, 2023, https://www.instagram.com/p/CsUL4HEu_bj/?hl=en.

8. Sidhbh Gallagher (drsidhbhgallagher), "More patients are choosing to add in torso masculinization…," Instagram, April 5, 2023, https://www.instagram.com/p/Cqp7_RUMq2M/?hl=en.

9. "Staff: Neasa Gallagher," Gallagher Plastic Surgery, https://gallagherplasticsurgery.com/staff.

10. Luka Hein, telephone interview by the author.

11. Scott Mosser, "Double Incision," Gender Confirmation Center, https://www.genderconfirmation.com/gallery/double-incision-ftm-chest-surgery.

12. Scott Mosser, "Realistic Top Surgery Outcomes," Gender Confirmation Center, https://www.genderconfirmation.com/ftm-top-surgery-results.

13. Sidhbh Gallagher (drsidhbhgallagher), "Happy Pride Month!!…," Instagram, June 1, 2023, https://www.instagram.com/p/Cs8od2Iu3u8/?hl=en.

14. Kelsey Bolar, "Mentally Ill Teen Betrayed by Health Professionals Who Recommended Testosterone and 'Top Surgery,'" Independent Women's Forum, https://www.iwf.org/identity-crisis-stories/prisha-mosley.

15. Prisha Mosley, telephone interview by the author, December 22, 2022.

16. Bolar, "Mentally Ill Teen Betrayed."

17. Prisha Mosley, telephone interview by the author.

18. Bolar, "Mentally Ill Teen Betrayed."

19. Prisha Mosley, telephone interview by the author.

20. Ibid.

21. Bolar, "Mentally Ill Teen Betrayed."

22. Prisha Mosley, telephone interview by the author.

23. Gallagher (drsidhbhgallagher), "More patients are choosing to add."

24. Bolar, "Mentally Ill Teen Betrayed."

25. Prisha Mosley, telephone interview by the author.

26. Chloe Cole, interview by the author, Washington, D.C., January 9, 2023.

27. See Complaint for Medical Negligence and Jury Trial Demand, *Chloe E. Brockman a/k/a Chloe Cole, an Individual, Plaintiff, v. Kaiser Foundation Hospitals, Inc., a California Corporation, the Permanente Medical Group, Inc., a California Corporation, Lisa Kristine Taylor, M.D., an Individual, Hop Nguyen Le, M.D., an Individual, Susanne E. Watson, Ph.D., an Individual, and Does 1 through 50, Inclusive, Defendants,* Superior Court of the State of California, filed February 22, 2023, 18, available at https://libertycenter.org/wp-content/uploads/2023/02/Complaint1.pdf.

28. "Breast Augmentation in Teenagers," American Society of Plastic Surgeons, June 2015, https://www.plasticsurgery.org/documents/Health-Policy/Positions/policy-statement_breast-augmentation-in-teenagers.pdf.

29. Ibid.

30. Complaint, *Chloe E. Brockman v. Kaiser Foundation Hospitals,* 18.

31. Ibid., 19.

32. Ibid., 19–20.

33. Ibid., 20.

34. Ibid., 21.

35. Ibid.

36. Ibid.

37. Chloe Cole, interview by the author.

Chapter 6: Realization

1. Luka Hein, telephone interview by the author, December 27, 2022. See also Complaint for Medical Malpractice, Waiver of Panel Review, and Demand for Jury Trial, *Luka Hein, Plaintiff, v. UNMC Physicians, the Nebraska Medical Center, Nahia J. Amoura, M.D., Perry Johnson, M.D., Stephan Barrientos, M.D., and Megan Smith-Sallans, Defendants,* District Court of Douglas County, Nebraska, filed September 13, 2023, available at https://libertycenter.org

/wp-content/uploads/2023/09/Luka-Hein-District-Court-Complaint-9-13-23-filed .pdf.

2. "Hysterectomy," Yale Medicine, https://www.yalemedicine.org/conditions /hysterectomy.

3. "The FOLX Guide to Hysterectomies," FOLX Health, July 27, 2022, https://www .folxhealth.com/library/hysterectomies-guide.

4. "Phalloplasty for Gender Affirmation," Johns Hopkins Medicine, https://www .hopkinsmedicine.org/health/treatment-tests-and-therapies/phalloplasty-for-gender -affirmation.

5. "The FOLX Guide to Hysterectomies."

6. "Phalloplasty for Gender Affirmation."

7. Prisha Mosley, telephone interview by the author, December 22, 2022.

8. Alexander L. Chapman, "Dialectical Behavior Therapy: Current Indications and Unique Elements," *Psychiatry (Edgmont)* 3, no. 9 (September 2006): 62–68, https://www.ncbi.nlm.nih.gov/pmc/articles/PMC2963469.

9. Prisha Mosley, telephone interview by the author.

10. Kelsey Bolar, "Mentally Ill Teen Betrayed by Health Professionals Who Recommended Testosterone and 'Top Surgery,'" Independent Women's Forum, https://www.iwf.org/identity-crisis-stories/prisha-mosley.

11. Helena Kerschner, "By Any Other Name," prude posting (Substack), February 19, 2022, https://lacroicsz.substack.com/p/by-any-other-name.

12. Chloe Cole, telephone interview by the author, January 13, 2023.

13. See Complaint for Medical Negligence and Jury Trial Demand, *Chloe E. Brockman a/k/a Chloe Cole, an Individual, Plaintiff, v. Kaiser Foundation Hospitals, Inc., a California Corporation, the Permanente Medical Group, Inc., a California Corporation, Lisa Kristine Taylor, M.D., an Individual, Hop Nguyen Le, M.D., an Individual, Susanne E. Watson, Ph.D., an Individual, and Does 1 through 50, Inclusive, Defendants*, Superior Court of the State of California, filed February 22, 2023, 21, available at https://libertycenter.org/wp-content/uploads/2023/02 /Complaint1.pdf.

14. Chloe Cole, telephone interview by the author; Complaint, *Chloe E. Brockman v. Kaiser Foundation Hospitals*, 21.

15. Hannah Grossman, "Former Trans Kid Shares Agony of Side Effects from 'Mutilating' Medical Transition: 'I've Gotten No Help,'" Fox News, February 3, 2023, https://www.foxnews.com/media/former-trans-kid-shares-pain-suffering -mutilating-gender-affirming-care-ive-gotten-no-help.

16. Complaint, *Chloe E. Brockman v. Kaiser Foundation Hospitals*, 22.

17. Chloe Cole, telephone interview by the author.

18. Complaint, *Chloe E. Brockman v. Kaiser Foundation Hospitals*, 22.

19. Chloe Cole, telephone interview by the author.

20. Ibid.

Chapter 7: Detransition

1. Luka Hein, telephone interview by the author, December 27, 2022. See also Complaint for Medical Malpractice, Waiver of Panel Review, and Demand for Jury Trial, *Luka Hein, Plaintiff, v. UNMC Physicians, the Nebraska Medical Center, Nahia J. Amoura, M.D., Perry Johnson, M.D., Stephan Barrientos, M.D., and Megan Smith-Sallans, Defendants*, District Court of Douglas County, Nebraska, filed September 13, 2023, available at https://libertycenter.org/wp-content/uploads/2023/09/Luka-Hein-District-Court-Complaint-9-13-23-filed.pdf.

2. Prisha Mosley, telephone interview by the author, December 22, 2022.

3. Prisha (@detransaqua), "I've already put my mom through so much…," (thread), Twitter, April 26, 2023, 8:47 p.m., https://twitter.com/detransaqua/status/1651387580875677698?s=20.

4. Prisha (@detransaqua), "I've arrived. My mom picked me up. She brought me to their house and we ate…," Twitter, June 4, 2023, 3:06 p.m., https://twitter.com/detransaqua/status/1665434947585179650.

5. Prisha Mosley, telephone interview by the author.

6. Helena Kerschner, telephone interview by the author, February 9, 2022.

7. Helena, "By Any Other Name: The Story of My Transition and Detransition," prude posting (Substack), February 19, 2022, https://lacroicsz.substack.com/p/by-any-other-name.

8. Ftmconfusedashell, "Anyone else know/speculate that their hormones were off before transitioning?" Reddit, r/detrans, July 2023, https://www.reddit.com/r/detrans/comments/14mlyn8/anyone_else_knowspeculate_that_their_hormones.

9. Inner-Ad-Throwaway, "Question for those who are detrains demales and had testicular implants," Reddit, r/detrans, September 2023, https://www.reddit.com/r/detrans/comments/165utj3/question_for_those_who_are_detrans_females_and.

10. SoeiEnso, "Muscle atrophy and achieving an athletic body," Reddit, r/detrans, September 2023, https://www.reddit.com/r/detrans/comments/163hxc9/muscle_atrophy_and_achieving_an_athletic_body.

11. Fleshjerky, "I genuinely don't know how to cope with this kind of grief," Reddit, r/detrans, https://www.reddit.com/r/detrans/comments/1628f1i/i_genuinely_dont_know_how_to_cope_with_this_kind.

12. Naro (@N4R0G8), "One year ago this month I had a noose tied in my closet…," Twitter, June 23, 2023, 3:18 p.m., https://twitter.com/N4R0G8/status/1672323148291661824.

13. Josh Milton, "Reddit Just Banned Its Viciously Transphobic 'Gender Critical' Page amid Vigorous Crackdown on Hate Speech," PinkNews, June 29, 2020, https://www.thepinknews.com/2020/06/29/reddit-bann-transphobia-gender-critical-page-hate-speech-donald-trump-steve-huffman.

14. Lisa Littman, "Parent Reports of Adolescents and Young Adults Perceived to Show Signs of a Rapid Onset of Gender Dysphoria," *PLOS One* 14, no. 3 (August 16, 2018), https://journals.plos.org/plosone/article?id=10.1371/journal.pone.0202330.

15. Helena, "By Any Other Name."

16. See Complaint for Medical Negligence and Jury Trial Demand, *Chloe E. Brockman a/k/a Chloe Cole, an Individual, Plaintiff, v. Kaiser Foundation Hospitals, Inc., a California Corporation, the Permanente Medical Group, Inc., a California Corporation, Lisa Kristine Taylor, M.D., an Individual, Hop Nguyen Le, M.D., an Individual, Susanne E. Watson, Ph.D., an Individual, and Does 1 through 50, Inclusive, Defendants,* Superior Court of the State of California, filed February 22, 2023, 24, available at https://libertycenter.org/wp-content/uploads/2023/02/Complaint1.pdf.

17. Ibid., 5.

18. Ibid., 23.

19. Ibid., 24.

20. Chloe Cole, telephone interview by the author, June 2023.

Chapter 8: He

1. Ritchie (@TullipR) "I want to tell everyone what they took from us…," (thread), Twitter, June 13, 2022, 2:57 p.m., https://twitter.com/TullipR/status/1536422533230206976?s=20.

2. Ritchie (@TullipR), "Before I disappear for a while…," (thread) Twitter, April 6, 2023, 8:56 p.m., https://twitter.com/TullipR/status/1644142155500498944.

3. Walt Heyer, "The 'Sex Change' I Had 40 Years Ago Was a Scam, Not Medicine," The Federalist, March 23, 2023, https://thefederalist.com/2023/03/23/the-sex-change-i-had-40-years-ago-was-a-scam-not-medicine.

4. Mary Margaret Olohan, "'It Destroyed My Body': Here's Why This Former Trans Woman Regrets His Gender Transition," The Daily Caller, February 23, 2020, https://dailycaller.com/2020/02/23/walt-heyer-gender-transition.

5. Walt Heyer, "In the Past 5 Years, the Transgender Explosion Has Wounded More and More People," The Federalist, January 13, 2020, https://thefederalist.com/2020/01/13/in-the-past-5-years-the-transgender-explosion-has-wounded-more-and-more-people.

6. Sex Change Regret, https://sexchangeregret.com.

7. Olohan, "'It Destroyed My Body.'"

8. Heyer, "The 'Sex Change' I Had 40 Years Ago Was a Scam."

9. "Abel Garcia," telephone interviews by the author, January 27, 2023, and April 3, 2023.

10. Ibid.

11. Ibid.

12. "Male to Female (MTF) Procedures for Transgender Women," UVA Health, https://uvahealth.com/services/transgender/transgender-mtf-surgery.

13. "Vaginoplasty for Gender Affirmation," Johns Hopkins Medicine, https://www
.hopkinsmedicine.org/health/treatment-tests-and-therapies/vaginoplasty-for
-gender-affirmation.

14. "Ask a Clinician: How Long Do You Have to Dilate after Bottom Surgery?," FOLX
Health, January 3, 2023, https://www.folxhealth.com/library/how-long-do-you
-have-to-dilate-after-bottom-surgery.

15. "Vaginoplasty for Gender Affirmation."

16. Brandon Showalter, "Eunuchs, 'Frankenstein Level Stuff' and ISIS: This Trans
Sci-Fi Horror Story Is Real," The Christian Post, April 28, 2023, https://www
.christianpost.com/voices/eunuchs-frankenstein-level-stuff-and-isis-this-story-is
-real.html; Vera L. Negenborn et al., "Lethal Necrotizing Cellulitis Caused by
ESBL-Producing E. Coli after Laparoscopic Intestinal Vaginoplasty," *Journal of
Pediatric & Adolescent Gynecology* 30, no. 1 (February 2017): e19–e21, https:
//www.jpagonline.org/article/S1083-3188(16)30174-7/fulltext.

17. Showalter, "Eunuchs, 'Frankenstein Level Stuff' and ISIS"; Elon Musk
(@elonmusk), "I agree. This is super messed up…," Twitter, April 25, 2023, 8:47
a.m., https://twitter.com/elonmusk/status/1650843875622232064.

Chapter 9: The Aftermath: Dealing with Betrayal

1. Helena, "By Any Other Name: The Story of My Transition and Detransition,"
prude posting (Substack), February 19, 2022, https://lacroicsz.substack.com/p/by
-any-other-name.

2. Helena, "An Update," prude posting (Substack), July 17, 2022, https://lacroicsz
.substack.com/p/an-update.

3. Helena Kerschner, email interview by the author, April 10, 2023.

4. Do No Harm, https://donoharmmedicine.org.

5. Chloe Cole, telephone interview by the author, June 2023.

6. Ibid.

7. Kelsey Bolar, "'Detransitioners' Are Being Abandoned by Medical Professionals
Who Devastated Their Bodies and Minds," The Federalist, February 10, 2023,
https://thefederalist.com/2023/02/10/detransitioners-are-being-abandoned-by
-medical-professionals-who-devastated-their-bodies-and-minds.

8. Prisha (@detransaqua), "I have my appointment with Plume tomorrow…," Twitter,
January 29, 2023, 8:22 p.m., https://twitter.com/detransaqua/status
/1619868535966289920?s=20.

9. Prisha (@detransaqua), "Plume ghosted me…," Twitter, January 30, 2023, 1:15
p.m., https://twitter.com/detransaqua/status/1620123460080111616?s=20.

10. Susana (@detransfemcel), "When I detransitioned I realized how 'good' trans
people have it…," (thread) Twitter, February 4, 2023, 6:36 p.m., https://twitter
.com/detransfemcel/status/1622016263986810886?s=20.

11. Mary Margaret Olohan, "PhRMA, Pfizer Funded LGBT Index Scoring Hospitals
for Promoting Gender Ideology," The Daily Signal, May 24, 2023, https://www

.dailysignal.com/2023/05/24/phrma-pfizer-funded-lgbt-index-scoring-hospitals-promoting-gender-ideology.

12. "HEI Scoring Criteria," Human Rights Campaign, https://www.thehrcfoundation.org/professional-resources/hei-scoring-criteria.

13. Mary Margaret Olohan, "EXCLUSIVE: Leaked Policy Exposes Fox News Stances on Woke Ideology," The Daily Signal, May 22, 2023, https://www.dailysignal.com/2023/05/22/exclusive-leaked-policy-exposes-fox-news-stances-on-woke-ideology.

14. Dana Kennedy, "Inside the CEI System Pushing Brands to Endorse Celebs like Dylan Mulvaney," *New York Post*, April 7, 2023, https://nypost.com/2023/04/07/inside-the-woke-scoring-system-guiding-american-companies.

15. "Best Places to Work for LGBTQ+ Equality 2022," Human Rights Campaign, https://www.hrc.org/resources/best-places-to-work-for-lgbtq-equality-2022.

16. Jessica Guynn, "Bud Light Maker Stripped of LGBTQ+ Rating for Caving to Dylan Mulvaney Backlash," *USA Today*, May 18, 2023, https://www.usatoday.com/story/money/2023/05/18/bud-light-loses-lgbtq-score-after-dylan-mulvaney-transgender-campaign/70229893007.

17. "Fox Corporation Recognized with Highest Rating in 2022 Human Rights Campaign Corporate Equality Index," Fox, January 27, 2022, https://investor.foxcorporation.com/news-releases/news-release-details/fox-corporation-recognized-highest-rating-2022-human-rights.

18. Olohan, "EXCLUSIVE: Leaked Policy Exposes Fox News Stances."

19. Chloe Cole, telephone interview by the author.

20. Luka Hein, telephone interview by the author, December 27, 2022. See also Complaint for Medical Malpractice, Waiver of Panel Review, and Demand for Jury Trial, *Luka Hein, Plaintiff, v. UNMC Physicians, the Nebraska Medical Center, Nahia J. Amoura, M.D., Perry Johnson, M.D., Stephan Barrientos, M.D., and Megan Smith-Sallans, Defendants*, District Court of Douglas County, Nebraska, filed September 13, 2023, available at https://libertycenter.org/wp-content/uploads/2023/09/Luka-Hein-District-Court-Complaint-9-13-23-filed.pdf.

21. NewsNation, "Full Episode: Discussing Transgender Health Care for Minors: CUOMO," YouTube, December 16, 2022, https://www.youtube.com/watch?v=btBg9oHDrhU.

22. Luka Hein, telephone interview by the author.

23. Ibid.

24. Prisha Mosley, telephone interview by the author, December 22, 2022.

Chapter 10: The Future

1. Watson (@ImWatson91), "Another day on Twitter: I post a heartfelt thread about how I've been insulted and threatened for being a detransitioner...," Twitter,

August 29, 2021, 4:37 p.m., https://twitter.com/ImWatson91/status/143208000 8630214664?s=20.

2. Helena (@lacroicsz), "Every time the media reports on sex offenders...," Twitter, February 17, 2022, 2:57 p.m., https://twitter.com/lacroicsz/status/1494400 619972632587.

3. Helena (@lacroicsz), "Trans people have to accuse me of being paid off and puppeteered by Big Terf...," (thread) Twitter, May 27, 2022, 3:06 p.m., https://twitter.com/lacroicsz/status/1530264270822416385?s=20.

4. Mary Margaret Olohan, "DeTransitioners Flood Social Media with Testimony, Photos: 'The Darkest Time in My Life,'" The Daily Wire, March 12, 2022, https://www.dailywire.com/news/detransitioners-flood-social-media-with-testimony -photos-the-darkest-time-in-my-life.

5. Chloe Cole, "DETRANSITIONER Chloe Cole Speaks at The End Child Mutilation Rally in NASHVILLE," YouTube, October 21, 2022, https://www.youtube.com/watch?v=ARP_XmPRhzc.

6. Jon Brown, "Detransitioning Rally Turns Violent When Antifa Shows Up, Participants Left 'Afraid' to Speak Out: Organizer," Fox News, March 15, 2023, https://www.foxnews.com/us/detransitioning-rally-turns-violent-antifa-shows-up -participants-left-afraid-speak-out-organizer.

7. Cole, "DETRANSITIONER Chloe Cole Speaks."

8. Prisha, "Ohio HB68," Prisha's Substack (Substack), April 27, 2023, https://detransaqua.substack.com/p/ohio-hb68.

9. Christina Buttons, "Detransitioner Chloe Cole Announces Official Lawsuit against Kaiser Permanente for 'Medical Negligence,'" The Daily Wire, February 23, 2023, https://www.dailywire.com/news/detransitioner-chloe-cole-announces-official -lawsuit-against-kaiser-permanente-for-medical-negligence.

10. Complaint for Medical Negligence and Jury Trial Demand, *Chloe E. Brockman a/k/a Chloe Cole v. Kaiser Foundation Hospitals, Inc., a California Corporation, the Permanente Medical Group, Inc., a California Corporation, Lisa Kristine Taylor, M.D., an Individual, Hop Nguyen Le, M.D., an Individual, Susanne E. Watson, Ph.D., an individual, and Does 1 through 50, Inclusive, Defendants*, Superior Court of California, filed February 22, 2023, 2–4, available at https://libertycenter.org/wp-content/uploads/2023/02/Complaint1.pdf.

11. Ibid., 4.

12. Ibid., 25.

13. Maggie Astor, "How a Few Stories of Regret Fuel the Push to Restrict Gender Transition Care," *New York Times*, May 16, 2023, https://www.nytimes.com /2023/05/16/us/politics/transgender-care-detransitioners.html. See also Francesca Paris, "Bans on Transition Care for Young People Spread across U.S.," *New York Times*, April 15, 2023, https://www.nytimes.com/2023/04/15/upshot/bans -transgender-teenagers.html; Azeen Ghorayshi, "Many States Are Trying to Restrict Gender Treatments for Adults, Too," *New York Times*, April 22, 2023, https://www.nytimes.com/2023/04/22/health/transgender-adults-treatment-bans .html; Jeff Victor, "Lawmakers Nix Anti-Trans 'Chloe's Law' amid Warnings of

an Insurance Crisis," Wyoming Public Media, February 23, 2023, https://www
.wyomingpublicmedia.org/news/2023-02-23/lawmakers-nix-anti-trans-chloes
-law-amid-warnings-of-an-insurance-crisis.

14. Complaint for 1. Medical Negligence 2. Medical Negligence-Hospital/Medical
Group Jury Trial Demanded, *Kayla Lovdahl, an Individual Plaintiff, v. Kaiser
Foundation Hospitals, Inc., a California Corporation, the Permanente Medical
Group, Inc., a California Corporation, Lisa Kristine Taylor, M.D., an Individual,
Winnie Mao Yiu Tong, M.D., an Individual, Susan E. Watson PHD., an
Individual, Mirna Escalante, M.D., an Individual, and Does 1 through 50,
Inclusive.* . . . Superior Court of the State of California, in and for the County of
San Joaquin-Stockton Branch, filed June 14, 2023, available at https://libertycenter
.org/wp-content/uploads/2023/06/1.-Complaint-1.pdf.

15. Ibid., 2, 4, 5–6.

16. Ibid., 2, 3, 10, 12, 13, 15.

17. Ibid., 22.

18. Ibid., 9–12.

19. Ibid., 13–14.

20. Ibid., 13–14, 25–26.

21. "Missouri Attorney General Andrew Bailey Confirms Launch of Multi-Agency
Investigation into St. Louis Transgender Center for Harming Hundreds of
Children," Missouri Attorney General, February 9, 2023, https://ago.mo.gov
/missouri-attorney-general-andrew-bailey-confirms-launch-of-multi
-agency-investigation-into-st.

22. Jamie Reed, "I Thought I Was Saving Trans Kids. Now I'm Blowing the Whistle,"
The Free Press, February 9, 2023, https://www.thefp.com/p/i-thought-i-was-saving
-trans-kids.

23. Bari Weiss, "Resignation Letter," https://www.bariweiss.com/resignation-letter.

24. Jamie Reed, "Affidavit of Jamie Reed," Missouri Attorney General, February 7,
2023, 1, https://ago.mo.gov/wp-content/uploads/2-07-2023-reed-affidavit-signed
.pdf.

25. Ibid., 2.

26. Ibid., 22.

27. Ibid., 15.

28. Ibid., 21.

29. Ibid., 13.

30. Ibid., 19.

31. Ibid., 17.

32. Ibid., 8.

33. Ibid., 7.

34. Ibid., 14.

35. Ibid., 18.

36. Ibid., 19.

37. "Missouri Attorney General Andrew Bailey Confirms Launch."
38. "Attorney General Bailey Launches Tip Line for Reports of Questionable Gender Transition Interventions," Missouri Attorney General, March 23, 2023, https://ago.mo.gov/home/news/2023/03/23/attorney-general-bailey-launches-tip-line-for-reports-of-questionable-gender-transition-interventions.
39. "Hawley Outlines Investigation of Washington University Transgender Center at St. Louis Children's Hospital: 'Accountability Is Coming,'" Josh Hawley Senate, February 9, 2023, https://www.hawley.senate.gov/hawley-outlines-investigation-washington-university-transgender-center-st-louis-childrens-hospital.
40. Ibid.; Jessica Chasmar, "Children's Hospital Advised School District Not to Require Disclosure of Students' Chest-Binding to Parents," Fox News, January 17, 2023, https://www.foxnews.com/politics/childrens-hospital-advised-school-district-not-require-disclosure-students-chest-binding-parents.
41. Josh Hawley (@HawleyMO), "I spoke to the Chancellor of Washington University in St. Louis today…," Twitter, February 9, 2023, 2:33 p.m., https://twitter.com/HawleyMO/status/1623767144562401280?s=20.
42. Kacen Bayless, "Planned Parenthood Sues Missouri AG Bailey for Investigating Its Gender-Affirming Care," *Kansas City Star*, March 31, 2023, https://www.kansascity.com/news/politics-government/article273821510.html.
43. "Transgender Care," Planned Parenthood of the St. Louis Region and Southwest Missouri, https://www.plannedparenthood.org/planned-parenthood-st-louis-region-southwest-missouri/patients/our-services/transgender-care.
44. Andrew Bailey, telephone interview by the author, May 3, 2023.
45. "Vaginoplasty for Gender Affirmation," Johns Hopkins Medicine, https://www.hopkinsmedicine.org/health/treatment-tests-and-therapies/vaginoplasty-for-gender-affirmation.
46. Amanda Prestigiacomo, "'Huge Money Maker': Video Reveals Vanderbilt's Shocking Gender 'Care,' Threats against Dissenting Doctors," The Daily Wire, September 20, 2022, https://www.dailywire.com/news/huge-money-maker-video-reveals-vanderbilts-shocking-gender-care-threats-against-dissenting-doctors; Matt Walsh (@MattWalshBlog), "BREAKING: My team and I have been investigating the transgender clinic at Vanderbilt…," (thread including embedded video), Twitter, September 20, 2022, 3:54 p.m., https://twitter.com/MattWalshBlog/status/1572313369528635392.
47. Ibid.
48. "Trans Buddy Program," Vanderbilt University Medical Center, https://www.vumc.org/lgbtq/trans-buddy-program.
49. Matt Walsh (@MattWalshBlog), "In case the objectors hadn't gotten the memo, Vanderbilt unveiled a program called 'Trans Buddies'…," Twitter, September 20, 2022, 3:55 p.m., https://twitter.com/MattWalshBlog/status/1572313627008405504?s=20.

50. Matt Walsh (@MattWalshBlog), "After they have drugged and sterilized the kids...," (thread), Twitter, September 20, 2022, 3:56 p.m., https://twitter.com /MattWalshBlog/status/1572313708637962244?s=20.

51. Mary Margaret Olohan, "Vanderbilt University Medical Center under Fire after Videos Expose 'Big Moneymaker' Allegations about Transgender Surgeries on Kids," The Daily Signal, September 21, 2022, https://www.dailysignal.com/2022 /09/21/vanderbilt-tennessee-governor-lee-matt-walsh-transgender-surgeries -minors.

52. Sen. Marsha Blackburn (@MarshaBlackburn), "We are shocked by what we have seen in these videos...," Twitter, September 20, 2022, 6:43 p.m., https://twitter .com/MarshaBlackburn/status/1572355683861012480?s=20; Zach Jewell, "Gov. Bill Lee Calls for Investigation of Vanderbilt's Pediatric Transgender Clinic Following Matt Walsh Revelation," The Daily Wire, September 20, 2022, https: //www.dailywire.com/news/gov-bill-lee-calls-for-investigation-of-vanderbilts -pediatric-transgender-clinic-following-matt-walsh-bombshell.

53. Matt Walsh (@MattWalshBlog), "BREAKING: After my report, Vanderbilt's transgender clinic has deleted their entire website...," Twitter, September 20, 2022, 10:43 p.m., https://twitter.com/MattWalshBlog/status/15724161223807467 52?s=20.

54. Jewell, "Gov. Bill Lee Calls for Investigation."

55. Rep. Jason Zachary (@JasonZacharyTN), "Please see Vanderbilt Medical's response to the @tnhousegop...," Twitter, October 7, 2022, 3:57 p.m., https: //twitter.com/JasonZacharyTN/status/1578474545131888640?s=20; Mairead Elordi, "TN House GOP Formally Requests Vanderbilt Medical Halt Gender Surgeries on Minors," The Daily Wire, September 28, 2022, https://www.dailywire .com/news/tn-house-gop-formally-requests-vanderbilt-medical-halt-gender -surgeries-on-minors.

56. Leif Le Mahieu, "Vanderbilt Pediatric Gender Clinic Pausing Transgender Surgeries on Minors," The Daily Wire, October 7, 2022, https://www.dailywire.com/news /breaking-vanderbilt-pediatric-gender-clinic-pausing-transgender-surgeries-on -minors.

57. Christina Buttons, "Vanderbilt Insiders Fear Transgender Surgeries on Minors Will Resume," The Daily Wire, October 17, 2022, https://www.dailywire.com /news/vanderbilt-insiders-fear-transgender-surgeries-on-minors-will-resume.

58. Melissa Brown and Kelly Puente, "Vanderbilt Turns Over Transgender Patient Records to State in Attorney General Probe," Tennessean, June 21, 2023, https: //www.tennessean.com/story/news/health/2023/06/20/vanderbilt-university -m-turns-over-transgender-patient-medical-records-to-tennessee-attorney-general /70338356007.

59. "Tennessee Attorney General's Office Provides Statement Regarding VUMC Investigation," Jonathan Skrmetti, Attorney General & Reporter, June 21, 2023, https://www.tn.gov/attorneygeneral/news/2023/6/21/pr23-20.html.

Chapter 11: The Alternative

1. Juliette Fairley, "Trans Teen's Suicide Leads Mom to Sue LA County, Department of Children and Family Services," Southern California Record, March 28, 2022, https://socalrecord.com/stories/622458964-trans-teen-s-suicide-leads-mom-to-sue-la-county-department-of-children-and-family-services.
2. Virginia Allen, "This Mom Says Transgender Movement Took Her Daughter's Life," The Daily Signal, March 21, 2022, https://www.dailysignal.com/2022/03/21/this-mom-says-transgender-movement-took-her-daughters-life.
3. Jurisdiction/Disposition Report in the Matter of Yaeli Mozzelle Galdamez, Los Angeles County Department of Children and Family Services, September 15, 2016, 10.
4. Allen, "This Mom Says."
5. Jurisdiction/Disposition Report, 10.
6. Ibid., 12.
7. Ibid., 14.
8. Ibid.
9. Ibid.
10. Abby Martinez, telephone interview by the author, April 24, 2023.
11. Jurisdiction/Disposition Report, 12.
12. Ibid., 7–9, 12–13.
13. Ibid., 7.
14. Ibid., 8–9.
15. Ibid., 5.
16. Ibid., 7–9.
17. Ibid., 8.
18. Ibid., 9.
19. Ibid., 12.
20. Ibid.
21. Ibid., 12–13.
22. Ibid, 13.
23. Madeleine Kearns, "Children's Lives Depend on Parents' Rights," *Spectator World*, April 18, 2022, https://thespectator.com/topic/childrens-lives-depend-on-parents-rights.
24. Jurisdiction/Disposition Report, 15.
25. Abby Martinez, telephone interview by the author.
26. Jurisdiction/Disposition Report, 17.
27. Allen, "This Mom Says."
28. Ibid.
29. Kearns, "Children's Lives."
30. Status Review Report in the Matter of Yaeli Mozzelle Galdamez, Los Angeles County Department of Children and Family Services, July 10, 2017, 6.
31. Ibid, 7.

32. Ibid, 5.
33. Abby Martinez, telephone interview by the author.
34. Status Review Report, 8.
35. Josh Boswell, "EXCLUSIVE: 'I Knew the Hormones Wouldn't Work. Why Did They Play with Her Life?' Bereaved Mom Blames LA County for Her Teenage Daughter's Suicide, Claiming School Pushed Her to Transition to a Male Instead of Properly Treating Her Depression," *Daily Mail*, March 30, 2022, https://www.dailymail.co.uk/news/article-10612285/California-mom-claims-LA-school-encouraged-daughter-transition-blame-suicide.html.
36. Kearns, "Children's Lives"; "Another Florida School Board Sued over Concealing Gender Identity Counseling from Parents," Tallahassee Reports, January 30, 2022, https://tallahasseereports.com/2022/01/30/another-florida-school-board-sued-over-concealing-gender-identity-counseling-from-parents.
37. Allen, "This Mom Says."
38. "Examination Protocol: Jane Doe 67" (coroner's report on Yaeli Mozzelle Galdamez), County of Los Angeles, Department of the Medical Examiner, September 4, 2019.
39. Allen, "This Mom Says."
40. Ibid.
41. Hilda L. Solis, "Responding to the Immediate Need to Support Foster Youth Who Identify as LGBTQ+," Los Angeles County, September 24, 2019, https://file.lacounty.gov/SDSInter/bos/supdocs/140611.pdf.
42. Los Angeles Department of Children and Family Services, email to the author, April 19, 2023.
43. Hank Berrien, "'I'm Broken': CA Mom Whose Daughter Committed Suicide after 'Transitioning' Blames School," The Daily Wire, March 18, 2022, https://www.dailywire.com/news/im-broken-ca-mom-whose-daughter-committed-suicide-after-transitioning-blames-school.
44. Jurisdiction/Disposition Report, 17.
45. Philip Browning, telephone interview by the author, April 19, 2023.
46. Allen, "This Mom Says."

INDEX